Gendered Futures
in
Higher Education

Gendered Futures
in
Higher Education

Critical Perspectives for Change

Becky Ropers-Huilman, editor

State University of New York Press

Published by
State University of New York Press, Albany

For information, address State University of New York Press,
90 State Street, Suite 700, Albany, NY 12207

Production by Michael Haggett
Marketing by Anne M. Valentine

Library of Congress Cataloging-in-Publication Data

Gendered futures in higher education : critical perspectives for change /
Becky Ropers-Huilman, editor.
    p. cm.
  Includes bibliographical references and index.
  ISBN 0-7914-5697-8 (alk. paper) — ISBN 0-7914-5698-6 (pbk. : alk.
paper)
    1. Sex discrimination in higher education—United States.   2. Women
in higher education—United States.   I. Ropers-Huilman, Becky.

LC212.862 .G46 2003
378'.0082—dc21

                                                             2002042639

10 9 8 7 6 5 4 3 2 1

To Anson, Stephanie,
and the Memory of Erika.

Contents

PART III
DECONSTRUCTING THE PRESENT:
FACULTY LIVES

PART IV
RE-CONCEIVING THE FUTURE

Acknowledgments

This text would not have been possible without the help of many people. First, I wish to thank the chapter authors who quickly agreed to participate in this emerging project some years ago. I have learned much from their insights and questions. Second, several graduate students and faculty members at Louisiana State University have helped me in the preparation of this document. While many have contributed to the concepts and concerns presented in this text, Monisa Shackelford, Laura Carwile, Petra Munro, Laura Hensley, and Nina Asher have directly aided its production by reading various drafts and making suggestions for improvement. Finally, my friends and family both in Louisiana and the Midwest are invaluable to my academic work. Particularly to Brian and Anson, I am deeply grateful. Thanks to them, I am able to stay grounded in what matters.

Gender in the Future of
Higher Education

Becky Ropers-Huilman

Monday, February 5, 2001. Again, the Chronicle of Higher Education's news briefs are waiting for me on my e-mail. I am not encouraged. From following related links, I learn that at the University of Cambridge, "66 percent of women said they had felt undervalued or excluded at some point. Only 6 percent of Cambridge's full professors are female . . . [and] males recorded the highest levels of satisfaction with the university" (Walker, 2001). Another article details that

> *A federal district court judge has decided that a woman can sue her former professor for sexual harassment for calling her "Monica Lewinsky." In his ruling, Judge Hurd noted that Professor Young "observed that the plaintiff wore the same color lipstick as Monica Lewinsky, and made comments such as, 'How was your weekend with Bill?' and 'Shut up, Monica. I'll give you a cigar later,'" in front of the entire class in the fall of 1998. . . . Professor Young, who has since retired, admits to making the references because he thought Ms. Hayut looked like Monica Lewinsky, but denies that his comments were anything other than making fun. "He feels bad that it may have been tasteless or politically incorrect, but he certainly had no intention of making it a sexual thing," said Kenneth Kelly, his lawyer. "It was joking and teasing." (Kellogg, 2001)*

From one day's news briefs, I am reminded that gender is still very much a part of higher education.

As readers begin to engage with the dialogues and debates included in this volume, they might ask themselves: Have we moved beyond the need for gendered discussions? Are conversations such as those included in this book really relevant to higher education in current times? As the authors illustrate, the roles that participants at all levels of higher education play are crafted and performed

1

within an environment that is indeed gendered, and conversations related to this gendering process are both relevant and urgently needed.

The purpose of this volume is twofold. First, by focusing on historical knowledge, contemporary experience, and future visions, this book identifies and describes several key gender issues currently taking shape in higher education environments. Second, each contributor applies critical perspectives to suggest needed change. Despite evidence that often paints a dark picture of current realities, the authors both draw on the accomplishments of the past and suggest clear ways to improve in the future.

Underlying this volume is the feminist belief that gender takes shape in, and is shaped by, teaching, learning, and leadership practices, and in relations between students, faculty, administrators, and communities. At the same time, neither gender nor feminism is construed as a static concept uninfluenced by context. For example, as the authors collectively point out, the concept of "gender" is interpreted in many different ways depending on social dynamics related to race, sexual orientation, and other cultural markers. I envision this volume as being widely useful for students, scholars, and practitioners who are interested in learning about, and perhaps becoming a part of, the gender-related conversations that promise to continue influencing higher education environments.

WHY GENDER?

Girls and boys, men and women, are reminded of their proper sex roles through both formal and informal education. Through the interactions in many contexts, *gender is constructed.* Although we are each born with a biological sex that is more or less determined, the ways in which our sex is expressed through social practices is known as *gender.* For example, the ways in which one female chooses to be a woman can vary greatly from how others choose to construct themselves and interact with their environments.

It is also important to remember in this volume that *gender is constructed through interactions with others.* From the beginning, when boys are encouraged to be active and told not to cry, when girls are praised for their appearance and their quiet and polite behavior, when both boys and girls are given gender-specific toys that implicitly teach them what each gender is "supposed" to find pleasurable, gender is formed. However, gender is not formed only during the early years of our lives. Instead, in our interactions throughout our lives, we subtly (and sometimes not so subtly) let others know what we expect from them as gendered beings.

The chapters in this volume illustrate that gender is a social construction. This has two important implications. First, gender is an expression of social context. Thus, depending on various elements of context, people will express—by choice, coercion, and force—their genders in a variety of different ways. To be a woman or a man does not mean the same thing to all people in all situations in all cultures. As such, as the chapters in this volume persuasively argue, we need to continually look at the multiple ways in which gender is expressed, and the manifestations and implications of those expressions. Second, because gender is socially constructed, it can also be deconstructed. Specifically, we can work to understand the ways in which gendered norms and expectations have a variety of effects on teaching, learning, and leading in higher education.

Given the identities that each of us embodies, gender is certainly not the sole characteristic that influences our lives. As Taunya Lovell Banks (1997) writes, "My life stories influence my perspective, a perspective unable to function within a single paradigm because I am too many things at one time" (p. 99). We each come from a location set, in part, by the categories in which we place ourselves—and into which we are placed by others. Our race, class, sexual orientation, geographic location, family composition, and other identity factors are significant in shaping opportunities, challenges, and interpretations of our lives. In various ways, gender is also a salient characteristic that significantly shapes our experiences in social settings. For example, we know that men and women tend to have different communication styles (Tannen, 1991), learning styles (Belenky, Clinchy, Goldberger, & Tarule, 1986; Hayes & Flannery, 2000), and leadership preferences (Chlinwiak, 1997). This discussion of differences is not to negate the obvious similarities in the ways women and men live their lives. It is, however, to suggest that the existing differences have meaningful effects on our interactions with each other and the opportunities that are readily available to those of either gender.

WHY HIGHER EDUCATION?

Higher education has far-reaching consequences for the construction of our society. With technological advancements that allow institutions of higher learning to reach more and more people, this nation's more than 4,000 colleges and universities offer educational experiences to over 14 million students (Chronicle, 2001). Hundreds of thousands of administrators, faculty, and staff support those students as well as produce scholarship and engage in service to the community. Because higher education both reinforces and resists society's norms, what we do in these teaching and learning environments has the potential to exacerbate, replicate, or challenge gender constructions that exist in society writ large.

And what have our choices yielded thus far? In many respects the numbers are improving, suggesting that equity between women and men is possible. For example, feminist faculty members, administrators, and students have developed

Women's and/or Gender Studies programs at over 800 campuses in the United States (National Women's Studies Association, personal communication, February 2, 2001). Further, women and men are approaching parity in many aspects of their college participation. Indeed, women comprise over half of all students and, even at the doctoral level, make up approximately 42% of students. Yet, while some disciplines are close to achieving parity, others are far from that goal. For example, at the undergraduate level, only 18% of all students in engineering are women, and only 25% of all students in education are men. At the doctoral level, male participation increases in both cases. In engineering, only 12.3% of all students are women, whereas men constitute 36.8% of doctoral students in education (Chronicle, 2001).

Analyses of numbers related to faculty provide further evidence of disparities, particularly when considering salaries and ranks. In material terms, women faculty members earn less than men faculty members, even when rank, productivity, and years in service are taken into account (Hagedorn, 1996, 2000). And, while women constitute 50% of all instructors, their numbers decrease to 20% at the highest, tenured level of full professor (Chronicle, 2001). Clearly, gender matters both in our interactions and in how our work is valued.

This is true not only in the United States. For example, as several recent volumes have pointed out, although the concept of egalitarianism pervades higher education, somehow that concept does not translate into equal opportunities and experiences for women and men in the United Kingdom, New Zealand, or Australia (Brooks, 1997; Morley, 1999). And although Women's Studies courses have become relatively established in many Western countries, they have been more recently developed in countries such as China, India, South Africa, and Mexico (Morley, 1999). The international literature on topics such as feminism in the academy, women's experiences as students, faculty, and leaders, and the emerging understandings of "equal opportunity" in academic settings require that we understand that women are situated in a wide variety of ways, and that there is no monolithic or static understanding of gender in academic settings.

And yet, numbers and research affirm that gender does matter, albeit in many different ways. Much educational research has suggested that administrators, teachers, and students—for better or worse—are actively involved in the construction of gender in higher education. For example, in classrooms, men tend to speak more frequently and for longer periods, suggesting the importance of their ideas (Lewis, 1993; Lewis & Simon, 1986). Faculty members often do not combat—or even notice—this occurrence, thereby reinforcing its appropriateness (Griffin, 1992). Additionally, some faculty members are expected to behave in certain ways, often as mother or father, expert or facilitator, depending in part on their gender (Griffin, 1992; Jipson, 1995; Martin, 2000; Ropers-Huilman, 1998; Thorne & Hochschild, 1997). Others come to recognize the ways in which discrimination negatively affects their work environment and devalues their contributions (MIT Faculty Newsletter, 1999; Park, 1996). Women leaders, particularly those who are identified as change agents, experience difficulty in establishing their credibility and longevity as leaders (Clark, Garner, Higonnet, & Katrak, 1996; Schmuck, Hollingsworth, & Lock, 2002; Kolodny, 1998). And women and men who embody intersecting identity characteristics that have not readily been accepted in higher education environments face both challenges and unique opportunities on multiple levels (Neumann & Peterson, 1997; Ng, 1997). Our interactions with each other and the ways in which we value each other all continue to shape gender in higher education environments. And these actions have dramatic effects.

Each of the authors contributing to this text has experienced multiple roles in society. In this volume, they turn their attention toward higher education and the ways in which gendered realities get played out in colleges and universities. These authors, who represent both beginning and seasoned scholars, take a range of perspectives about what higher education should look like as we approach the upcoming century. They utilize a variety of approaches and assumptions in framing their arguments. Some make suggestions to gradually improve our current system (by improving student services or creating more representative curricular offerings). Others suggest immediate and substantial changes to university structures (by eliminating fraternities, changing well-entrenched policies, or engaging in advocacy education). While these authors may not agree on the necessary strategies to improve higher education environments, they do agree that those environments are currently deeply and problematically gendered.

A particular strength of this work is the acknowledgment that gender is not a static concept that can be uniformly understood, addressed, and forgotten. Instead, the authors suggest that although gender in itself is important, the intersection of gender with other identities and situations creates unique challenges and opportunities for understanding—and acting to improve—the gendered nature of higher education. Through their analyses, the authors convey the urgency of both conversation and action.

GENDERED LESSONS IN HIGHER EDUCATION

This text is meant as an introduction of issues related to gender in higher education. As Mary Catherine Bateson (1997) wrote, "One of the questions that is often asked about research of this kind is whether the voices we hear are 'representative.' This is a false question, since they offer a range of possibility, not a statistical sample" (p. viii). Each chapter author has her or his own vision for the future of higher education. These chapters, and the analyses they offer, are not meant to be comprehensive in their examination of gender issues on campus. Instead, they provide many different visions of higher education, gender, and feminism. They might be most useful when viewed as case studies that illustrate the multiple ways that participants involved in higher education environments negotiate gender. As such, some of the chapters focus on women explicitly, while others focus on the construction of gender for men and women, as well as the effects of those constructions. The majority of the chapters also include an analysis of the ways gender intersects with other dimensions of identity, such as race, sexual orientation, and class.

In the first section, on "Learning from the Past," the chapters review what we can learn from the successes of our predecessors in our attempts to create a better future for higher education. Specifically, this section begins with a historical analysis reminding us of the importance of looking at history as a framework from which to consider options for the future. Jana Nidiffer provides a history of women's participation in higher education in her chapter entitled, "From Whence They Came: The Contexts, Challenges, and Courage of Early Women Administrators in Higher Education." Within this history, she situates men and women as having differential access to resources and opportunities, as well as having different expectations placed on their behavior in higher education. Nidiffer particularly emphasizes the role that early women administrators had in shaping women's participation as students and leaders in higher education. She urges that "We no longer should assume that the traditional, male-oriented nature of institutions is the norm to which women must respond." Instead, higher education should value the lessons that our foremothers taught us through their leadership and activism about how to create female-friendly institutions.

The second chapter in this section is Lisa Wolf-Wendel's "Gender and Higher Education: What Should We Learn From Women's Colleges?" In this chapter, Wolf-Wendel describes the lessons that women's colleges have to offer to other higher education environments. She describes the various factors that make women's colleges successful in promoting women's intellectual and social development and asserts that there are distinct practices and policies that, when enacted, could have positive effects on women's involvement in coeducational higher education as well. Wolf-Wendel writes of the importance of "taking women seriously" such that they are able to develop their full potential for contributing to society. She challenges us to develop policies and practices that: (1) clarify and communicate a mission that puts women at the center; (2) [illustrate a belief that] women can achieve, and hold them to high expectations; (3) make students feel like they matter; (4) provide strong, positive role models; (5) provide ample opportunities for women to engage in leadership activities; (6) include women in the curriculum; and (7) create safe spaces where women can form a critical mass. These chapters offer a strong reminder that there have been success stories in our past. We are not starting anew in our quest for a gender-fair educational environment. In learning from the past, we can identify powerful models to guide our understandings of the present and our planning for the future.

The second section of this book focuses on "Deconstructing the Present." In this section, the authors turn their attention to deconstructing—for the purpose of better understanding—present experiences of students and faculty. These chapters rightly acknowledge that the context in which students and faculty are expected to engage in scholarly pursuits drastically affects their abilities to do so. This section is divided into two parts. The first part considers how certain social norms and expectations have gendered effects in college students' lives. As Laura Hensley points out in "Stepping Off the Scale: Promoting Positive Body Image in College Students," gendered norms and expectations can show up in physical ways on the bodies of individuals, including those of college students. In this chapter, Hensley asserts that although issues related to ideal body image for men and women are not necessarily created on campus, there are many ways those in student affairs, counseling, and other forms of leadership can combat the harmful effects that unrealistic expectations for body image can have on students. She suggests that in order to challenge the harmful causes and sometimes deadly effects of eating disorders, college personnel would be wise to embrace factors that lead toward the resiliency of college of students. Specifically, Hensley suggests that we challenge the media-generated "slender ideal," model and develop in others a sense of interdependency, move beyond typical sex-role prescriptions, encourage an internally derived sense of self-worth, develop broader definitions of beauty, and make sure that students find places and people in their higher education environments through which they feel supported and empowered.

The second chapter, William Pinar's "The Gender of Violence on Campus," focuses on another physical manifestation of gendered expectations and norms: violence on campus. He suggests that the violence permeating our larger society has indeed found root on our college campuses. In his work, which critiques practices and customs associated with hazing, athletics, and other college experiences, he describes the ways in which violent acts on campus serve to reify masculinity and femininity with often hurtful consequences. After careful review of several incidents of, and precursors to, violence in higher education, he asserts that to create safer environments for both male and female students, social fraternities should be closed and "big-time" sports should be substantially changed in their orientation and focus. Finally, he suggests that students would gain important understandings through involvement in Women's and Gender Studies courses—understandings that have the potential to reduce the likelihood for violence on college campuses. As such, he recommends that Women's and Gender Studies courses should be a general education requirement.

The second part of this section turns to a deconstruction of faculty experiences. Judith Glazer-Raymo's "Women Faculty and Part-Time Employment: The Impact of Public Policy" focuses on the unintended consequences of policy related to part-time faculty work and illustrates the complexities of policies that attempt to be sensitive to gender. In her chapter, she expresses a concern that policies made in past and current educational settings do not take into consideration the differential effects that they may have on women and men, and on people of color. Like many of the authors, she urges that we look to the ways that gender intersects with other identities to create situations that are uniquely effected by seemingly neutral policies. With this analysis, Glazer-Raymo argues that "women must become agents of social change and advocates for women's concerns," and that women should be encouraged to seek high-level administrative posts so that they can begin to change the "rules of the game" that are detailed in higher education policy. Finally, she emphasizes the importance of women serving as mentors and advocates for each other.

The second chapter in this part, "Future Prospects for Women Faculty: Negotiating Work and Family," illustrates the ways those faculty members who are involved in dual-career relationships or are currently parenting children experience additional challenges to participating fully in faculty life. In this chapter, Lisa Wolf-Wendel and Kelly Ward illustrate how the typical career trajectory for faculty conflicts with typical family responsibilities for women. Through a discussion of dual-career families and parenthood, this analysis suggests that more positive working environments for working parents would ultimately benefit the institution by leading to greater institutional loyalty, faculty satisfaction, and productivity. However, the authors argue that to better accommodate the interests of both academic institutions and the persons who perform their core work, many changes are in order. First, Wolf-Wendel and Ward urge those who are in positions to hire faculty to redefine the meanings of quality in faculty work and the ways in which it is found and fostered. Second, they encourage an ongoing examination of institutional policies and point to the ways tenure clocks and biological clocks simultaneously demand much of people, especially women. Finally, they emphasize that policies and practices that underscore men's roles in family life must be addressed. In this way, higher education can begin to change social norms that reinforce family-making as "women's work."

The last chapter in this part focuses on feminist faculty. In this chapter, entitled "Negotiating Identities and Making Change: Feminist Faculty in Higher Education," Becky Ropers-Huilman and Monisa Shackelford discuss the ways feminist faculty members create professional identities in climates that are not always conducive to feminist beliefs. In their analysis, the authors consider how feminist faculty negotiate their feminist identities in light of their other responsibilities as faculty members. They describe both their struggles to be change agents and their strategies for integrating their various identities into a professional persona. Further, they suggest that those in academic settings need to take into account the multiple identities that faculty members bring to their professional roles. Structural changes, such as those that reward scholarship and teaching that is deemed as "outside the mainstream," are needed to ensure that feminist faculty remain in academic settings and continue to promote positive changes to campus climates. Additionally, collaboration and networking among feminist faculty members is crucial to the support of this important ongoing work.

The final section of this book focuses on the ways participants in higher education might engage in "Re-conceiving the Future." Specifically, the two chapters in this section consider how teaching and learning environments and scholarly work might be changed if we purposefully attempted to acknowledge the importance of identities. Entitled "Advocacy Education: Teaching, Research, and Difference in Higher Education," the first chapter in this section focuses on what students and teachers can do together to construct better environments for teaching and learning. In their work, Becky Ropers-Huilman and Denise Taliaferro define advocacy education as education that intertwines teaching, research, and advocacy among participants. The authors emphasize that advocacy education can be enacted by all participants in higher education in various ways. The complexities that arise in this form of education, however, require that participants "foster dialogic communities in which we can see, hear, and feel (at least partially) the material effects of each other's life experiences." Taking both feminist and womanist approaches, Ropers-Huilman and Taliaferro present the complexities involved in engaging in advocacy education because of the multiple identities involved. They suggest that despite the complexities, faculty members have a responsibility to be university citizens— and advocates—to improve higher-education environments.

The second chapter in this section is Ana Martínez Alemán's "Gender, Race and Millennial Curiosity." In her work, Alemán asserts that gender is not fixed or stable, but rather changes, depending on context and interpretation. Additionally, she stresses the importance of seeing race and gender as intersecting identities, rather than as separable variables, when researching and analyzing participants' experiences in higher education. As Alemán suggests, higher education scholarship and research have the potential to inform practice in meaningful ways—in classrooms, in student affairs, and in research. She argues that because race plays such an important role in shaping social interactions both historically and today, discussions of gendered futures in higher education must include dialogue about race. Similarly, discussions about a "raced" future in higher education must consider the effects of gender. The "curiosities" of race, gender, sexual orientation, class, and other identities need to be taken into consideration when crafting research that has the potential to shape practice.

FINAL THOUGHTS

Higher education is one of the primary institutions that shape culture. While those of us who participate in that institution cannot take the blame, credit, or responsibility for current gender relations, we can insist that gender discrimination will not be perpetuated in the very institutions that hold promise for developing both knowledge and people—a development that is certainly stymied by gender discrimination. Now is the time to shape our collective future. And, as the authors in this volume assert, clear—if complex—strategies exist to guide that action. The works presented in this volume invite students, staff, faculty, administrators, and community members to participate in the shaping of our collective gendered future in higher education.

As readers engage with this volume, they might find it useful to ask the question: What would higher education look like if the authors' perspectives were enacted? Through that question, readers may better understand how each of the topics presented in this text are intertwined. Gender is holistic and permeates higher education. Yet, constructions of gender respond to evolving social contexts and will, therefore, change over time. The strength of this volume, then, is not in positing the right answers. Rather, its strength lies in its illustration of a process of asking meaningful questions and suggesting solutions to improve the gendered future of higher education. With this in mind, I invite readers to engage fully in the critical dialogue initiated by this text.

REFERENCES

Banks, T. L. (1997). Two life stories: Reflections of one Black woman law professor. In A. K. Wing (Ed.), *Critical race feminism* (pp. 96–100). New York: New York University.

Bateson, M. C. (1997). Foreword. In A. Neumann & P. Peterson (Eds.) *Learning from our lives: Women, research, and autobiography* (pp. vii–viii). New York: Teachers College.

Belenky, M. F., Clinchy, B. M., Goldberger, N. R., & Tarule, J. M. (1986). *Women's ways of knowing: The development of self, voice, and mind.* New York: Basic Books.

Brooks, A. (1997). *Academic women.* Bristol, PA: Open University Press.

Chlinwiak, L. (1997). *Higher education leadership: Analyzing the gender gap.* ASHE-ERIC Higher Education Report Vol. 25, No. 4. Washington, DC: George Washington University, Graduate School of Education and Human Development.

Chronicle of Higher Education. (2001). *Almanac.* Retrieved August 1, 2002, from <http://chronicle.com/free/almanac/2001>

Clark, V., Garner, S. N., Higonnet, M., & Katrak, K. H. (1996). *Anti-feminism in the academy.* New York: Routledge.

Griffin, G. B. (1992). *Calling: Essays on teaching in the mother tongue.* Pasadena, CA: Trilogy Books.

Hagedorn, L. (1996). Wage equity and female faculty job satisfaction: The role of wage differentials in a job satisfaction causal model. *Research in Higher Education, 37*(5): 569–598.

Hagedorn, L. (2000). Gender differences in faculty productivity, satisfaction, and salary: What really separates us? Presented at *Women in higher education: The unfinished agenda. Women's lives, women's voices, women's solutions: Shaping a national agenda for women in higher education*. St. Paul, MN.

Hayes, E., & Flannery, D. D. (2000). *Woman as learners: The significance of gender in adult learning*. San Francisco: Jossey-Bass.

Jipson, J. (1995). Teacher-mother: An imposition of identity. In J. Jipson, P. Munro, S. Victor, K. F. Jones, & G. Freed-Rowland (Eds.) *Repositioning feminism and education: Perspectives on educating for social change* (pp. 21–36). Westport, CT: Bergin & Garvey.

Kellogg, A. P. (2001, February 5). Professor may be sued for calling student "Monica Lewinsky," judge rules. *Chronicle of Higher Education*. Retrieved February 4, 2001, from <http://chronicle.com/daily/2001/02/2001020505n.htm>

Kolodny, A. (1998). *Failing the future: A dean looks at the 21st century*. Durham, NC: Duke University Press.

Lewis, M. G. (1993). *Without a word: Teaching beyond women's silence*. New York: Routledge.

Lewis, M., & Simon, R. (1986). A discourse not intended for her: Learning and teaching within patriarchy. *Harvard Educational Review, 56*(4), 457–472.

Martin, J. R. (2000). *Coming of age in academe: Rekindling women's hopes and reforming the academy*. New York: Routledge.

MIT Faculty Newsletter. (1999). A study on the status of women faculty in science at MIT. *11*(4). Retrieved August 1, 2001, from <http://web.mit.edu/fnl/women/women.html>

Morley, L. (1999). *Organising feminisms: The micropolitics of the academy*. New York: St. Martin's Press.

Neumann, A. & Peterson, P. (1997). *Learning from our lives: Women, research and autobiography in education*. New York: Teachers College.

Ng, R. (1997). A woman out of control: Deconstructing sexism and racism in the university. In S. de Castell & M. Bryson (Eds.) *Radical in(ter)ventions: Identity, politics, and difference/s in educational praxis* (pp. 39–57). Albany: State University of New York Press.

Park, S. M. (1996). Research, teaching, and service: Why shouldn't women's work count? *Journal of Higher Education, 67*(1): 46–84.

Ropers-Huilman, B. (1998). *Feminist teaching in theory and practice: Situating power and knowledge in poststructural classrooms*. New York: Teachers College.

Schmuck, P., Hollingsworth, S., & Lock, R. (2002). Women administrators and the point of exit: Collison between the person and the institution. In C. Reynolds (Ed.) *Women and school leadership: International perspectives* (pp. 93–110). Albany: State University of New York.

Tannen, D. (1991). *You just don't understand: Women and men in conversation*. New York: Ballantine.

Thorne, B., & Hochschild, A. R. (1997). Feeling at home at work: Life in academic departments. *Qualitative Sociology, 20*(4), 517–520.

Walker, D. (2001, February 5). Consultants call U. of Cambridge's culture "macho" and "insular." *Chronicle of Higher Education*. Retrieved February 5, 2001, from <http://chronicle.com/daily/2001/02/2001020507n.htm>

Part I

Learning from the Past

From Whence They Came

The Contexts, Challenges, and Courage of Early Women Administrators in Higher Education

Jana Nidiffer

It is likely that most people are familiar with the old adage that dooms a society that ignores its history to subsequently repeat it. Although this adage is quite hackneyed, it nevertheless holds an element of truth. So I have rephrased it, conveying what for me is its essence. My version states: "From history we gain insight, and from insight we have a *chance* at wisdom for the future." It is in this spirit that I offer a chapter on the contexts, challenges, and courage of early women administrators in higher education. This chapter begins with a review of women's opportunities for participation in higher education over the past two centuries. It then turns specifically to the opportunities and actions of early women administrators. Finally, it urges readers to insist on structures that support the experiences of women who participate in higher education at all levels.

TOUGH AS ROOTS—BARRIERS TO WOMEN'S EDUCATION

Over time, higher education has become a national stage on which social attitudes about women and gender are dramatized. Although a full history of women's education is beyond the scope of this chapter (see Gordon, 1990; McCandless, 1999; Nidiffer, 2001b; Rosenberg, 1982; Solomon, 1985), a review of the various arguments opposing women's education places the work of female administrators in perspective. This history also illustrates the strategies and struggles of some of the first change agents for women's participation in higher education.

At the time of the American Revolution, a powerful barrier to white women's higher education was based on Anglo-Saxon tradition. In fact, the cornerstone of resistance was the very Judeo-Christian heritage on which the country was founded. Laws and social practices were informed by the pan-Protestantism of the era that proclaimed a divinely ordained world order. God's plan called for women to be subservient and generally confined to the domestic sphere of life, while men were part of the political, economic, and social spheres of their communities (Rosenberg, 1982). The "cult of true womanhood" demanded piety, obedience, purity, and domesticity, and dictated life for many middle-class white women (Welter, 1976). Thus, it was impractical to educate women. If the colonial colleges chiefly prepared young men to enter the ministry, politics, or academic life, the idea of women attending college was absurd. They could never be ministers, politicians, statesmen, or farmers.

Not only would college serve no useful purpose for a woman, but common wisdom also dictated that she lacked the intellectual capacity to handle the rigors of the classical curriculum. In the antebellum era, the dominant curriculum consisted of classical studies with an emphasis on language study, literature, and philosophy as the pinnacle (Rudolph, 1962). Much of the new science was relegated to the margins of established colleges such as Harvard and Yale. Ironically, early women's academies tended to emphasize science (Shmurak & Handler, 1992; Tolley, 1996). Another accommodation to women's perceived intellectual inferiority was offering higher education limited to the "finishing arts" or the "Ladies Course" provided at Oberlin College (Solomon, 1985). Both curricula were less rigorous than the curriculum offered to men and emphasized women's likely domestic role.

By the middle of the nineteenth century, a new justification for limiting women's education entered the national discourse. Science, specifically biology, was used to justify the differences between the genders. It was commonly assumed that the body was a closed biological system in which the expenditure of energy in one part necessarily deprived another part. It was further believed that the conclusions of Charles Darwin could be applied to the full range of human activities—that "specialization of function" was critical to both social and biological evolution (Rosenberg, 1982). Therefore, a biologically based justification for limiting women's education and therefore her encroachment into previously male roles emerged from the medical community.

In 1873, a former member of the Harvard Medical School faculty, Dr. Edward H. Clarke, published his views on women's education in a small book entitled *Sex in Education; or, a Fair Chance for the Girls.* Clarke believed that biology was destiny, women's brains were less developed than men, and women could not tolerate intense levels of mental stimulation. More importantly, Clarke linked concentrated brain activity with the potential malfunction of the reproductive "apparatus," especially if women were overtaxed during the "catamenial function" (menstruation) (p. 48). Clarke feared for women's ruined health.

Clarke's book had a tremendous impact and was extensively used by opponents of women's education. Yet, its biological argument waned in favor of one of social undesirability (Gordon, 1979). Throughout the 1870s and 1880s, the discomfort surrounding changing gender roles was often expressed as a fear of "masculating" or "un-sexing" women, making them unfit for marriage. After the turn of the nineteenth century, a version of this argument resurfaced as the notion of "race suicide." Anxiety regarding acceptable sex roles combined with increasing xenophobia and anti-immigration sentiments and condemned women's education as grievously harmful to the larger society. College-educated women married later, if at all, and had fewer children than their less-educated contemporaries. Of course, the only "race" of concern in this argument was that of white, native-born, middle-class Americans (Gordon, 1990).

Yet another criticism emerged during the Progressive Era: coeducation was feminizing male students and even the institutions themselves. At the turn of the century, the popular press, reflecting society's preoccupation with feminization, encouraged American men to be more manly, athletic, and aggressive (Gordon, 1990). Some social commentators feared that increasing industrialization and urbanization were rendering men too soft, but other critics considered higher education the real culprit. They charged that coeducation was responsible for the loss of manly verve. The fact that such a charge conferred enormous power on women and depicted men in quite unfavorable terms seemed lost on the critics. Such criticism was, in fact, a response to the growing prevalence of coeducation, especially to the impressive academic success of women students (Rosenberg, 1982). For example, at the University of Chicago between 1892 and 1902, women earned 46% of the baccalaureate degrees but 56.3% of the Phi Beta Kappa keys (Gordon, 1979).

When the nineteenth century drew to a close, American higher education was profoundly different from what it had been just 50 years previously. As the mission, purpose, curriculum, and structure of universities had changed, the antagonism toward women's education took on new nuances. Within the academy, Americans passionately embraced science. The various scientific disciplines replaced classical study and philosophy as the pinnacle of the curriculum (Veysey, 1965). Clear gender distinctions emerged even within departments. One common division separated the theoretical (considered masculine) from the practical (feminine). Thus, a relatively new stereotype took hold—a belief that women were incapable of learning science and were skilled only in the humanities, languages, and possibly applied social sciences—which conveniently ignored the previously held and diametrically opposed belief.

Along with a zeal for science came an enthusiasm for all that was rational and empirical, with a concurrent disdain for the emotional and unscientific. Not surprisingly, the belief that men were rational while women were emotional reinforced the privileged status of men at the universities. "Feminized" became a demeaning epithet and prestige hierarchies of disciplines and professions were established which remain today. The professional schools of law, medicine, business, and divinity were dominated by male students with a social ethos that women did not belong. Universities hurried to add graduate and professional programs frequented by men and resisted those in the "feminized" occupations, encouraging four-year colleges to train the nurses, social workers, and teachers. At many universities, it was reasoned that establishing more male-oriented professional schools would increase the number of men on campus and elevate a coeducational university to the status of the all-male Ivy League. An economist at the University of Chicago summed up the thinking of the era in 1902:

> The congestion of numbers [of women students] is now largely due to the fact that the undergraduate courses are practically used by women as an advanced normal school to prepare for teaching. Just so soon as proper support and endowments are given to work which offers training for careers in engineering, railways, banking, trade and industry, law and medicine, etc. the disproportion of men will doubtless remedy itself. (Rosenberg, 1982, pp. 48–49)

The criticism leveled at coeducation spoke volumes about the changing nature of the relationship between higher education and the economy. As the twentieth century dawned, members of established professions were organizing, and members of nascent occupations were working hard to professionalize. Higher education became the gatekeeper to the professions and, consequently, the middle class (Bledstein, 1976). As more graduate schools opened and entry to high-status jobs depended less on family name, male students resented the places taken and honors won by women at the premier state universities. As higher education became associated with economic success, the privileged fought hard to limit broadening access (Barrow, 1992).

Despite this formidable collection of barriers, women's colleges were founded and other colleges and universities became coeducational, although usually spurred by a mixture of economic and pragmatic necessity, rather than any feminist sentiment. Morrill Act–funded colleges and their sister state institutions experienced serious financial pressures in their early years from the 1860s through the 1880s (Nevins, 1962; Rudolph, 1962). When it was discovered that families would pay tuition for daughters as well as for sons, colleges opened their doors to women, but often maintained their disdain. External economic demands also influenced the cause. At various times, the economy needed teachers or nurses, for example, and women's opportunities increased. Occasionally, coeducation resulted from a sense of fairness or even from the persuasive rhetoric of the early women's rights movement. Yet, as historian Lynn Gordon sardonically commented, colleges and universities were rarely "overwhelmed by egalitarian considerations" and, on the whole, did not admit women enthusiastically (1990, p. 21).

The resistance toward women's entry into higher education did not magically disappear once admission was granted. The legal barriers of exclusion proved easier to surmount than attitudinal ones, so resentment and prejudice lingered. But despite the social, political, ideological, and economic arguments against them, women successfully obtained educations. The early female academies provided the first opportunities. By the 1830s and 1840s, Oberlin and Antioch Colleges experimented with both coeducation and integrated education. After the Civil War, more women's colleges were founded and female students were admitted to many public universities, especially in the Midwest. By the turn of the twentieth century, women's participation in higher education was secured, but equality of treatment was an elusive goal. Early women administrators opened the first doors, and the second wave improved conditions for admitted students. The many women administrators who continue this battle today are their legacies.

REMEMBER THE LADIES

The intellectual and political fomentation surrounding the American Revolution, especially the conviction that all human beings were inherently rational, led some women to question their lack of educational opportunity. Abigail Adams exclaimed, "If you complain of neglect of Education in sons, what shall I say with regard to daughters, who every day experience the want of it?" and asked her husband, John, to please "remember the ladies" in the new political system being created (Solomon, 1985, p. 1). Other feminists such as Mercy Otis Warren, Judith Murray, and Mary Wollstonecraft agitated for more education and greater political participation and recognition for women (Solomon, 1985). Sadly, the revolutionary zeal that inspired the Founding Fathers to seek more freedom and opportunity for themselves and their sons did not extend to women.

There were a few eighteenth-century experiments with women's education. Timothy Dwight, sympathetic to the need for women's education, opened a small coeducational academy in Greenfield Hill, Connecticut in 1773. In 1797, the Young Ladies' Academy of Philadelphia, co-founded by Benjamin Rush, opened. Sarah Pierce began her "respectable academy" in Litchfield, Connecticut four years later. But women's higher education made little progress until the 1830s (Solomon, 1985).

Grudgingly, male educators accepted the idea of women's higher education, but narrowly, and only if it satisfied specific pragmatic or economic needs. One such need was "Republican Motherhood," an idea championed by Benjamin Rush. Rush believed women should be educated so they could, in turn, school their sons in ways judged advantageous by the leaders of the new Republic (Kerber, 1980). While Republican Motherhood may have been deemed noble, other issues were considered more urgent (Nash, 1997). The expansion of common (elementary) schooling produced a need for teachers at a time when a growing mercantilism gave young men new career opportunities that made teaching less attractive. The Second Great Awakening, a period of tremendous religious fervor, created a need for missionaries. These two developments only minimally expanded the edges of the female sphere because within them, women remained obedient Christians and nurturers of children (Solomon, 1985). This heritage permeated the academies and the curriculum remained overwhelmingly pious. However, it was a workable social contract—women found intellectual and professional fulfillment without violating social expectations and provided services that were genuinely needed, and society did not condemn them.

A more radical catalyst for women's education was the first women's movement. In the late 1830s and 1840s, Susan B. Anthony, Elizabeth Cady Stanton, and other women's rights advocates included women's education in the *Declaration of Sentiments* at the first Women's Rights Convention in Seneca Falls, New York in 1848 (Gurko, 1976). Although the social and political progressives of the 1840s asked women to put their educational aspirations on hold to concentrate on the more urgent issue of abolition, a few steadfast pioneers created academies for women.

All over the country, but especially in the northeast and south, these new women educators had different expectations for their students (Farnham, 1994). The principal leaders of the academy movement were Emma Willard, Catherine Beecher, Zilpah Grant, Mary Lyon, and Almira Phelps. As Barbara Solomon (1985) characterized them:

> Each in her own way appeared to accept the social constraints placed on women and yet drew on Enlightenment republican thought and on evangelical sentiment to enlarge the scope of women's higher education. Women, pioneering in new roles, founded schools where the female student became the focus of academic purpose. (p. 17)

Emma Willard's Troy Seminary (1821) in upstate New York and Mary Lyon's Mount Holyoke Seminary (1837) in western Massachusetts exemplify the movement. The early curriculum created by the founding presidents was as demanding as many of the other antebellum colleges for men, especially in the sciences. The academies often emphasized intellectual accomplishment, teacher training, and self-reliance for students. A considerable number of presidents' administrative duties and responsibilities would be familiar to college presidents today. The founders had to generate political support for their schools, raise funds, market the colleges, handle admissions, design the curricula, discipline students, hire, control, and fire the faculty members, deal with community leaders, and fend off antagonists. The majority of these academies closed and became teachers' colleges or even secondary schools. The exception was Mount Holyoke, which emerged after the Civil War as one of the eastern, elite, women's liberal arts colleges known as the "Seven Sisters."

The latter half of the nineteenth century was a critical era in American higher education. Strong undergraduate colleges and academies matured, offering more sophisticated curricula and becoming the liberal arts colleges of today. Other institutions added graduate training and metamorphosed into research universities. Simultaneously, higher education diversified—before the century was over, separate colleges had been created for African Americans, future teachers or engineers, and women.

A PLACE FOR WOMEN

Historian Geraldine Clifford (1989) commented on the historical correlation between the number of women students attending an institution and the number of adult women employed there. In coeducational institutions, women faculty were most frequently found in "women's" departments such as education, social work, or home economics. Women rarely became senior administrators except when charged to care for women students in roles such as physical educators, doctors, or deans of women. However, the women's colleges offered new opportunities. Several of the single-sex institutions hired women faculty in many disciplines and in administrative positions at various levels, including president.

Today, women's colleges are found in every region of the country. They range in quality, target population (historically African American or predominantly white), and affiliation (either sectarian, especially Catholic, or independent) (Harwarth, Maline, & DeBra, 1997). In the nineteenth century women's colleges were most common in the Northeast. In comparison, Southern higher education was often single-sex, but lagged behind the North in the number of students enrolled, while the Midwest was dominated by coeducation. The most well known of the prestigious Northeastern colleges were the Seven Sisters—Mount Holyoke (1837), Vassar (1865), Smith (1875), Wellesley (1875), Bryn Mawr (1884), and the coordinate colleges of Barnard (1889) and Radcliffe (1894). Of these, Wellesley and Bryn Mawr were led by women presidents early in their history.

Alice Freeman of Wellesley and M. Carey Thomas of Bryn Mawr personified women's administrative authority at the turn of the century (Bordin, 1993; Brown, 2001; Horowitz, 1984, 1994). As Cynthia F. Brown (2001) noted, their leadership was fraught with symbolism and potential for future women leaders. Both women had to reconcile notions of the "old woman" (pious, domestic, subservient) with the "new woman" (intellectual, accomplished, public) in ways that placated conservative members of the community while pushing their vision of the college forward. They had to attract and please male mentors and benefactors, support and encourage women faculty, and provide women students with quality education. Brown argues that Freeman, who became president of Wellesley in 1881, was more successful at this balancing act than Thomas, whose passion and strong-headedness frightened and alienated many conservative critics (see also Horowitz, 1994). Freeman's personal style was more accommodating and her board of trustees was less antagonistic than the board of trustees at Bryn Mawr. Thanks to Freeman's persistence in "challenging the waning tenets of Victorian culture and suggesting ways that old and new woman could merge identities," Brown states, "the 'girl president' successfully liberalized curriculum, college life, and faculty expectations" (2001, p. 40). Yet, despite their different personal styles, both leaders created strong women's colleges with clear, intellectual missions.

Catholic women's colleges represented another type of single-sex institutions at the turn of the century. Between 1896 and 1918, fourteen Catholic women's colleges opened their doors (Introcaso, 2001). Unlike their independent counterparts, Catholic women's colleges expected female leadership from the founding religious order. But the women religious who ran the colleges faced several dilemmas. First, leaders of these institutions had to decide how "Catholic" the curriculum would be. In other words, would they model Vassar, or become an extension of Catholic secondary education? Second, these leaders had to reconcile social attitudes about women, as well as church views on women's authority, with their own sense of ambition and mission for the colleges (Brown, 2001).

Whether in Catholic or independent colleges, the pioneering women presidents "confronted the task of aligning social, personal, and intellectual expectations for their young institutions" (Brown, 2001, p. 56). At times, this meant challenging such formidable foes as the cultural ideas about the place of women and the centrality of religion. Although the majority of American women today choose coeducational environments, the women's colleges played a critical role in the history of women's education. Only at these colleges was women's intellectuality a foregone conclusion, and only there did women assume senior administrative authority before the latter half of the twentieth century.

"CO"-EDUCATION IS NOT "EQUAL" EDUCATION

Single-sex colleges offered students an environment in which the intellectual capacity of women was assumed rather than doubted, yet these institutions were too few in number to educate all women who wanted a college degree. Even among the so-called "first generation" women (those attending college between 1870 and 1890; see Solomon, 1985), coeducation was the more popular choice. Out of all 18–21 year old women in the U.S. during this era, only

2.2% went to college. However, among all college students, women comprised 35% of those enrolled. Slightly over 70% of all first-generation students were in coeducational institutions (Newcomer, 1959, p. 46).

Today the climate of coeducational campuses is described as "chilly" for women (Sandler, Silverberg, & Hall, 1996). By comparison, the climate in the late nineteenth century was downright frigid. Many male professors, administrators, and students were openly hostile (Gordon, 1990). Male students made it difficult for women to enter their preserve. Photographs of lecture halls of the era reveal a pattern of strict gender segregation (Rosenberg, 1988). Women were ridiculed under the guise of humor as misogynistic cartoons and stories filled campus newspapers, literary magazines, and yearbooks. "Coeds," as they came to be called, were excluded from clubs, dining halls, music groups, honorary societies, and most activities associated with campus prestige (Gordon, 1979).

This antagonism toward women students was tangibly manifested in the inequitable distribution of resources that universities bestowed on them. In general, coeducational universities did not provide women with housing, medical care, or physical education facilities, despite the fact that such facilities existed for men by the 1870s. Access to a gymnasium was considered especially important because of the concerns regarding the health and fitness of women students. Ordinarily, universities barred women from the gyms initially and then gradually relented to granting limited access because of pressure applied by women students and their allies. However, the access granted was often at times assumed less desirable by men, during the dinner hour, for example. Antagonism toward women students was also apparent in the extreme paucity of scholarship money available to women. In response, local club women, YWCA members, and faculty wives raised money for scholarships and other, nonacademic needs (Nidiffer, 2000; Solomon, 1985). But the capacity of local club women to make permanent changes at the universities was limited. Instead, two new types of administrators took it upon themselves to improve the academic, material, and physical well being of women students: physical educators and deans of women.

One cadre of new administrators were the physical educators. Male college administrators were quite nervous about the "dangerous experiment" (McGuigan, 1970) of coeducation, particularly with respect to women's health. They engaged the services of physical educators or female doctors to ensure that college did not ruin the students' health. The first physical educators usually had teaching duties in addition to their administrative responsibilities, but were rarely afforded full academic rank. Commonly, these women combined teaching gymnastics or physical culture with history, English composition, Latin, or elocution. Physical education teachers also served as registrars, librarians, or the presidential assistants (Paul, 2001). They faced many obstacles, the most pervasive being the lack of academic respect and sneers of other educators who believed physical training was antithetical to mental training. They also dealt with seriously inadequate facilities, the controversy over gymnasium costumes, and the stigma of masculinity (Paul, 2001).

Regardless, these women were dedicated to overseeing students and directing their conduct. As historian Joan Paul (2001) noted:

> Some of the most powerful and dominant women in education were the physical educators. . . . From the time they entered the halls of academia, they assumed responsibility for their young female charges by governing almost every aspect of their lives. Out of concern for their physical well-being, they supervised their women students' diets, the amount of rest they received, regulated their exercise, monitored their weight, and worked to improve their posture. . . . [The physical educators also] monitored [students'] behavior in and out of class, prescribed proper dress, neatness, and cleanliness. . . . Health, as the perceived outcome, was an encompassing notion that comprised physical, mental, and social behavior. From mid-nineteenth to mid-twentieth century, these women educators were strong agents of social control in their perceived role as the guardians of women's health. (p. 183–184)

These early women leaders dramatically shaped the higher education environments and experiences available to women.

The second group of early administrators on coeducational campuses were deans of women. The position of dean of women is intriguing because it was the first systemic, administrative response in higher education to cope with a new, and essentially unwelcome, population (Nidiffer, 2001a). Deans of women were initially employed in the first coeducational colleges of the 1830s and 1840s: Oberlin and Antioch. Propriety required the close supervision of unmarried young women. The president and faculty quickly recognized such "problems which demanded the presence and supervision of an older woman" (Holmes, 1939, p. 109). The first woman administrator in a coeducational college was Mrs. Marianne Parker Dascom of Oberlin, who held the title of "Lady Principal of the Female Department" (Kehr, 1938, p. 6).

By the late 1880s, however, the growing concern about coeducation at the newly expanding universities changed the nature of the nascent profession of deans of women. At a few universities, women students, their parents, and occasionally community members, insisted the universities offer some living arrangements for the women students. Without supervised housing, middle-class parents and families who lived long distances from the campuses expressed reluctance to send daughters to college (Gordon, 1990). Instead of hiring dormitory matrons as the early colleges had, the universities of the late nineteenth century began hiring professional deans of women. The first and most influential of these women was Marion Talbot of the University of Chicago, who left Boston for the "woolly" West in 1892 (Talbot, 1936).

Talbot was influential for myriad reasons. First, Chicago at the turn of the century was a vibrant and exciting community, especially for women interested in the emerging field of settlement work, the forerunner of modern social work. Talbot linked the students with interesting women such as Jane Addams of Hull House, and assembled a broad intellectual community. As a result, other deans interested in improving the academic life and job prospects of women students looked to Talbot as a model. Second, Talbot was a born organizer and gathered her fellow deans for a meeting in 1903. This Conference of Deans of the Middle West was the first professional meeting for women college administrators. Third, Talbot was a social scientist of some note and helped lay the intellectual foundation on which the work of pioneering deans rested. In her book, *The Education of Women,* Talbot (1910) stated unequivocally, "women have proved their ability to enter every realm of knowledge. They must have the right to do it. . . . Unhampered by traditions of sex, women will naturally and without comment seek the intellectual goal which they think good and fit" (p. 22). She used her academic training to document the success of women at the university, refusing to let women's accomplishments go unnoticed (Fitzpatrick, 1989).

Following Talbot's lead, deans of women at Berkeley, Cornell, Indiana, Minnesota, Michigan, and Wisconsin developed a raison d'être—to improve the material and intellectual experience of women on campus. To do so, they created career centers and job opportunity fairs, and introduced students to professional women in the community. The deans built women's centers, instituted innumerable programs for social and academic enrichment, and agitated for adequate on-campus housing. They also helped women learn valuable skills for post-college success such as leadership and supervision, and how to develop a sense of community. The deans were disciplinarians and were sometimes at odds with their charges, but the student diaries and records that survive indicate these women made life at coeducational universities bearable (Nidiffer, 2000).

MAKING ADMINISTRATION A PROFESSION

By the early twentieth century, a symbiotic relationship between universities and the middle class solidified (Bledstein, 1976). American faith in science as a remedy for medical *and* social ills created a growing dependence on, and respect for, expertise. The moniker "professional" came to describe members of selected occupations who were entrusted to care for their "clients." As Burton Bledstein described, professionals were endowed with middle-class status (and the resulting economic security) and universities became the gatekeepers. The alliance of the middle class, the professions, and the universities proved powerful and appealing. Numerous occupations struggled to gain the attributes of a profession, including the emerging field of university administration (Hawkins,

1992). For women, it was the deans who took the first steps toward professionalization (Nidiffer, 2000).

By the early twentieth century, a sense of what comprised a "profession" emerged. In general, professions had a unique and significant niche of expertise, based on an identifiable knowledge base. Members were responsible for policing the profession, usually through the auspices of a professional organization. These organizations maintained standards, issued or revoked licenses, enforced codes of ethics, lobbied for practitioner benefits, and negotiated with universities to train aspirants (Nidiffer, 2000). As a result, professional organizations had significant control over the supply and demand for professionals and the consequent remuneration and status of practitioners. The quintessential model was the relationship between the American Medical Association and the nation's medical schools. Professionalism, with its implied expertise and authority, also indicated a dedication to one's profession above all else—an ethos that violated the family-first expectations placed on women. Thus, women faced the additional burden of either exclusion from professions or gender-role conflict if they participated (Antler, 1977).

The early deans sought to create a profession of university administration for women. In this effort, Marion Talbot was especially pivotal. After convening the first conference of deans in 1903, she oversaw the continuation of these meetings on a biennial basis. Additionally, she helped define the intellectual foundation for deaning in her 1910 book, *The Education of Women*. On the eve of World War I, Lois Mathews of the University of Wisconsin added two other elements by teaching courses designed to introduce aspiring women to the profession of university administration and writing the first book exclusively for the profession, *The Dean of Women* (1915). What the deans of women did not have was a formal organization. Instead, the early deans at the Midwestern universities were meeting at their conferences and joining the conferences of the Association of Collegiate Alumnae (ACA).

In the summer of 1915, Kathryn Sisson McLean, dean of women at State Teachers College, Chadron, Nebraska, initiated an informal discussion among deans of women who were taking graduate courses at Teachers College, Columbia University. McLean and her colleagues realized that

> neither professional training, while essential, nor informal professional organizations such as the Conference of Deans of Women, while valuable, could foster national connections among deans of women. To achieve this end, the profession needed an official professional society which served deans of women across the country. (Bashaw, 2001a, p. 163)

In the summer of 1916, McLean learned that the National Education Association was holding its annual meeting in New York City and asked that the

Teachers College graduate students be allowed to hold an organizational meeting for deans of women. NEA officials agreed and the National Association of Deans of Women (NADW) was born (Bashaw, 2001a).

During the 1920s the nature of these organizations changed, but the overlapping memberships and the web of interconnection persisted. The biennial conferences of deans continued until 1922, when they became a division of the NADW. NADW established permanent headquarters in Washington, D.C. in 1926. The ACA merged with the Southern Association of Collegiate Alumnae in 1921 to form the American Association of University Women (AAUW), the "most long-lived, significant, and complex" of women's organizations (Bashaw, 2001b, p. 250). Both organizations provided women with professional support when many of the other organizations for university administrators ignored or prohibited women's participation. However, their support was granted only to white women. Because of racist attitudes and practices, African American professionals were forced to form a parallel structure.

A relatively small number of African American students were educated in northern institutions prior to the mid-twentieth century; most attended Historically Black Colleges and Universities (HBCUs). Analogous to the experience of women at male-dominated colleges, African American professionals had few opportunities at predominantly white institutions. The first African American dean of women, Lucy Diggs Slowe, worked at Howard University (Anderson, 1989). From the beginning of her career in 1922, Slowe defined herself as an expert in women's education, not a matron. Like her pioneering white counterparts, Slowe was dedicated to making a viable women's community on Howard's campus. In 1924, she became the first president of the National Association of College Women (NACW), an organization for African American women that closely paralleled the AAUW whose restrictive practices made most African American women ineligible for membership. Eventually, the NACW became the National Association of University Women. It merged in 1954 with the National Association of Personnel Deans of Negro Educational Institutions, an organization for both men and women (Davis & Bell-Scott, 1989).

In 1922, Slowe became the first African American woman to join the NADW. The NADW did not formally exclude African American women from membership, but their practices effectively eliminated participation. The NADW often held their annual meetings in restrictive hotels so African American women were neither accommodated nor served meals. Slowe protested, but the NADW did not change. In response, she gathered her African American peers at a Conference of Deans and Advisors of Women on Howard's campus in 1929. The Conference was run under the auspices of the Standards Committee of the NACW until 1935, when it became an organization in its own right, the Association of Deans of Women and Advisers to Girls in Negro Schools (ADWAGNS). Slowe provided vital leadership from the first Conference in 1929 until her death in 1937 (Anderson, 1989; Davis &

Bell-Scott, 1989). Not until the late 1960s and early 1970s did slightly greater numbers of African American women hold administrative positions in predominantly white institutions and gain, for the first time, leadership positions in the NADW (Nidiffer, 2000).

The NADW and the AAUW sustained white professional administrators throughout the Depression years and war years, but the ensuing years brought considerable change to both groups. The Supreme Court decision of *Brown v. Board of Education of Topeka Kansas* resulted in some integration of the groups. Two other, coeducational organizations dedicated to student affairs became more central to the profession, especially the American College Personnel Association (ACPA) and the National Association of Student Personnel Administrators (NASPA—the outgrowth of the first organization for deans of men, NADM). Women were also achieving limited recognition in organizations for other types of professionals (such as admission officers or registrars) and feminist activists questioned the necessity of single-sex organizations (Bashaw, 2001b). And finally, women students, several student affairs professionals, and other senior administrators were suggesting that deans of women were not essential, perhaps even anachronistic (Nidiffer, 2000).

In response, the NADW broadened the types of professionals it served and changed its name accordingly. In 1956, it became the National Association of Women Deans and Counselors (NAWDC); in 1973, the National Association of Women Deans, Administrators, and Counselors (NAWDAC); and finally in 1991, the National Association for Women in Education (NAWE). However, it was unable to recapture its position as the leading professional organization for women administrators. Sadly, the NAWE closed its doors completely in 1999.

THE NEW WOMEN ON CAMPUS

Perhaps the struggle of whether to pursue separate or integrated structures was most obvious in the domain of women's athletics. Physiology may always dictate a certain amount of separation between male and female sports, but inequities in resources and opportunities for women athletic administrators have more to do with gender bias than sex differences.

Linda Carpenter and Vivian Acosta (2001) discussed the catalyst for a separate women's athletic organization in a recent essay. They noted:

> in the 1950s and 1960s intercollegiate competition for women was informal and predominantly social. . . . No championships were held, and colleges provided little, if any, support. Female physical educators volunteered as coaches, . . . athletes bought their own uniforms, packed brown bag lunches, and paid their own transportation and motel bills. (p. 209)

Women athletes and coaches looked to amateur sports groups for help, but soon realized that a formal organization was needed. Yet, the female athletic administrators were worried about following the male model, with its inherent flaws (Carpenter & Acosta, 2001). So, in 1966, the Division of Girls and Women in Sport (DGWD), part of the former American Association for Health and Recreation, created the Commission on Intercollegiate Athletics for Women (CIAW).

CIAW's primary purpose was "to sanction intercollegiate athletic events and to establish, conduct, and promote national championships for women" (Carpenter & Acosta, 2001, p. 210). The CIAW was replaced by the Association for Intercollegiate Athletics for Women (AIAW) in October, 1971 in a move to improve the financial backing of women's sports. By design, the AIAW was different and, in the minds of the participating women, better than the male-dominated NCAA (Carpenter & Acosta, 2001). Women of AIAW worked for the passage of Title IX, the 1972 civil rights legislation, which states that women shall not be denied participation in, or the benefits of, educational programs receiving federal assistance.

The NCAA initially fought to exclude athletics from the purview of Title IX. Then, after losing that battle, fought to exclude "revenue" sports such as men's basketball and football. The courts voted against the NCAA, but it was a Pyrrhic victory for women. Deciding its interests were best served by incorporating women's athletics under its auspices, the NCAA pushed to eliminate the AIAW and encouraged institutions to subsume women's sports under the control of the existing athletic director. The result was a staggering loss of jobs for women who had served as coaches and directors of separate women's athletic programs. To date, the losses have not been recouped and the majority of new hires in women's athletics are men (Carpenter & Acosta, 2001).

In other administrative positions, women tend to compete in any venue, not only in single-sex settings. In the first study of its kind, Karen Doyle Walton and Sharon McDade (2001) surveyed women Chief Academic Officers (CAOs). The CAO position is important on its own, but as an acknowledged stepping stone to a presidency, it is key to women's advancement. Walton and McDade found that women occupy approximately 15% of all CAO positions. Of those, most female CAOs preside at baccalaureate and liberal arts colleges (37%), while slightly fewer than 13% serve at Research I or II universities— about the same percentage who work at women's colleges. Like most other administrative positions, more white women serve than women of color and the salaries of women CAOs are lower than men's. Although these data are disheartening, they represent a significant increase from just twenty years ago.

Women account for approximately 16% of all college presidents or CEOs. Women presidents least often lead elite research universities and are generally paid less than male presidents (American Council on Education, 1998; Touchton, Shavlik, & Davis, 1993; Walton, 1996). Women presidents may belong to a host of institutional, professional, or even discipline-based organizations that are coeducational. Yet, in 1990 the Office of Women in Higher Education sponsored a single-sex group that provides a forum for discussing the issues unique to women presidents (Nidiffer, 2001c).

As the new millennium dawns, it is time to refocus the efforts of all administrators in higher education. Rather than asking whether women are better served in single-sex or coeducational (but male-dominated) structures, it is time to make more concerted efforts to thwart the sexism that makes women-only spaces so necessary. It is also time to reframe the question. We no longer should assume that the traditional, male-oriented nature of institutions is the norm to which women must respond.

CONCLUSION

What is the historical legacy of women administrators? These pioneers combined tenacious activism and savvy pragmatism to attain genuine access to a full college life for women students and, in the process, created professional opportunities for themselves (Bashaw & Nidiffer, 2001). They identified opportunities and pursued them. They founded secular and religious women's colleges; they helped students on coeducational campuses find opportunities and acceptance; they demanded that colleges enforce gender-equity legislation. They attended to women's health, material well-being, and intellectual growth. And they proved to a skeptical society that women are capable leaders and managers.

From the pioneers of post-revolutionary America to the presidents of major universities today, women administrators have accepted the challenges of creating institutions, ensuring access, and easing the way for women. In many ways, they have redefined women's higher education. These women were administrators, but more important, they were educators, reformers, and fighters, whose actions provide guidance to enable positive change in higher education.

NOTE

I wish to thank my co-editor and colleague, Carolyn Terry Bashaw, and SUNY Press for their support with making references to material from *Women Administrators in Higher Education: Historical and Contemporary Perspectives*. I also wish to thank the contributors to that volume for their insights and information.

REFERENCES

American Council on Education. (1998). *The American college president: A 1998 edition*. Washington, DC: ACE.

Anderson, K. (1989). Brickbats and roses: Lucy Diggs Slowe, 1883–1937. In G. J. Clifford (Ed.) *Lone voyagers: Academic women in coeducational universities, 1870–1937* (pp. 281–307). New York: Feminist Press.

Antler, J. (1977). *The educated woman and professionalization: The struggle for a new feminine identity, 1890–1920.* Unpublished doctoral dissertation, State University of New York at Stony Brook.

Barrow, C. W. (1992). *Universities and the capitalist state: Corporate liberalism and the reconstruction of American higher education, 1894–1928.* Madison: University of Wisconsin Press.

Bashaw, C. T. (2001a). "Reassessment and Redefinition": The NAWDC and higher education for women. In J. Nidiffer & C. T. Bashaw (Eds.) *Women administrators in higher education: Historical and contemporary perspectives* (pp. 157–182). Albany: State University of New York Press.

Bashaw, C. T. (2001b). "To Serve the Needs of Women": The AAUW, NAWDC and persistence of academic women's support networks. In J. Nidiffer & C. T. Bashaw (Eds.) *Women administrators in higher education: Historical and contemporary perspectives* (pp. 249–270). Albany: State University of New York Press.

Bashaw, C. T., & Nidiffer, J. (2001). Women administrators in higher education today and in the future. In J. Nidiffer & C. T. Bashaw (Eds.), *Women administrators in higher education: Historical and contemporary perspectives* (pp. 271–278). Albany: State University of New York Press.

Bledstein, B. J. (1976). *The culture of professionalism: The middle class and the development of higher education in America.* New York: Norton.

Bordin, R. (1993). *Alice Freeman Palmer: The evolution of a new woman.* Ann Arbor, University of Michigan Press.

Brown, C. F. (2001). Patterns of leadership: The impact of female authority in four women's colleges. In J. Nidiffer & C. T. Bashaw (Eds.) *Women administrators in higher education: Historical and contemporary perspectives* (pp. 37–66). Albany: State University of New York Press.

Carpenter, L. J., & Acosta, V. (2001). Let her swim and climb mountain peaks: Self-sacrifice and success in expanding athletic programs for women. In J. Nidiffer & C. T. Bashaw (Eds.) *Women administrators in higher education: Historical and contemporary perspectives* (pp. 207–230). Albany: State University of New York Press.

Clarke, E. H. (1873). *Sex in education: Or, a fair chance for the girls.* Boston: James R. Osgood.

Clifford, G. J. (Ed.) (1989). *Lone voyagers: Academic women in coeducational institutions, 1870–1937.* New York: Feminist Press.

Davis, H. A., & Bell-Scott, P. (1989, Summer). The Association of Deans of Women and Advisers to Girls in Negro Schools, 1929–1954: A brief oral history. *Sage, 6,* 40–44.

Farnham, C. (1994). *Education of a southern belle.* New York: New York University Press.

Fitzpatrick, E. (1989). For the "Women of the university": Marion Talbot, 1858–1948. In G. J. Clifford (Ed.) *Lone voyagers: Academic women in coeducational universities, 1870–1937* (pp. 85–124). New York: Feminist Press.

Gordon, L. D. (1979). Co-education on two campuses: Berkeley and Chicago, 1890–1912. In M. Kelley (Ed.) *Woman's being, woman's place: Female identity and vocation in American history* (pp. 171–193). Boston: Hall.

Gordon, L. D. (1990). *Gender and higher education in the Progressive Era.* New Haven: Yale University Press.

Gurko, M. (1976). *The ladies of Seneca Falls: The birth of the woman's rights movement.* New York: Schocken Books.

Harwarth, I., Maline, M., & DeBra, E. (1997). *Women's colleges in the United States: History, issues, and challenges.* Washington, DC: National Institute on Postsecondary Education, Libraries, and Lifelong Learning, U.S. Department of Education.

Hawkins, H. (1992). *Banding together: The rise of national associations in American higher education, 1887–1950.* Baltimore: Johns Hopkins University Press.

Holmes, L. (1939). *A history of the position of dean of women in a selected group of co-educational colleges and universities in the United States.* New York: Teachers College, Columbia University, Bureau of Publications.

Horowitz, H. L. (1984). *Alma mater: Design and experience in the women's colleges from their nineteenth century beginnings to the 1950s.* New York: Knopf.

Horowitz, H. L. (1994). *The power and passion of M. Carey Thomas.* New York: Knopf.

Introcaso, C. (2001). Determination in leadership: Pioneering Roman Catholic women presidents. In J. Nidiffer & C. T. Bashaw (Eds.) *Women administrators in higher education: Historical and contemporary perspectives* (pp. 67–84). Albany: State University of New York Press.

Kehr, M. (1938, January). The pioneer days of the dean of women. *The Journal of the National Education Association, 27,* 6–7.

Kerber, L. (1980). *Women of the republic: Intellect and ideology in revolutionary America.* Chapel Hill: University of North Carolina Press.

Mathews, L. K. (1915). *The dean of women.* Boston: Houghton Mifflin.

McCandless, A. T. (1999). *The past in the present: Women's higher education in the twentieth century American south.* Tuscaloosa: University of Alabama Press.

McGuigan, D. G. (1970). *A dangerous experiment: 100 years of women at the University of Michigan.* Ann Arbor: Center for the Continuing Education of Women.

Nash, M. (1997). Rethinking Republican Motherhood: Benjamin Rush and the Young Ladies' Academy of Philadelphia. *Journal of the Early Republic, 17(2),* 171–191.

Nevins, A. (1962). *The state universities and democracy.* Urbana: University of Illinois Press.

Newcomer, M. (1959). *A century of higher education for American women.* New York: Harper & Row.

Nidiffer, J. (2000). *Pioneering deans of women: More than wise and pious matrons.* New York: Teachers College Press.

Nidiffer, J. (2001a). Advocates on campus: Deans of women create a new profession. In J. Nidiffer & C. T. Bashaw (Eds.) *Women administrators in higher education: Historical and contemporary perspectives* (pp. 135–156). Albany: State University of New York Press.

Nidiffer, J. (2001b). Crumbs from the boy's table: The first century of coeducation. In J. Nidiffer & C. T. Bashaw (Eds.) *Women administrators in higher education: Historical and contemporary perspectives* (pp. 13–36). Albany: State University of New York Press.

Nidiffer, J. (2001c). New leadership for a new century: Women's contribution to leadership in higher education. In J. Nidiffer & C. T. Bashaw (Eds.) *Women administrators in higher education: Historical and contemporary perspectives* (pp. 101–134). Albany: State University of New York Press.

Nidiffer, J. & Bashaw, C. T. (Eds.). (2001). *Women administrators in higher education: Historical and contemporary perspectives.* Albany: State University of New York Press.

Paul, J. (2001). Agents of social control: The role of physical educators as guardians of women's health, 1860–1960. In J. Nidiffer & C. T. Bashaw (Eds.) *Women administrators in higher education: Historical and contemporary perspectives* (pp. 183–206). Albany: State University of New York Press.

Rosenberg, R. (1982). *Beyond separate spheres: The intellectual roots of modern feminism.* New Haven: Yale University Press.

Rosenberg, R. (1988). The limits of access: The history of coeducation in America. In J. M. Faragher & F. Howe (Eds.) *Women and higher education in American history* (pp. 107–129). New York: Norton.

Rudolph, F. (1962). *The American college and university: A history.* New York: Knopf.

Sandler, B. R., Silverberg, L. A., & Hall, R. M. (1996). *The chilly climate: A guide to improve the education of women.* Washington, DC: National Association for Women in Education.

Shmurak, C. B., & Handler, B. S. (1992). "Castle of Science": Mount Holyoke College and the preparation of women in chemistry. *History of Education Quarterly, 32(3),* 315–342.

Solomon, B. M. (1985). *In the company of educated women.* New Haven: Yale University Press.

Talbot, M. (1910). *The education of women.* Chicago: University of Chicago Press.

Talbot, M. (1936). *More than lore: Reminiscences of Marion Talbot.* Chicago: University of Chicago Press.

Tolley, K. (1996). Science for ladies, classics for gentlemen: A comparative analysis of scientific subjects in the curricula of boys and girls secondary schools in the United States, 1794–1850. *History of Education Quarterly, 36(2),* 129–154.

Touchton, J., Shavlik, D. & Davis, L. (1993). *Women in presidencies: A descriptive study of women college and university presidencies.* Washington, DC: ACE, OWHE.

Veysey, L. R. (1965). *The emergence of the American university.* Chicago: University of Chicago Press.

Walton, K. D. (1996). *Against the tide: Career paths of women leaders in American and British higher education.* Bloomington, IN: Phi Delta Kappa Educational Foundation.

Walton, K. D., & McDade, S. A. (2001). At the top of the faculty: Women as chief academic officers. In J. Nidiffer & C. T. Bashaw (Eds.) *Women administrators in higher education: Historical and contemporary perspectives* (pp. 85–100). Albany: State University of New York Press.

Welter, B. (1976). *Dimity convictions: The American woman in the nineteenth century.* Athens: Ohio University Press.

2

Gender and Higher Education

What Should We Learn from Women's Colleges?

Lisa Wolf-Wendel

In the last decades of the twentieth century, women have made great progress in higher education. They have achieved majority status on most college and university campuses, they are increasingly earning graduate degrees in a variety of fields, and they are gradually attaining positions within the ranks of the faculty and within the administrative lattice of many institutions of higher education. Concurrent with this progress has been a shift from single-sex education to coeducation, which began in earnest in the 1960s and the 1970s. During this time period, the most prestigious exclusively male colleges and universities began to admit women, many women's colleges also became coeducational, and many of the women's colleges that decided not to admit men closed due to financial exigency. As a result, the number of women's colleges, which peaked at approximately 300 institutions in 1960, declined to fewer than 80 institutions by 1999 (National Center for Education Statistics, 1999).

Today, women's colleges educate fewer than one percent of all women attending post-secondary institutions and award one percent of all degrees conferred, approximately 25,000 degrees in 1998 (National Center for Education Statistics, 1999). Although these numbers are quite small, the future importance of women's colleges outweighs these figures. Indeed, the women's colleges that maintained their mission to educate women students serve as models to other institutions, in terms of their resilience as well as in terms of the outcomes their graduates have achieved.

The goal of this chapter is to describe what we can learn from the successes of women's colleges to better support the teaching and learning experiences of women. In doing so, this chapter will not argue that women's colleges are better than coeducational institutions, or that all women would be best served by attending a single-sex institution. Instead, the chapter will demonstrate the ways in which women's colleges can serve as models to other institutions for how to take women seriously. Further, this chapter suggests that although a move toward coeducation has provided women with greater access to education, the critical issue to examine in the future is the quality of that access.

WHAT ARE THE CHARACTERISTICS OF TODAY'S WOMEN'S COLLEGES?

Today, there are approximately 80 women's colleges still in existence. These institutions tend to be small, ranging in size from 94 full-time students to 5,000 full-time students. While women's colleges are private institutions, more than half of the existing women's colleges have a religious affiliation, most often with the Catholic Church (33%). In terms of geographic location, almost half of the women's colleges are located in the northeastern United States, while 33% are located in the South (Harwarth, Maline, & DeBra, 1997). There are three women's colleges in California, and the rest are scattered around the country.

While the most selective women's colleges, those known as the "Seven Sisters,"[1] receive the most attention in the media and in the research literature, women's colleges represent a diverse array of institutions. For example, women's colleges include two historically black institutions and six two-year institutions. In addition, women's colleges represent four of the Carnegie Classifications of Institutions of Higher Education.[2] In one category (Baccalaureate I), 18 four-year women's colleges enrolled 20,700 students, 16% of all women in that category. These institutions enrolled a higher proportion of nontraditional-aged students, part-time students, African Americans, Hispanics, Asians, and nonresident aliens compared to coeducational institutions in this category. Additionally, women's colleges awarded a higher proportion of bachelor's degrees to women in the fields of mathematics, computer sciences and physical sciences when compared with coeducational institutions in this category (Harwarth, Maline, & DeBra, 1997).

There are 29 Baccalaureate Granting II institutions classified as women's colleges; these institutions represent eight percent of the institutions in this category. These women's colleges enrolled 29,500 students in fall 1993, which represents 10% of the total female undergraduate enrollment at institutions of this kind. As with the Baccalaureate I institutions, women's colleges enroll a higher proportion of female undergraduates over the age of 25, and more Asian female undergraduates. They also award a higher proportion of bachelor's degrees in the following areas: agricultural sciences, communications, psychology, public administration, social sciences, health professions, and visual and performing arts compared to comparable coeducational institutions (Harwarth, Maline, & DeBra, 1997).

Thirteen women's colleges are classified as Master's Granting I institutions, representing seven percent of the 182 institutions in this category. The women's colleges in this category enroll 20,300 students, or seven percent of the female students in this category. Again, the women's colleges enroll a higher proportion of nontraditional-aged students and black women than do comparable institutions. The women's colleges in this category grant a higher proportion of degrees in mathematics, education, health home economics, liberal arts, biological sciences, public administration, social sciences and history, and visual arts than their coeducational counterparts (Harwarth, Maline, & DeBra, 1997).

Finally, there are four women's colleges classified as Master's Granting II institutions, representing six percent of the institutions in this classification. The women's colleges in this category enroll 6,500 undergraduates, or eight percent of the women undergraduates in this category. As with other institutional types, the women's colleges in this category enroll higher percentages of women over the age of 25, a higher percentage of African American and Asian American students, and a higher proportion of part-time students than comparable coeducational institutions. In addition, the women's colleges grant a higher proportion of degrees to women in the fields of sciences, English language, health, and public administration than comparable coeducational institutions (Harwarth, Maline, & DeBra, 1997).

Although women's colleges do not represent a single mold, they do share some common traits. Women's colleges, for example, seem to serve women of color and nontraditional-aged women in higher proportions than comparable coeducational institutions (National Center for Education Statistics, 1999). The explanation for this is twofold. First, serving women, in all their diversity, is a major component of the mission of many women's colleges. Second, for the existing women's colleges to survive with their original missions still intact, many had to be creative in attracting and retaining women students. Because fewer than five percent of high school women will even consider applying to a women's college, this means that many women's colleges have had to focus their attention on attracting older women, part-time students, and transfer students (Tidball, Smith, Tidball, & Wolf-Wendel, 1999). It is also clear that women's colleges are more likely than their coeducational counterparts to grant undergraduate degrees to women in the more male-dominated fields compared to similar coeducational institutions.

ARE WOMEN'S COLLEGES REALLY STILL NECESSARY?

To many, the replacement of single-sex education with coeducation was seen as part of women's attainment of equality with men. In fact, many believe that the shift away from single-sex institutions to coeducational ones served both sexes better. According to Lasser (1987), "advocates and critics alike unquestioningly held equal education for women and men to be synonymous with coeducation" (p. 2). Indeed, many people are uncomfortable with the idea that separate education may be better for women than coeducation. Pundits argue, for example, that people could use information about the contribution of women's colleges as a way to hurt the status of women (Talbot, 1994). Specifically, they argue that if one believes that women should attend women's colleges, it somehow implies that women are different from or inferior to men. Others argue that women who attend single-sex institutions do not learn to deal with men and are therefore less ready to compete and function in the "real world." These arguments, however, are based in part on the assumption that coeducation means that men and women have the same or at least comparable experiences when they enroll at the same institutions.

As more institutions have become coeducational, research indicates that women's experiences at coeducational institutions are not always equal to the experiences of their male counterparts. In other words, though men and women can attend the same institution, they do not necessarily experience the institution in the same way and are not necessarily treated equitably either within the classroom, on the campus, or by their peers. In fact, researchers have described the campus climate for women at coeducational colleges as "chilly" both in and outside the classroom (Hall & Sandler, 1982, 1984). Studies of classroom interaction in coeducational environments conclude, for example, that men are called on more often in class than women, and that men's comments are taken more seriously (American Association of University Women, 1991; Krupnick, 1985; Sadker & Sadker, 1994). Similarly, in Boyer's (1987) study of undergraduate education he concluded:

> We were especially struck by the subtle, yet significant differences in the way men and women participated in class. . . . In many classrooms, women are overshadowed. Even the brightest women often remain silent. . . . Not only do men talk more, but what they say often carries more weight. (p. 150)

Holland and Eisenhart (1990) discovered that the peer culture within co-educational environments emphasizes the value of romantic relationships for women, while emphasizing the value of academics, athletics and other achievements for men. These authors argue that the emphasis on social life impedes women's academic progress in coeducational environments, which can lead to women "not being taken seriously as students" and can have "dire consequences for learning" (p. 203). Another study concluded that the coeducational collegiate experience is gendered in that there are still profound differences by gender in the characteristics, attitudes and values of women and men as they start college and as they change through college. Specifically, although both men's and women's self-confidence improves over time in college, men start out more confident than women and that difference increases over the four years of college (Smith, Morrison, & Wolf, 1994).

Measuring the existence of the chilly climate outside the classroom has become more difficult because the obvious barriers to access have been removed and all that remains are the more subtle forms of gender discrimination. Pascarella et al. (1996) conducted a national longitudinal study of first-year students to determine if the chilly climate existed. They concluded that although its effect might not be pervasive, the chilly climate was present and had a small effect on self-reported gains in academic preparation for a career. Although the impact of the chilly climate might not be the result of overt hostility to women, a campus that is merely neutral to women may indeed demonstrate an absence of positive intent concerning women's education.

A recent research project conducted by Tidball and Tidball (1994) demonstrates what can happen at coeducational institutions that operate under the guise of gender neutrality. Specifically, the authors compared the baccalaureate origins of all the men and women who earned doctorates through 1991 and who earned their undergraduate degrees between 1970 and 1979. The results demonstrate that after controlling for institutional selectivity, women's colleges had the greatest productivity of women who earned doctorates. Further, institutions that graduated larger numbers of men who earned doctorates, graduated smaller numbers of women who earned doctorates. These results led the authors to conclude that "even though an institution appears to have sufficient material supports and encouragement for men students' achievement, these advantages are not necessarily available to women in the same degree" (p. 53).

In addition to the research about coeducational environments having potentially negative outcomes for women, there is another body of literature that demonstrates that women's colleges have something important to teach other segments of higher education. Specifically, a wide array of qualitative and quantitative research projects have demonstrated that women's colleges are among the most accessible and promoting environments wherein women are taken seriously and ultimately experience success. Specifically, a significant body of research literature suggests that women's colleges have a direct, positive impact on their students. Compared to women at coeducational institutions, for example, students at women's colleges are more satisfied with their overall college experience (Astin, 1977, 1985, 1992; Smith, 1990); are more likely to major in nontraditional fields (Bressler & Wendell, 1980; Riordan, 1992; Scheye & Gilroy, 1994; Sebrechts, 1993; Solnick, 1995); and express higher levels of self-esteem and leadership skills (Astin, 1977, 1985; Kim & Alvarez, 1995; Kuh, Schuh, & Whitt, 1991; Riordan, 1992). In addition, researchers have found that students who have attended women's colleges are more likely to graduate, to have high expectations of themselves, to attend graduate school, and to be successful in their adult lives (Astin, 1977, 1992; Riordan, 1994; Wolf-Wendel, 1998).

In all fairness, it is important to note that there exists some skepticism regarding the effects of attending a women's college, especially with regard to the impact on career and post-graduation outcomes. Critics tend to focus on those studies that use institutions rather than individuals as the unit of analysis and that, therefore, cannot adequately control for individual student background characteristics. In addition, some researchers suggest that the relative success of graduates of women's college may be a dated phenomenon. In other words, when women students began to have access to prestigious men's colleges, did claims about women's colleges remain true? This question assumes that the success of women's colleges is due to the fact that the "best" women students could not attend the "best" schools in the country. It also assumes that studies of women's colleges focus on the most elite of these institutions. A third critique about the research on women's colleges is that it fails to account for the self-selection of students. In other words, some suggest that women who choose to attend women's colleges are predestined to be successful and that one cannot credit the institution at all for the outcomes produced.

The best way to confront such critiques is to examine the literature on women's colleges in its totality rather than to look at one study at a time. Research is most powerful when conclusions are drawn from a wide variety of studies using different methods, sources of data, and time periods. In reviewing the literature, it is clear that the majority of studies on women's colleges, including those that control for both institutional and individual characteristics of students, come to the same conclusion. As such, although it is impossible to randomly assign students to attend either a women's college or coeducational college, the self-selection argument appears specious. Further, it is not only dated studies that make claim to the outcomes associated with women's colleges: current studies using contemporary college attendees also come to the same conclusions. Given the totality of the research on women's colleges, Tidball, Smith, Tidball, and Wolf-Wendel (1999) conclude:

> Despite these differences [between methodologies and approach] the extent of overlap, the consistency, and the corroboration in the research findings are so great as to warrant the conclusion that women's colleges are among the most accessible and promoting environments wherein women are taken seriously. (p. 31)

Similarly, based on a thorough review of the literature on college impact, Pascarella and Terenzini (1991) assert:

> Even with student background characteristics and institutional selectivity held constant, a woman attending an all-women's college, compared with her coeducational counterpart, is more likely to emerge with higher educational aspirations, to attain a higher degree, to enter a sex-atypical career, and to achieve prominence in her field. (pp. 638–39)

WHAT LESSONS CAN WOMEN'S COLLEGES
TEACH THE REST OF HIGHER EDUCATION?

The Carnegie Commission on Higher Education's Opportunities for Women in Higher Education in 1973 noted: "These accomplishments of the graduates of women's colleges are worthy of emphasis, not only as they bear on decisions of women's colleges . . . but also—and far more significant in terms of potential influence—as they suggest how changes in policies and faculty attitudes in coeducational institutions could affect the accomplishments of their women students" (p. 74). Despite this early call to take women's colleges seriously, they typically remain invisible because they represent such a small proportion of the higher education community and because of their small size as individual institutions. They may only educate a small proportion of women—but they have lessons to offer the rest of higher education.

Based on case studies at women's colleges[3] and an extensive review of the literature on the environments found at women's colleges, seven institutional traits stand out as being descriptive of how women's colleges facilitate the success of their women students. These traits are presented below as lessons that other institutions might follow if they wish to learn from women's colleges how to create environments that facilitate the success of women students. These lessons include:

1. Clarify and communicate a mission that puts women at the center;
2. Believe women can achieve and hold them to high expectations;
3. Make students feel like they matter;
4. Provide strong, positive role models;
5. Provide ample opportunities for women to engage in leadership activities;
6. Include women in the curriculum;
7. Create safe spaces in which women can form a critical mass.

CLARIFY AND COMMUNICATE A
MISSION THAT PUTS WOMEN AT THE CENTER

The power of a strong, focused mission and its effect on educational quality has been discussed often in the literature (Astin 1985; Clark, 1991; Gardener, 1989; Kuh et al., 1991). For example, Chickering and Reisser (1993) state that "a strong sense of shared values and purpose is the foundation for institutional coherence and integrity" (p. 480). Women's colleges typically have focused missions that permeate the culture, the institution's values, decisions, physical environment, rituals and history. The education of women is central to this mission and is intentionally reflected in curriculum decisions, publications, and at numerous decision-making points day-to-day and over the long term. For women's colleges, the singular focus on meeting the educational needs of a particular group of students puts these campuses in an advantageous position compared to many other post-secondary institutions. Women are an explicit part of the mission at these institutions. As one professor explained, "The starting place for anything . . . is to be very clearheaded about where you want to end up and where you want to go." Similarly, another professor stated, "The clearer the mission, the better you can do it." Many institutions do not have the luxury of being able to focus exclusively on women. Nonetheless, by purposefully considering the needs of women, coeducational, predominantly white institutions may be better able to serve students from traditionally disenfranchised groups.

BELIEVE WOMEN CAN ACHIEVE AND HOLD THEM TO HIGH EXPECTATIONS

Just as women's colleges were initially established to refute the notion that women could not succeed in serious academic pursuits, today's women's colleges continue to demonstrate the importance of holding women students to high academic standards and believing in the capacity of women students' success. Indeed, having high expectations and encouraging students to achieve is one of the main characteristics of women's colleges that is worthy of emulation. The research literature supports the idea that high academic expectations are related to student success (e.g., Ayres, 1983; Green, 1989; Kannerstein, 1978; Whitt, 1992). In *Involving Colleges*, for example, Kuh et al. (1991) found the presence of faculty members who "assume that all students can learn anything given the proper circumstances" (p. 284) to be a trait common to successful institutions. Further, the authors of *Involving Colleges* emphasize the ethic of membership, which is translated to mean "because you have chosen us . . . we will do everything we can to help you succeed" (p. 56).

The psychological theory of attribution (Kelley, 1973) also supports the importance of high expectations by suggesting that when one credits success to effort rather than ability (likewise when one credits failure to insufficient effort rather than to low ability), self-esteem is enhanced as is a willingness to approach challenging tasks. According to Sanford (1962), challenge is a necessary component to enhance student learning and personal development. The high expectations conveyed by faculty members at women's colleges provide such a challenge by introducing students to new skills, new experiences, and a more complex self-understanding.

At women's colleges, the most common approach to getting students to "aim high" involved faculty telling students that they have potential, telling them that they are capable, and telling them what is expected of them. The notion most frequently repeated by respondents in the case studies was, "If I tell you long enough that you are the greatest, then you are going to believe it." A student elaborated on this point eloquently:

> If you are continually told that you are stupid or ignorant you will begin to perform to that capacity. If you are told you are phenomenal, excellent, then you will perform on that level. And, I truly believe that is what these young women hear night and day. "You are phenomenal women. You are exceptional. You operate in a spirit of excellence." This is continually told . . . I think that puts them in a mind to see themselves that way.

Respondents at women's colleges stressed the idea that students were not "allowed" to use their backgrounds as an excuse for failure. For example, faculty members talked about how it was unacceptable for students to claim that women can't "do math." Just as students should not use their backgrounds as an excuse for failure, faculty members suggested the importance of not giving up too early on students who are having academic difficulties. This is especially true in male-dominated fields, where faculty members reiterated the notion that, as women, students are capable of achieving success in all fields, even those that are considered traditionally male. One professor stated: "The emphasis is placed on helping students succeed, not on screening out the ones that shouldn't be here." Similarly, a science professor added:

> One of the differentiators is that the expectation at a majority school is that you have the "right stuff" from day one. . . . Their orientation is distinction, differentiation, grooming the best. . . . [Here] if you have the interest and some ability, you are going to find some level of success and then you can slug it out in the higher-level courses to see if you really have the right stuff. . . . Where you cut people off is further along.

Although the cutoff point for failure might be later, one of the points brought up consistently was that the faculty would not accept substandard work. This comment from a professor was typical: "[We] take in a lot of students who probably wouldn't get into other colleges based on their SAT scores and their grade point averages. . . . But when they leave [here] they are going to be prepared to compete with everybody else out there who has gotten a bachelor's degree."

Make Students Feel Like They Matter

Respondents at women's colleges frequently mentioned that one factor underlying the success of graduates was the support and caring that students received from faculty and administrators. Support from constituents at women's colleges includes not only guidance related to academic issues, but also guidance and advice on personal matters. Not surprisingly, research demonstrates that some degree of personal support on a campus is pivotal for student success. Schlossberg's (1989) theory of mattering puts the importance of support into perspective. Mattering, which is measured by student perceptions, occurs when students feel that they are noticed, that what they say or do is important, and that they are appreciated. Mattering further suggests that students must feel appreciated for who they are and what they do if they are to grow, develop, and succeed in college. The *Involving Colleges* (Kuh et al., 1991) study also identified the importance of mattering. Specifically, a characteristic of involving colleges is that students perceive "that faculty care and are interested, responsible, and available" (p. 286).

In talking about support, respondents at women's colleges used words like "one-on-one," "mentoring," and "hand holding" to describe relationships between faculty members and students. As a professor explained, "I feel a strong sense of responsibility for the success of my students." Faculty and administrators at the case study sites talked about the institutional commitment to provide students with the support they need. Respondents, for example, mentioned that teaching and working directly with students was an important factor in determining promotion and pay raises at all of the institutions. A professor indicated, "It is not in your job description. You either bring it with you, or you intuit that is what is needed and you either say 'okay' . . . or you decide this is not what I want to do and you find a job somewhere else."

While support is extremely important, respondents also expressed the idea that support should be tempered because ultimately students are responsible for themselves. A faculty member explained that they "try very hard to be helpful, supportive and encouraging to them . . . but . . . we are not going to be holding their hands through every step of the way. We expect a certain maturity and initiative on their part." As another professor explained, "I try to make it clear to my students there is going to be a grade at the end of the semester. That is something they have to live with, but I am going to apply as much support and encouragement over the course of the semester as I can and be as understanding of students that are coming up to speed as I can without compromising academic integrity."

PROVIDE STRONG, POSITIVE ROLE MODELS

When asked to explain the success of alumnae, respondents at women's colleges are quick to mention the importance of role models. It is often assumed that being able to interact with successful people who are "like you" will further one's chances of success and improve one's self-concept. That individuals learn by observing another person in a similar situation to their own is at the heart of this belief (Bandura & Walters, 1963). Yet, research on the importance of role modeling is sparse and yields differing results. In a review of literature, Speizer (1981) found no conclusive evidence that female professors directly influenced their female students. She stated, "We must take it on faith that knowing a woman academician and being close enough to see something of the reality of her life and action will help the young intellectual woman to concretize her role concept" (p. 702).

Case studies of women's colleges offer one more piece of evidence about the importance of role models. Specifically, respondents at women's colleges identified alumnae, current students, campus visitors and lecturers, administrators, support staff, and faculty members as role models. Role models were considered important because they conveyed to students, "I can do that too." In particular, the presence of women faculty and administrators was mentioned as important for women students. Respondents noted that having women in positions of power within the institution helped women students deal with "balancing the parenting and career thing" and also to "create a visual correlation between image and possibility." As an administrator explained:

> I think it's just terribly exciting to young women to come to an institution where the portraits on the wall are women, where the people teaching them are women, where the president is a woman. . . . Young women at a very impressionable time in their development are in an institution where women have taken on the burdens and pleasures of leadership equally or with something of an advantage. And that is so different from the world most of them have known, and that has a lot more influence than they are conscious of.

By the composition of their employees, women's colleges communicate clearly that the options for women are varied and the doors of possibility are open wide. In contrast, at institutions where women do not hold positions of authority, a significant statement is made about whether women should be in those positions, whether they can succeed in such positions, and whether women students should aspire to such positions. That is, an absence of women in leadership roles and within the faculty communicates a great deal about gendered options and choices.

PROVIDE AMPLE OPPORTUNITIES FOR WOMEN TO ENGAGE IN LEADERSHIP ACTIVITIES

One of the things that is most noteworthy about women's colleges is that they provide a variety of opportunities for women to be involved in the life of the campus, both in and outside of class. These opportunities help students develop strong leadership skills, keep them active in their institutions, and facilitate their overall success. At women's colleges, women were obligated to hold all of the available leadership positions. As a professor stated, the fact that there are "fewer men around, that in the school organizations there are all women . . . [this] enables young women . . . to gain confidence. This place is very much a proving ground so that skills and experience are fostered." Similarly, an administrator stated, "Women have an opportunity to be creative, to develop their leadership skills without having to compete with men until they get to the larger society. And, by that time they are pretty well equipped to do that." Similarly, a student explained, "If it needs to be done, it's a given that women will do it." Of all of the factors listed, the area of involvement opportunities has been given the most attention in the wider literature. Involvement, as defined by Astin (1977), entails the investment of psychological and physical energy in tasks, people, and activities. Involvement is said to be associated with a variety of positive educational outcomes (Astin, 1992; Pascarella & Terenzini, 1991). As such, it is not surprising that institutions that expect women students to be involved and active members of the community are likely to graduate successful students.

INCLUDE WOMEN IN THE CURRICULUM

Constituents at women's colleges mentioned the benefits of including gender issues in the formal and informal curriculum. At the same time, however, constituents across the institutions did not call for the dissolution of the "traditional" curriculum. As a faculty member explained, generally the curriculum is fairly mainstream because "we need to prepare them to know the same material as other students so they can do well on the standardized tests." Women's colleges often infuse women into the general curriculum via classroom examples, lectures, and assigned readings. In addition, topics pertaining to women can be found as a major part of extracurriculum—presented through planned (and often required) lectures, speaker series, and discussion groups. Regardless of the form it takes, respondents agreed that providing opportunities for students to learn about themselves and about others who have been historically marginalized is important because it provides "students with role models and knowledge about where they come from."

A review of the literature on the impact of diversity initiatives indicates some positive outcomes associated with addressing issues of race, gender, and social class in the curriculum (Appel, Cartwright, Smith, & Wolf-Wendel, 1996; Smith & Associates, 1997). It was not surprising, therefore, to find that many respondents mentioned the importance of learning about gender issues in both the formal and informal curriculum. Respondents emphasized the importance of exposing their students to diverse women's history, literature and backgrounds as a means to help students become aware of racism, sexism, and classism faced by those in the "real world." Expanding the curriculum to educate *all* students to live in a multicultural society, according to Smith (1995), is the best way for institutions to deal proactively with the changing demographics of society. Including the voices of women is not something one does merely to enhance the self-esteem of underrepresented students. Instead, the infusion of diversity into the curriculum helps all students understand how to succeed and how to fight societal discrimination and injustice.

CREATE SAFE SPACES WHERE WOMEN
CAN FORM A CRITICAL MASS

Constituents at women's colleges emphasized the benefits of having a supportive peer culture that both created a safe space for students and served as a motivating force. Respondents discussed how the campus peer cultures influence women students to succeed. Generally, responses fell into two general categories: having a "driven, high-achieving" peer culture, and having a culture that emphasizes peer support. At one college, for example, respondents described the peer climate as one that "rewards academic achievement." Respondents also discussed how supportive students were of each other. In the words of a student: "You battle, but you always try to support."

Although there were similarities between the institutions in terms of the importance of peer culture, the importance of the climate factor was different for white women than for women of color. Specifically, although white women are a numerical majority on most college campuses, respondents at a white women's college suggested that there was something "powerful for women about being at a place that is theirs. . . . They identify with the culture and see the culture as taking them seriously and really being invested in them." A student, for example, explained "I felt like I belonged here . . . I was struck by being in a community of women." Further a faculty member talked about the importance of having a place where intellectual women "find camaraderie and colleagueship of other women who are trying to do the same thing . . . it creates a gendered intellectual density." At women's colleges, this type of women-centered peer culture comes naturally.

Respondents at a historically black women's college frequently used the term "critical mass" as they discussed the peer culture and its effect on the success of women of color. Unlike white women who are in the majority at many campuses, women of color rarely find themselves surrounded by driven, motivated, talented students who come from similar backgrounds. An administrator explained that students "get the chance to be surrounded by African American women who all have similar achievement goals. . . . This is the first and only time that this will happen in their lives and it has a powerful effect."

The fact that women students represent the majority at most institutions of higher education creates an interesting conundrum—why is it that many women students do not feel a strong sense of peer support and community on coeducational campuses (AAUW, 1995; Hall & Sandler, 1984; Pascarella et al., 1996)? This is an area worthy of more research and exploration. Research suggests that the proportion of different types of individuals within an institution impacts both how they are viewed by the organization as well as how they fit in (Kanter, 1976; Tidball, 1983). It would appear, however, that critical mass means more than just "adding more" students from a particular group; it also means consciously paying attention to the needs of that group and providing a supportive climate. It means fostering an effective community, as described by Gardner (1989), which entails, among other things, incorporating diversity, creating a shared culture, and promoting caring, trust and teamwork. According to respondents at women's colleges, being around peers who share certain characteristics makes one feel comfortable, safe, supported, and included. In contrast, the absence of this supportive peer culture makes one feel isolated and limited.

CONTEXTUALIZING THE LESSONS

At first glance, the characteristics of women's colleges mirror those described in the literature connected to student-centered institutions for both men and women. In fact, there is evidence from the wider literature that having a focused mission, high expectations, support, role models, a supportive peer culture of high-achieving students, opportunities for extracurricular involvement, and inclusion of women and people of color in the curriculum, are all traits associated with institutions that facilitate the success of students. What sets women's colleges apart from other student-friendly institutions is the purposefulness with which these institutions respond to the needs of their women students. The success of women is central to the values held by campus constituents. This belief undergirds much of the actions of both the institutions and the individual campus constituents. These are environments in which the situation for women is not only favorable, but also empowering: colleges where there is a critical mass of women faculty, colleges where women are nurtured and challenged, colleges where woman-related issues dominate campus discussions. Taking women seriously requires intentionality, manifest in a living history and a legacy for larger purposes.

Women's colleges carry out these traits in different ways, exemplifying the idea that "successful" colleges are not all alike. Differences in race, ethnicity, social class, and other experiences influence what students need from their campuses and how campuses should respond. Although separate examinations of the characteristics of each institution are illuminating, it is important to understand that the whole of these institutions is greater than the sum of their parts—one cannot look at a single element in isolation. Instead, it is the combination of characteristics, the ethos of these institutions, which makes them unique and able to facilitate the success of their students. What women's colleges do that sets them apart from other campuses is that they are purposeful in their adoption of structures, policies, practices and curriculum that are attuned to the needs of women.

THE FUTURE OF WOMEN'S COLLEGES

What is the future of women's colleges? The heyday of women's colleges is long past. One should not expect to see an increase in the number of women's colleges nor should one expect to see large increases in the proportion of women who decide to attend the remaining women's colleges. No matter how well women's colleges do at nurturing, encouraging, supporting and taking women seriously, there will always be relatively few college students who see this as more valuable than attending a college with a more traditional social life.

Yet, despite these facts, women's colleges do have a future. Women's colleges will continue to provide an excellent educational environment for those women who choose to attend. In particular, they will continue to attract and serve nontraditional-aged women and younger women who choose to put academic pursuits before the more traditional conceptions of campus life. Women's colleges can serve as models for other institutions that want to create academic communities that take women seriously. It is in this way that the legacy of women's colleges can most greatly affect the future of women's education.

NOTES

1. The Seven Sisters, the oldest and most selective of the women's colleges, include: Barnard, Bryn Mawr, Mount Holyoke, Smith, Wellesley, Vassar, and Radcliffe. The last two on the list are no longer women's colleges.

2. The Carnegie Classifications are a recognized typology of American colleges and universities that groups institutions that share related missions, programs and purposes together.

3. The following data and quotations are based on the author's visits to several campuses that were identified as having been particularly successful at granting undergraduate degrees to white women and women of color who subsequently earned doctorates. The researcher interviewed students, faculty, administrators, and alumnae of these campuses and asked them to describe what about their campus facilitated the success of women students. A more detailed description of the methodology and the results can be found in the *Review of Higher Education, 23*(3) 319–346.

REFERENCES

American Association of University Women (AAUW). (1995). *How schools shortchange girls.* New York: Marlowe.

American Association of University Women (AAUW). (1991). *Shortchanging girls, shortchanging America.* Washington, DC: AAUW.

Appel, M., Cartwright, D., Smith, D., & Wolf-Wendel, L. (1996). *The impact of diversity on students: A preliminary review of the research literature.* Washington, DC: American Association of Colleges and Universities.

Astin, A. W. (1977). *Four critical years: Effects of college on beliefs, attitudes and knowledge.* San Francisco: Jossey-Bass.

Astin, A. W. (1985). *Achieving educational excellence.* San Francisco: Jossey-Bass.

Astin, A. W. (1992). *What matters in college? Four critical years revisited.* San Francisco: Jossey-Bass.

Ayres, Q. W. (1983). Student achievement at predominantly black and predominantly white universities. *American Educational Research Journal, 20,* 291–304.

Bandura, A., & Walters, R. (1963). *Social learning and personality development.* New York: Holt, Rinehart & Winston.

Boyer, E. L. (1987). *College: The undergraduate experience in America.* The Carnegie Foundation for the Advancement of Teaching. New York: Harper & Row.

Bressler, M., & Wendell, P. (1980). The sex composition of selective colleges and gender differences in career aspirations. *Journal of Higher Education, 51,* 650–653.

Carnegie Commission on Higher Education. (1973). *Opportunities for women in higher education: Their current participation, prospects for the future and recommendations for action.* New York: McGraw-Hill.

Chickering, A. W., & Reisser, L. (1993). *Education and identity.* (2d ed.). San Francisco: Jossey–Bass.

Clark, B. R. (1991). The organizational saga in higher education. In M. W. Peterson (ed.) *Organization and governance in higher education, an ASHE reader.* Needham Heights, MA: Ginn Press.

Gardener, J. W. 1989. Building community. *Kettering Review,* 73–81.

Green, M. F. (1989). *Minorities on campus: A handbook for enhancing diversity.* Washington, DC: American Council on Education.

Hall, R., & Sandler, B. (1982). *The classroom climate: A chilly one for women?* Project on the Status and Education of Women. Washington, DC: Association of American Colleges.

Hall, R., & Sandler, B. (1984). *The classroom climate: Still a chilly one for women?* Project on the Status and Education of Women. Washington, DC: Association of American Colleges.

Harwarth, I., Maline, M., & DeBra, E. (1997). *Women's colleges in the United States: History, issues, and challenges.* Washington, DC: U.S. Government Printing Office.

Holland, D.C., & Eisenhart, M. A. (1990). *Educated in romance: Women, achievement, and college culture*. Chicago: University of Chicago Press.

Kannerstein, G. (1978). Black colleges: Self-concept. In C.V. Willie & R. R. Edmonds (Eds.) *Black colleges in America: Challenge, development, survival* (pp. 29–50). New York: Teachers College Press.

Kanter, R. M. (1976). Numbers: Minorities and majorities. *Men and women of the corporation* (pp. 206–242). New York: Basic Books.

Kelley, H. E. (1973). The processes of causal attribution. In *American Psychologist*. Washington, DC: American Psychological Association.

Kim, M., & Alvarez, R. (1995). Women-only colleges: Some unanticipated consequences. *Journal of Higher Education, 66*, 641–669.

Krupnick, C. G. (1985, May). Women and men in the classroom: Inequality and its remedies. *On Teaching and Learning*, 18–25.

Kuh, G. D., Schuh, J. H., Whitt, E. J., & Associates. (1991). *Involving colleges: Successful approaches to fostering student learning and development outside the classroom*. San Francisco: Jossey-Bass.

Lasser, C. (Ed.). (1987). *Educating men and women together: Coeducation in a changing world*. Urbana: University of Illinois Press.

National Center for Education Statistics. (1999). *Digest of Education Statistics*. Washington DC: Department of Education.

Pascarella, E. T., & Terenzini, P. T. (1991). *How college affects students: Findings and insights from twenty years of research*. San Francisco: Jossey-Bass.

Pascarella, E. T., Whitt, E. J., Edison, M., Nora, A., Hagedorn, L. S., Yeager, P. M., & Terenzini, P. T. (1996). *Women's perceptions of a "chilly climate" and their cognitive outcomes during the first year of college*. Paper presented at the Annual Meeting of the Association for the Study of Higher Education, Memphis, TN.

Riordan, C. (1992). Single- and mixed-gender colleges for women: Educational, attitudinal, and occupational outcomes. *The Review of Higher Education, 15*(3), 327–346.

Riordan, C. (1994). The value of attending a women's college: Education, occupation and income benefits. *Journal of Higher Education, 65*, 486–510.

Sadker, M., & Sadker, D. (1994). *Failing at fairness: How our schools cheat girls*. New York: Simon & Schuster.

Sanford, N. (1962). *The American college: A psychological and social interpretation of the higher learning*. New York: John Wiley & Sons.

Scheye, P. A., & Gilroy, F. D. (1994). College women's career self-efficiency and educational environments. *Career Development Quarterly, 42*, 244–251.

Schlossberg, N. K. (1989). Marginality and mattering: Key issues in building community. In D. C. Roberts (Ed.) *Designing campus activities to foster a sense of community: New directions for student services*. (Vol. 48). San Francisco: Jossey-Bass.

Sebrechts, J. S. (1993). Cultivating scientists at women's colleges. *Initiatives, 55*(2), 45–52.

Smith, D. G. (1990). Women's colleges and coed colleges: Is there a difference for women? *Journal of Higher Education, 61*(2), 181–197.

Smith, D. G. (1995). Organizational implications of diversity in higher education. In M. Chemers, S. Oskamp, & M. Costanza (Eds.) *Diversity in organizations.* Thousand Oaks, CA: Sage.

Smith, D. G., Gerbick, G., Figueroa, M., Watkins, G. H., Levitan, T., Moore, L. C., Merchant, P., Beliak, H. D., & Figueroa, B. (1997). *Diversity works: The emerging picture of how students benefit.* Washington, DC: Association of American Colleges and Universities.

Smith, D., Morrison, D., & Wolf, L. E. (1994). College as a gendered experience: An empirical analysis using multiple lenses. *Journal of Higher Education, 65*(6), 696–725.

Solnick, S. J. (1995). Changes in women's majors from entrance to graduation at women's and coeducational colleges. *Industrial and Labor Relations Review, 48*(3), 505–514.

Speizer, J. (1981). Role models, mentors, and sponsors: The elusive concept. *Signs, 6,* 176–182.

Talbot, M. (1994, November 20). The gender trap. Are women's colleges bad for women? *Washington Post Magazine.*

Tidball, M. E. (1983). The ideal gas, a critical mass, and homeostasis. *Women's Studies Quarterly, 11*(2), 5–7.

Tidball, E., Smith, D., Tidball, C., & Wolf-Wendel, L. (1999). *Taking women seriously: Lessons and legacies for higher education from women's colleges.* Phoenix, AZ: ACE/Oryx Press.

Tidball, M. E., & Tidball, C.S. (1994). *Population demographics and the search for gender equity.* Paper presented at Women's College Coalition Conference, Mount Holyoke College, South Hadley, MA.

Whitt, E. J. (1992). *Taking women seriously: Lessons for coeducational institutions from women's colleges.* Paper presented at the Annual Meeting of the Association for the Study of Higher Education, Minneapolis, MN.

Wolf-Wendel, L. E. (1998). Models of excellence: The baccalaureate origins of successful African American, European American and Hispanic women. *The Journal of Higher Education, 69*(2), 144–172.

Wolf-Wendel, L. E. (2000). Women friendly campuses: What five institutions are doing right. *The Review of Higher Education, 23*(3), 319–345.

Part II

Deconstructing the Present

Student Lives

3

Stepping off the Scale

Promoting Positive Body Image in College Students

Laura Hensley

In my work as a college counselor and educator, I hear the stories of many women whose self definition rests solely on their physical appearance. Although they may be successful in other areas of their lives, they place primary importance on their body size, weight, and overall physical appearance; if they are not thin and beautiful, then they do not believe they are acceptable. Given the bombardment of messages about thinness and beauty they receive, it is not surprising that many college women place these mainstream cultural expectations on themselves. Societal pressures to attain a "thin ideal" are magnified on college campuses and research shows that the ideal portrayed in the media is accepted as a sociocultural norm among college women (Media Report to Women, 1999). The intensive college setting paired with pressing developmental issues for students creates a ripe environment for the occurrence of negative body image, which in turn is strongly related to depression, low-self-esteem, and disordered eating in college women (Brazelton, Greene, Gynther, & O'Mell, 1998; Streigel-Moore, Silberstein, & Rodin, 1986; Weiderman & Pryor, 2000). The embodied experiences of college women are necessary to consider when attempting to understand the gendered nature of higher education.

It is estimated that 50% of all women are dissatisfied with their overall physical appearance (Cash & Henry, 1995). Body image dissatisfaction, weight preoccupation, and unhealthy weight management are prevalent even among college women of normal weight (Schwitzer, Bergholz, Dore, & Salimi, 1998; Springer, Winzelberg, Perkins, & Barr-Taylor, 1999). During their first year of college, up to 65% of college women display behavioral and psychological characteristics associated with disordered eating, such as chronic dieting, bingeing, or purging (Mintz & Betz, 1988). One-quarter of college women feel that their eating is out of control, and six percent report using laxatives or self-induced vomiting after eating (Koszewski, Newell, & Higgins, 1990). Thirty percent of students are extremely worried about body image, and 25% are extremely worried about weight control (Derlene & Bragowicz, 1990). Another study found that approximately 70% of college women engage in binge-eating practices, and 50–61% of college women are involved in regular or chronic dieting (Thombs, Rosenberg, Mahoney, & Daniel, 1996). These statistics are alarming given the research that consistently shows a relationship between negative body image and lowered self-esteem, depression, obsessive thoughts about weight and appearance, and interference with overall physical and psychological functioning (Mintz & Betz, 1988; Weiderman & Pryor, 2000).

The statistics are not surprising, however, given the environmental and developmental stressors present in the college setting. Several authors note that campus environments magnify the already powerful sociocultural pressures for thinness by creating a climate that serves to shape women's choices about the importance of weight and adhering to the prescribed "ideal" (Lee, 1989; Schulken, Pinciaro, Sawyer, Jensen, & Hoban, 1997; Streigel-Moore, Silberstein, & Rodin, 1986). Especially for traditional students, environmental stressors such as leaving home and transitioning to campus life, living in residence halls with limited access to food services, facing financial or academic stresses, and residing in an environment in which dating and social acceptance are emphasized lead many women to focus on dieting, weight, and the pursuit of an ideal body type (Lee, 1989).

Further, developmental issues that emerge for women students during the college years are often expressed through a focus on diets and disordered eating. At a time in which students are establishing identity—including comfort with their bodies and appearances, sexual orientation, and overall self-concept—they are also striving to individuate from parents and acquire autonomy (Chickering & Reisser, 1993). This process is not as complex for men because they are socialized from an early age to be independent and autonomous. Girls, however, receive strong messages regarding the importance of pleasing others, often at the expense of self. In the college setting, women may be confused when asked to be both independent and dependent upon others. According to Josselson (1987), a key issue in college student women's development is identity achievement, a process in which the individual experiences pressure to give up comforts of what is currently known about the self (generally prescribed by parents) only to face unknown and unpredictable future possibilities (Evans, Forney, & Guido-DiBrito, 1998). Facing the unknown without a guaranteed safety net, women often have difficulty in adult autonomy struggles during the college years. It is interesting to note that research demonstrates that women college students experiencing contradictory messages regarding independence and dependence are also likely to develop eating disorders (Meyer & Russell, 1998). When experiencing uncertainty in individuation from parents and others and in developing an autonomous identity, women may focus on weight, dieting, and body size to regain some sense of power and control in their lives (Meyer & Russell, 1998). They often feel it is safer to rechannel energy into reaching a number on a scale than to face the uncertainty of an unfamiliar and often unsupportive campus and/or community climate. The strong sociocultural pressures that serve to reinforce these attitudes and behaviors perpetuate the "normative discontent" that many college women have with their bodies (Rodin, Silberstein, & Streigel-Moore, 1985).

It is important for higher education faculty, staff, and other personnel to understand the belief systems that underlie this pervasive discontent. Those individuals who internalize the body type ideals portrayed to them in U.S. culture, and who place primary importance on physical appearance in evaluating their overall self-esteem, will spend vast amounts of energy and time in attempts to attain these ideals. In so doing, they often develop negative body image and disordered eating practices.

As professionals in higher education, we must begin to recognize the negative effects these belief systems have on women's performance in our colleges and universities. Might a woman with negative body image be less willing to speak out in class, to question her ability to pursue leadership positions, or lack the confidence to assert herself in activities? Might she spend energy on dieting and achieving a certain weight that could be rechanneled into developing other aspects of herself? The answers are clear: women who are frequently dieting and who are dissatisfied with their bodies experience extreme appearance anxiety, even as they spend time, energy, and money in attempts to attain the cultural ideal for attractiveness. Until we gain awareness of and actively address this pervasive problem, many women will continue to struggle to meet unrealistic expectations, to question their inadequacy when they do not "measure up," and to then define themselves according to these feelings of inadequacy. What would happen on our campuses if we supported students in developing broader, more flexible definitions of what is considered attractive? What if students were able to reject sociocultural pressures to attain a thin ideal? What would happen if they were fully able to refocus energy away from only the number on a scale and instead devote energy to balanced development in all spheres of the self—the intellectual, emotional, spiritual, and the physical?

In this chapter, I examine the construct of body image, U.S. sociocultural ideals regarding attractiveness, and resulting sex-role conflicts for college women. Further, I describe the consequences of internalization of U.S. sociocultural norms, the impact it has on higher educational settings, and what we as professionals who work with college students can do to begin to change this pervasive belief system that still exists on campuses. Specifically, I will examine some of the protective or resiliency factors that are present in women and men who do not experience problems with body image.

It is important to note that much of the research presented in this chapter was conducted with White college women (usually students in introductory psychology courses at major research universities). Although clinical eating disorders are more prevalent in this population, there is increasing evidence to suggest that these issues are not only "White women" issues. I will review a body of recent research that focuses on diverse cultural groups and body image. Findings indicate that women and men in any cultural group that internalizes Western sociocultural values for beauty and thinness will develop an increase in negative body image and eating disorders.[1] The normative discontent with body size and physical appearance is culture-bound (Barber, 1998).

What Is Body Image?

Body image is a multidimensional construct that involves self-attitude toward one's body size, shape, and aesthetics. Body image includes three aspects: evaluation, affect, and cognitive-behavioral investment (Cash, 1994). The evaluation component involves one's satisfaction or dissatisfaction with overall physical attributes. Body image affect refers to the emotional experiences that these self-evaluations may elicit. Cognitive behavioral investment is the extent to which one views appearance as a measure of overall self-evaluation, and also refers to the behaviors that involve the enhancement and management of appearance (Muth & Cash, 1997). Research overwhelmingly demonstrates that a negative body image is related to low self-esteem, depression, and disordered eating (Rodin, Silberstein, & Streigel-Moore, 1985; Weiderman & Pryor, 2000; Wolf, 1991). Excessive weight concerns, body image dissatisfaction, and disordered eating patterns are risk factors for the development of partial and full-syndrome eating disorders, including anorexia and bulimia (Springer et al., 1999).

In some respects, it is not surprising that there has been a dramatic increase in the prevalence of anorexia and bulimia on college campuses during the past several decades (Feingold & Mazzella, 1998). If U.S. college women live in a culture in which "normal" eating for most women is to be on a diet (Polivy & Herman, 1987) and unhealthy eating practices are common, we can conceptualize eating disorders at the end of a continuum of dieting and weight preoccupation. Eating disorders are then seen as extreme manifestations of normative, culturally acceptable behaviors (Barber, 1998). Instead of focusing on these disorders as pathology, it makes sense to examine the sociocultural pressures that all women face, and to delineate factors that predispose some women to internalize these standards to such an extent that they base their self worth on meeting these ideals. Some women resist these pressures; others develop negative body image but not disordered eating; others engage in unhealthy dieting and eating practices such as chronic dieting and purging; and a small minority develop full-blown eating disorder syndromes. Why are some women affected by these pressures to a greater extent than others?

THE INTERNALIZATION OF U.S. SOCIOCULTURAL IDEALS

Women are bombarded with messages about beauty, weight, and what is considered to be attractive. In Western societies, sociocultural ideals are based on a body type that is unattainable for the majority of women. Naomi Wolf argues in *The Beauty Myth* (1991) that the fashion industry has changed its ideals over time so that fewer and fewer women will ever be able to attain the ideal, no matter how much they diet, or how many beauty products they buy. Evidence of the changing ideal in the later twentieth century may be seen in the media portrayal of the female body as increasingly thin and decreasingly curvaceous (Barber, 1998). Research investigating the height, weight, and body measurements of *Playboy* centerfolds and Miss America Pageant contestants since the 1960s shows that their average weights have become increasingly lower than the average weight for U.S. women (Wiseman, Gray, Mosimann, & Ahrens, 1992). This finding has been replicated with publications such as *Ladies Home Journal* and *Vogue* (Barber, 1998). Interestingly, the majority of recent Playboy models and Miss America contestants weigh more than 15% less than the expected weight for their age and height category. Because a weight of 15% less than expected body weight is one of the criteria for anorexia nervosa (DSM-IV, American Psychiatric Association, 1994), the ideal body type portrayed in the media is an image of a woman at a dangerously low body weight. Why is the gap widening between how American women actually look and how the media tells them they should look? Who is most likely to subscribe to these ideals? Conversely, who is able to resist these pressures? These are important, complex questions, because the answers have a direct impact on the well-being of today's college women.

Recent research investigated the direct effects of fashion magazines on college women's body satisfaction. Turner, Hamilton, Jacobs, Angood, and Dwyer (1997) randomly assigned college women to two experimental conditions: one group read news magazines (control group), and the other group read women's fashion magazines (experimental group) prior to completing body image satisfaction surveys. Although there were no significant differences in height or weight between the experimental and control groups, those women who viewed the fashion magazines reported a lower ideal body weight and had greater body dissatisfaction than did women who were exposed to news magazines. The authors conclude that exposure to the "thin ideal" as portrayed in the media directly shapes social perceptions of the ideal body type for women (Turner et al., 1997). Because this body type is unattainable for the majority of women, those women who internalize this standard will develop negative body image, which undermines their physical and psychological well-being.

Given that the majority of college women have a negative view of their overall physical appearance, Showers and Larson (1999) examined the differences between college women with negative body image and nondisordered eating, and those women with negative body image and disordered eating. Specifically, they wanted to examine the self-concepts of women who held a negative body image but yet did not develop disordered eating practices. The authors found that women with disordered eating linked their assessment of their physical appearance to a wide range of other negative attributes about themselves, whereas the nondisordered eating group was able to compartmentalize beliefs about physical appearance. For women with nondisordered eating, beliefs about physical appearance did not spill over into their view of themselves in other life areas. The disordered eating group's physical appearance self-concept was extremely negative, and was rated as a highly important part of how they defined themselves. In contrast, the nondisordered group rated physical appearance as low in importance when evaluating their overall self-concept. The study demonstrates that it is possible for women to have a negative view of their body shape and size but to hold an overall positive self-concept. For women with disordered eating, however, beliefs about outward appearance impact all aspects of their lives, thus affecting overall self-esteem.

Women who believe that thinness will bring social acceptance and success (as is promised to them through U.S. sociocultural messages) are especially susceptible to significant negative consequences as a result of their beliefs. A study that examined the weight loss expectancies of college women found those who had the highest expectations for the effects of weight loss (i.e., increased social confidence and sense of self worth, positive performance, and social approval) had the highest scores on measures of bulimic symptomatology, including bingeing, body-image concerns, perceived lack of control of eating, and purging behaviors (Thombs, Rosenberg, Mahoney, & Daniel, 1996). When college women believe that thinness is the magic answer to solving their feelings of inadequacy, they may go to extreme measures to achieve this goal. The result may be starvation, bingeing, over-exercising, laxative abuse, dehydration, and overall lethargy. What is also disturbing are the ways these weight-loss expectancies are reinforced in U.S. culture: certainly the media promises happiness, success, and popularity with the attainment of the thin ideal. There is evidence that college students believe thinness is associated with greater attractiveness, social success and acceptance (Brazelton, Greene, Gynther, & O'Mell, 1998). Although weight loss is not problematic in itself, placing great importance on attaining an ultra-thin ideal results in body dissatisfaction. This dissatisfaction can lead to chronic dieting, which is strongly associated with the development of eating disorders.

College students susceptible to internalizing cultural messages regarding physical appearance may also be those who place an overemphasis on pleasing others, which often results in difficulties with intimacy and interpersonal relationships (Worobey, 1999). Meyer and Russell (1998) examined the codependency construct and how it may relate to disordered eating. The authors conceptualized the term "codependency" as an extreme focus outside the self, lack of open expression of feelings, and attempts to derive a sense of purpose through relationships (Spann & Fischer, 1990). Women with codependency and women with eating disorders display similar characteristics: a high need for control, distorted self–other boundaries, and the displacement of repressed feelings by way of self-destructive behaviors (Meyer & Russell, 1998). In their study of college women, Meyer and Russell (1998) found a significant relationship between codependency and disordered eating, and concluded that women who tend to deny or refrain from expressing their feelings are more susceptible to the development of disordered eating. These women hold their thoughts and feelings back to protect themselves and to please others. If their primary source of validation is through their physical appearance, a sense of inadequacy may pervade all aspects of their lives. Lacking a sense of power and self worth, they seek to regain control through striving to attain something within their grasp—a specific number on a scale. This finding has direct relevance for the college setting because many women with body image problems may stifle their voices, believing they have nothing of significance to contribute in or out of the classroom. Through validating women's experiences and listening carefully for their voices, we can encourage them to value and share their opinions and ideas. We can assist them in moving past an exclusive focus on dieting and weight, and instead urge them to value their unique gifts in all life areas.

THE SUPERWOMAN IDEAL

The changing roles of women in U.S. culture often create contradictory expectations, which lead to confusion for college women. College men also experience this double bind; they receive messages to be more sensitive and relationship-oriented (to develop their "feminine" side) but at the same time are encouraged to adhere to traditional masculine stereotypes that may be reinforced by certain social norms on campus (Archer & Cooper, 1998; see Pinar, chapter 4, this volume). Women often experience a conflict between being feminine and nurturing versus being self-reliant and high-achieving. They are simultaneously told to emphasize physical appearance and to attain an unrealistically thin body type ideal, in addition to becoming a caring nurturer who values relationships. At the same time, norms for women also include achievement in the workplace, self-reliance, and separation from parents (Hart & Kenny, 1997).

Many women who try to fulfill more traditional "feminine" role expectations experience pressure to be physically attractive, passive, and nurturing in their roles (usually as wives or mothers). Cash, Ancis, and Strachan (1997) found that women who reported conventional feminine role enactment in their relationships with men also placed great importance on physical appearance as part of overall self-image. The Meyer and Russell (1998) study described previously showed that women who refrain from expressing their feelings to please others are also more likely to develop negative body image and disordered eating. Does it follow, then, that the more importance a woman places on physical appearance and pleasing others in relationships, the more likely she is to be dissatisfied with her body and to engage in extreme behaviors related to weight control?

Researchers have investigated the link between adherence to traditional feminine ideals and disordered eating, hypothesizing that women with eating disorders may conform to a stereotype of femininity in which women are expected to be submissive, overly concerned with relationships, attractive, and thin. Specifically, they speculated that both men and women who have developed less stereotypical, rigidly defined gender roles would also be less likely to adhere to the thin ideal portrayed in U.S. culture; however, findings in this area have been inconsistent (Hart & Kenny, 1997). Studies indicate that even women and men with more nontraditional views of women's roles are not necessarily protected from accepting and internalizing cultural messages about appearance and weight. Lindner, Ryckman, Gold, and Stone (1995) classified college men and women as holding traditional or nontraditional gender role attitudes, and surveyed them regarding their "ideal male" and "ideal female" preferences. Contrary to their hypothesis, they found that college students' gender role attitudes did not significantly affect their ideal physique preferences. In a 1997 study, Cash, Ancis, and Strachan found that women who espoused a feminist ideology were no less likely to possess appearance-based criteria for self-evaluation, or to have a more favorable body image than did women who possessed more traditional gender role beliefs (Cash, Ancis, & Strachan, 1997). In both studies, the authors conclude that cultural messages which emphasize appearance are so deeply ingrained that even the development of a feminist ideology or nontraditional beliefs regarding sex roles does not protect one from their impact (Cash, Ancis, & Strachan, 1997).

Many college women today are confused: they are taught that to be a "woman" they must be curvaceous, attractive, and nurturing, but if they want to be perceived as competent in the workplace, they must also be independent, aggressive, and thin (i.e., noncurvaceous) (Barber, 1998). Often, students believe that women who are curvaceous are perceived as less competent and less likely to succeed (Keil, 1998). Obviously, it is unrealistic for women to attempt to meet these standards simultaneously, but it seems that many women continue to try. Unfortunately, these are also the women most at risk for eating disorders. Steiner-Adair (1986) proposed that women who experienced the most distress related to body dissatisfaction and eating were those who believed they must be tall, thin, beautiful, successful, and independent. In her research, Steiner-Adair (1986) found that the "superwoman" has three defining characteristics: she values the thin ideal, strives for success in multiple roles, and has insecure parental attachments that result in the devaluation of close relationships. To support the insecure parental attachment component of this hypothesis, psychologists and others posit that individuals who felt insecure in initial relationships with their primary caregivers are likely to have difficulty in forming a secure sense of self apart from the validation of others, which then leads to difficulties with both self-esteem and interpersonal relationships (Masterson, 1988). According to Steiner-Adair (1986), this insecurity paired with a strong need for success in multiple roles (including the need to achieve an ultra-thin body type), most often leads to body dissatisfaction.

Hart and Kenny (1997) tested the superwoman hypothesis in a study of college women. They found that students who strive for high achievement in multiple roles, who place high value on physical appearance, and who view their parental relationships as negative and discouraging of autonomy are likely to experience body dissatisfaction and other characteristics associated with disordered eating. This finding expands on Steiner-Adair's component of "insecure parental attachments" by focusing on the need for parental relationships to be both securely attached and encouraging of autonomy and exploration for a woman to develop optimally.

Hart and Kenny (1997) also found that women who report achievement strivings paired with secure parental attachments had low levels of body dissatisfaction and reported themselves to be socially competent. Many studies suggest that women college students can benefit from setting high standards in multiple life areas, as long as they do so in the context of emotionally supportive environments comprised of parents and others (Hesse-Biber, Marino, & Watts-Roy, 1999). Other research demonstrates that conflicts between dependency and independence are related to the development of eating disorders (Steiner-Adair, 1986). As an example, a longitudinal study of women diagnosed with bulimia while in college examined factors related to recovery. Those women who were able to recover from bulimia were more likely to have successfully balanced autonomy and relationships to establish a sense of interdependence (Hesse-Biber, Marino, & Watts-Roy, 1999). Those who had negotiated a balance between relating to others while maintaining a sense of independence had a more positive self-concept, which led to a healthier body image and a decrease in disordered eating symptoms.

Research indicates, therefore, that most women cannot thrive while being either separate from or dependent upon others; rather, the hallmark of adaptive development for women is interdependence (Hart & Kenny, 1997). Although college is a time wherein all students struggle with individuation and autonomy issues (Chickering & Reisser, 1993), the pressure to be both dependent and independent seems to create a conflict that manifests itself somatically through disordered eating symptoms in certain women. If the feelings around this tension are not faced, the attainment of interdependence may be delayed or foreclosed. As higher education professionals, we can promote interdependency in our students; research strongly indicates that this is a resiliency factor for college women that can protect against negative body image and disordered eating.

MULTICULTURAL RESEARCH

An examination of multicultural research yields rich data regarding the factors affecting an individual's ability to resist sociocultural injunctions for extreme thinness. Cross-cultural studies show that women and adolescent girls of Caucasian American descent report greater body dissatisfaction than women from other cultural groups both within and outside of the United States (Mukai, Kambara, & Sasaki, 1998). Research consistently demonstrates that the incidence of negative body image and disordered eating increases in non-Western women as they enter Western society and internalize its values regarding the importance of physical attractiveness. Further, as other societies become westernized, the incidence of eating-related problems increases in those societies as well (Lake, Staiger, & Glowinski, 2000). It is evident that the pervasive problem of body image dissatisfaction is culture-bound.

Women are socialized to attend to and internalize sociocultural pressures regarding beauty to a greater extent than are men, and the rates of eating disorders are lower for all cultural groups compared with White women and adolescents. Do White women internalize U.S. sociocultural pressures to a greater extent than do other cultural groups? What are the factors that enable members of certain cultural groups to maintain a positive body image, despite mainstream pressures for the attainment of narrowly defined beauty standards? In a national sample of Black and White men and women, Smith, Thompson, Raczynski, and Hilner (1999) found that women were more dissatisfied with body weight/shape and overall appearance than men. When examining effects for gender and ethnicity, White men were more dissatisfied with their appearance than Black men. Further, when controlling for age, body mass index, and education, White women were more dissatisfied with their size and appearance than were Black women. Black men and women were more invested in their appearances than White men and women, and women overall were more invested in their appearances than men.

One explanation for these differences is that Caucasian and African-American women hold differing beliefs regarding self-perception and beauty standards. As a group, African-American women adhere to standards of beauty that are more flexible and fluid, and Black women are less concerned with weight and dieting than are White women. Black women indicate that body image is less central to their self-evaluation and that they are more satisfied at higher body weights than White women (Molloy & Herzberger, 1998).

Molloy and Herzberger (1998) offer other explanations for these significant differences in body satisfaction. They found that race and ethnicity differences in body image between White and African-American women were primarily due to two factors: differences in the interpretation of their gender roles, and perception of what men desire as the ideal body type for women. African-American women who believed that men prefer larger body types, and who had higher scores on measures of masculinity (as defined by the Bem Sex Role Inventory; Bem, 1974) had higher levels of self-esteem and body satisfaction. The authors describe these "protective factors" as being less often present in Caucasian women (Molloy & Herzberger, 1998).

Lester and Petrie (1998) argue that African-American women are not invulnerable to body dissatisfaction and disordered eating, and report that they do suffer from clinically diagnosable eating disorders. Several studies indicate prevalence rates of eating disorders among African-American college women which are similar to rates for college women in general (Lester & Petrie, 1998). In their research, Lester and Petrie examined the bulimic symptomatology in African-American women, and investigated the relationships between body mass, body dissatisfaction, depression, self-esteem, internalization of U.S. cultural norms regarding attractiveness, and identification with the White culture. For the sample of African-American college students, body mass index, body dissatisfaction, and low self esteem were the best predictors of bulimic symptoms. These are also the risk factors associated with disordered eating in White women. In this study, the internalization of U.S. cultural beliefs about attractiveness and identification with White culture were not related to symptoms of bulimia. The internalization of cultural beliefs about beauty, however, was related to higher levels of depression, lower levels of self-esteem, and less overall satisfaction with both body size and shape. They conclude that identification with the White culture is a distinctly different process from internalizing mainstream cultural beliefs about appearance, with only the latter being associated with the correlates of disordered eating. If African-American women evaluate themselves according to the beauty ideal set by the dominant culture, then they too are at risk for the development of body dissatisfaction, which in turn may lead to disordered eating and full-blown eating disorders. It is important, then, to remain mindful of within-group differences regarding body dissatisfaction among members of all cultural groups, and to consider the extent to which group members internalize the standards of beauty espoused for women in Western cultures.

Japanese women are similar to American women in that they experience great pressure to be thin, and the rate of eating disorders among college women in Japan has increased in the past several decades (Mukai, Kambara, & Sasaki, 1998). With the Westernization of Japan during the past 40 years, a greater percentage of magazine articles and advertisements, many of which feature Caucasian models, have been dedicated to weight loss and the ultra-thin body ideal. Mukai, Kambara, and Sasaki (1998) argue that as Japanese women are increasingly bombarded with media images of tall, ultra-thin Caucasian models, the ideal body type for Japanese women has become increasingly similar to that for Caucasian women. Just as for Caucasian women, such a body type ideal is unattainable for the majority of Japanese women, and this leads to body dissatisfaction. A study of Japanese and American college women at Japanese and

U.S. universities compared levels of body dissatisfaction, eating disturbances, and need for social approval to determine differences between the two groups (Mukai, Kambara, & Sasaki, 1998). They found that although Japanese women were at lower body mass indexes, they were more likely to be dissatisfied with their bodies and to consider themselves as overweight than were American women. Further, need for social approval was associated with body dissatisfaction and disordered eating in the Japanese women; the authors suggest that for these women, social acceptability is considered synonymous with the attainment of thinness.

Other research has examined the relationship between sexual orientation and body dissatisfaction. In general, gay men and heterosexual women are the most dissatisfied with their bodies and more vulnerable to eating disorders. Between the two groups, there is a shared emphasis placed on pleasing men as well as on thinness and physical attractiveness. Research with gay men consistently shows they are more likely to be dissatisfied with their bodies than are heterosexual men (Beren, Hayden, Wilfley, & Grilo, 1996). As with women, this body image dissatisfaction is often related to disordered eating and depression. A study of eating disorders in males examined 135 men with a diagnosis of bulimia or anorexia (Carlat, Camargo, & Herzog, 1997). Forty-two percent of the bulimic men were either homosexual or bisexual, a percentage which is disproportionate to their representation in the general population. The authors conclude that homosexuality/bisexuality is a risk factor for males for the development of eating disorders, particularly bulimia.

It may be argued that if gay men and heterosexual women are particularly at risk for negative body image, then lesbian women may have higher levels of body satisfaction, since they place less emphasis on the importance of physical attractiveness, attracting men, and on adhering to traditional female norms (Ludwig & Brownell, 1999). Recent studies, however, have yielded varying findings. As with other cultural groups, it is the within-group differences that provide the most useful information regarding our understanding of negative body image. Ludwig and Brownell (1999) recruited lesbian and bisexual women to participate in a survey via e-mail and the Internet that examined within-group differences regarding body image. Women completed measures of demographics, sexual orientation, weight, how they described themselves in terms of masculinity/femininity, and attitudes regarding body satisfaction. Results show that the women who scored highest on levels of femininity had lower body satisfaction relative to the androgynous and masculine women. Further, women who had mostly lesbian and bisexual friends had higher levels of body satisfaction than those respondents with primarily heterosexual friends. The authors conclude that those who are surrounded by others who challenge cultural norms regarding the definition of physical attractiveness are more likely to be able to resist these pressures as well, and to subsequently maintain a higher level of satisfaction about their bodies.

There is a plethora of research on women, body image, and eating disorders; in other words, we understand what happens when women develop negative body image and disordered eating practices. In this chapter, the reviewed research on college women with body image problems indicates that they possess a drive for thinness, place high importance on physical appearance when evaluating self concept, develop high expectations for the effects of weight loss, overemphasize pleasing others, avoid intense feelings by focusing on dieting and weight, and experience conflicts between independence and dependence. However, it may be more helpful to focus our attention on the resiliency factors that seem to protect some individuals from problems with body image. Within-group differences among lesbian and bisexual women shed light on the specific resiliency factors that may buffer women and men from the development of a negative body image; these findings are also echoed in studies of within-group differences among African-American women. Such factors include: possessing traditionally "masculine" traits, placing low importance on attaining a certain standard of thinness to please men, developing a broad definition of beauty, and surrounding oneself with others who do not endorse U.S. sociocultural values regarding thinness. Further, valuing interdependency—balancing caring for one's own needs as well as for those of others—is another critical resiliency factor highlighted in the research. These themes provide directions for the prevention and treatment of body-image problems and disordered eating for all college students, regardless of race, gender, or sexual orientation.

CURRENT CAMPUS INTERVENTIONS

College counseling/mental health services and health and wellness centers have launched efforts to prevent college student reliance on societal messages regarding thinness, attractiveness, and dieting. Schwitzer, Bergholz, Dore, and Salimi (1998) suggest that any campus body image/eating disorders program should address three levels of intervention: prevention, developmental interventions, and psychotherapeutic interventions. Prevention models are targeted toward college students who may be susceptible to the development of dysfunctional behaviors in regard to eating, exercise, and weight management. As has been demonstrated in numerous studies, this group would include all college women (Mintz & Betz, 1988). Prevention efforts typically attempt to provide education to students to dispel myths, promote healthier behaviors, and to enhance women's body image. Counselors, nutritionists, health and wellness educators, and health science faculty may be involved in the implementation of these efforts through advertising campaigns, nutrition information in cafeterias, workshops, and "Awareness" weeks (Schwitzer et al., 1998).

One study investigated the effectiveness of introducing a credit-bearing course designed to improve the body image of class members (Springer et al.,

1999). The course, entitled "Body Traps: Perspectives on Body Image," provided opportunities for structured informational activities, group discussion, and journaling. Course content included the following topics: media influences, history of beauty, biological/evolutionary aspects of attractiveness, adolescent development, disability, aging, bodybuilding, cosmetic surgery, risk factors and consequences of anorexia and bulimia, obesity, and cultural differences. Students were challenged to identify current U.S. standards of beauty that are narrow, limiting, and unrealistic. They learned about the futility of restrictive dieting, and how frequent dieting often leads to binge eating and eating disorders. Pre- and post-evaluations of students' body image, eating attitudes, and self-esteem show that participants in the course improved significantly in their scores on measures of body image, eating attitudes, and eating behaviors. The introduction of an educational course format with group discussion and individual student reflection shows promise for changing the attitudes and behaviors of college students.

At the developmental level of intervention, the purpose is to assist students when a problem exists, causes some difficulties for the student, and has the potential to grow in frequency and intensity (Schwitzer et al., 1998). Workshops, structured counseling groups, and other interventions that provide education, challenge unrealistic beliefs, and develop skills are most useful.

Kaminski and McNamara (1996) designed a developmental group intervention for college women reporting chronic dieting, a known risk factor for the development of more serious eating disturbances. Measures of group outcomes show that, compared to a control group, participants reported significantly improved levels of self-esteem and body satisfaction. The following components were included in the group format design: discussion of realistic weight goals, the cycle of dieting, and healthy eating habits. Participants were challenged to change their negative thinking styles with regard to their bodies and overall physical appearance, and members brainstormed about how they might develop healthier ways of coping with emotions and stressors. They discussed the relationship between perfectionism, depression, and self-esteem. Members learned ways in which they have difficulty communicating directly, and practiced more assertive communication strategies. Finally, participants gained an awareness of the societal pressures and messages that contribute to the prevalence of dieting and low body image, and they learned ways to resist these pressures.

The training of students as paraprofessional peer educators can also be an effective developmental strategy (Schwitzer et al., 1998). Students paired with peer counselors have reported decreases in problematic eating behaviors and in perfectionism (Lenihan & Kirk, 1990). Newer students can benefit from being surrounded by large numbers of peer educators who possess realistic and positive attitudes about their bodies and physical attractiveness. According to Thombs et al. (1996), peer models can exemplify confidence, respect from others, and a sense of self-worth—the very traits that many women are seeking to achieve through weight loss. Women can learn that these qualities are not achieved through physical appearance, but through learning to value all aspects of themselves.

When problems with disordered eating intensify to cause significant impairment in a student's life, individual and group psychotherapy is recommended in addition to a wide range of adjunctive services. Treatment for anorexia and bulimia on campus ideally involves a collaboration between health and psychological services; multidisciplinary teams are recommended when possible (Schwitzer et al., 1998). Northern Illinois University developed a successful campus Eating Disorders Task Force, composed of a multidisciplinary team including counselors, a support-group leader, a physician, a psychiatrist, a nutritionist, and athletic trainers. The team meets bimonthly to consult regarding students with eating disorder problems (Archer & Cooper, 1998). At James Madison University in Virginia, the multidisciplinary eating disorders response team is composed of a health center physician, consulting psychiatrist, nurses, health educators, counseling center psychotherapists, nutrition specialists, and wellness center staff. When students are diagnosed with anorexia or bulimia, they receive both individual and group counseling at the counseling center, meet regularly with a doctor or nurse, and meet frequently with the nutritional specialist. Often, problems are so severe that off-campus services and inpatient treatment programs are recommended (Schwitzer et al., 1998).

IMPLICATIONS FOR THE FUTURE

So what can be done to change what Rodin, Silberstein, and Streigel-Moore (1985) term a "normative discontent" with women's bodies, which robs many college women of their strength, confidence, and vitality? How can we facilitate the necessary shift away from powerful, pervasive cultural messages regarding how students "should" look and feel? I propose that we rethink our focus on the problem (e.g., eating disorders, dieting) and rather focus on what does seem to be working for many individuals. An examination of resiliency factors present in college students who are able to resist strong cultural pressures provides some direction for shaping the future.

Resiliency Factor One:
Ability to Challenge the Media-generated "Slender Ideal"

What if we were all more aware of sociocultural messages regarding the "slender ideal"? Most media portrayals of beauty include only one body type as acceptable. As long as individuals strive to meet this standard, unattainable for most, they will never be satisfied with themselves as they are. If professionals in higher education encourage students to become aware of these powerful pressures as they observe media images, they can begin to question the rationality of starving themselves to meet an arbitrary and unhealthy ideal. The media promises great things for those who attain this ideal, but in reality, chronic dieting leads to malnourishment, irritability, lethargy, a lack of vitality, eventual weight gain, or even death by self-starvation (Kano, 1989). As professionals in higher education, we can encourage students to challenge conformity to destructive cultural norms. By facilitating conversations about challenging media images, we are also encouraging the development of students' critical thinking skills. Students will have more strategies for questioning what they are "fed" by the popular media broadly as they focus specifically on issues of beauty, thinness, and ideal body types.

Resiliency Factor Two:
Sense of Interdependency

Another resiliency factor identified in the research is a woman's sense of interdependency. When women feel the tension between independence and dependence and are unable to negotiate a balance between the two, they are at risk for the development of eating disorders. This tension is refocused on one area in which women believe they have control—their body size and weight. However, this control is illusory when the results of this pursuit of the ultra-thin ideal do not bring the power and sense of worth women seek; instead, they feel greater inadequacy and lack of esteem. This is a vicious cycle which can only be prevented through women's willingness to face these intense, conflictual feelings squarely. As highlighted in the reviewed research, women thrive most optimally in the context of emotionally supportive relationships through which they can fully express their feelings and nurture others—while also caring for themselves. Gilligan (1982) suggests that male developmental theorists traditionally view healthy development as moving away from parents toward increasing self-reliance, yet this model does not reflect the experiences of many women. Even college counselors traditionally encourage students to strive for individuation and independence (Archer & Cooper, 1998). We must be mindful, therefore, to respect interdependence as a hallmark of women's development, even though this value is not traditionally emphasized in higher education settings.

Resiliency Factor Three:
Moving Beyond Traditional Sex Role Prescriptions

A third resiliency factor includes a broader definition of what it means to be "feminine" or "masculine." What if we question what it means to be feminine, masculine, or androgynous in our culture? We can encourage students to deconstruct the idea that women should be "feminine" and men should be "masculine." According to research, those individuals who report high levels of androgyny have the highest levels of body satisfaction and overall self-esteem. If students are able to question and move beyond traditional sex-role prescriptions and instead express all aspects of themselves, they can then lead more authentic lives. As higher education professionals, we can model for students the ability to adhere to personally-defined values and goals.

Resiliency Factor Four:
Internally Derived Sense of Self-Worth

What if all students developed a healthy sense of self apart from external standards? Many women with negative body image and disordered eating place great emphasis on pleasing others, "attracting a man," and stifling their feelings in efforts not to offend others. Many women tend to deny that their thoughts and feelings are valid, believing instead that it is selfish to consider their own needs (Meyer & Russell, 1998). Higher education professionals can assist women in articulating aspects of their emotional lives that have been stifled or repressed by listening to and validating their feelings. They can also encourage women to speak of their ideas and opinions that they may have learned to devalue over time. If a woman looks to the opinions of others for reassurance of her acceptability, but is never reinforced for speaking, she may learn to remain silent. Instead, educators can promote and facilitate the free expression of all students' voices both in and out of the classroom.

Resiliency Factor Five:
Development of Broader Definitions of Beauty

As was highlighted in the literature on African-American women, a broader definition of what is considered attractive leads to fewer problems with body image. Higher education professionals can encourage the acceptance of all body types for men and women, since the human body naturally exists in a variety of shapes and sizes. Recent popular media (e.g., *Mode*) and Internet resources (e.g., *Real Women Project, Body Talk Magazine, Body Positive*) have been developed to support a broader view of beauty. Higher education professionals can turn to supportive literature and images while encouraging students to avoid those that espouse a limiting ideal for body shape and size. We can help all students question the mainstream media pressures to believe that only one body type is acceptable.

Resiliency Factor Six:
Support and Empowerment

What if all students felt empowered and supported? Women are promised that beauty (i.e., meeting U.S. sociocultural standards) will bring power, significance, and a sense of self-worth. Research consistently shows that individuals who hold these expectations are at risk for the development of negative body image, depression, low self-esteem, and disordered eating. The beauty ideal keeps changing and remains unattainable for the vast majority of people, so that they remain in a perpetual struggle to measure up. Instead of declaring war on themselves and viewing other women as competitors, we can encourage women to support one another. In an environment of support, it is clear that women can achieve a sense of power and significance. Women can encourage one another to reject unrealistic beauty ideals and empower others to refocus their energies on meaningful dreams and goals.

Sociocultural pressures will likely remain present on campus, yet responses at the university and even individual level can moderate their impact. On each campus, those who are interested in promoting a more positive body image for students can use the following questions as a guide. What programs may be instituted that encourage acceptance of multiple body shapes and sizes? Conversely, can programs that promote the objectification of women's bodies be eliminated or modified? What types of advertising are displayed on campus, and what impact do these images have on shaping campus norms? What can we do to enhance positive body image in groups that are particularly vulnerable to these types of sociocultural and campus pressures (e.g., sororities, women living in residence halls, athletes)? At the individual level of change, each participant on campus can make a difference. As a college counselor working individually with students regarding these issues, I have witnessed the power of a supportive, therapeutic relationship in facilitating change. One by one, women and men can learn to value themselves as well as others in all life areas.

I believe any changes in these areas will be met with strong resistance from those in the multimillion-dollar diet, beauty, and fashion industries who wish to maintain an unattainable beauty ideal for women. I also believe, however, that change can flow from the individual to societal levels. In any system, individual resistance to the status quo can throw the larger system into disequilibrium. I am hopeful, therefore, that if a significant number of individuals on campus support one another in building resiliency to problems with negative body image and dissatisfaction, higher education environments can be transformed. As this occurs, we can begin to envision what might happen on campus if all students truly felt empowered to achieve their fullest potential.

NOTE

1. In this paper, the terms "Western" and "U.S." cultural ideals are used interchangeably.

REFERENCES

American Psychiatric Association. (1994). *Diagnostic and statistical manual of mental disorders* (4th ed.). Washington DC: Authors.

Archer, J., & Cooper, S. (1998). *Counseling and mental health services: A handbook of contemporary practices and challenges.* San Francisco: Jossey-Bass.

Barber, N. (1998). The slender ideal and eating disorders: An interdisciplinary "telescope" model. *International Journal of Eating Disorders, 23,* 295–307.

Bem, S. (1974). The measurement of psychological androgyny. *Journal of Consulting and Clinical Psychology, 42,* 155–162.

Beren, S. E., Hayden, H. A., Wilfley, D. E., & Grilo, C. M. (1996). The influence of sexual orientation on body dissatisfaction in adult men and women. *International Journal of Eating Disorders, 20,* 135–141.

Brazelton, E. W., Greene, K. S., Gynther, M., & O'Mell, J. (1998). Femininity, bulimia, and distress in college women. *Psychological Reports, 83,* 355–363.

Carlat, D. J., Camargo, C. A., & Herzog, D. B. (1997). Eating disorders in males: A report on 135 patients. *American Journal of Psychiatry, 154*(8), 1127–1133.

Cash, T. F. (1994). The situational inventory of body-image dysphoria: Contextual assessment of a negative body image. *The Behavior Therapist, 17,* 133–134.

Cash, T. F., Ancis, J. R., & Strachan, M. D. (1997). Gender attitudes, feminist identity, and body images among college women. *Sex Roles: A Journal of Research, 36*(7), 433–448.

Cash, T. F., & Henry, P. E. (1995). Women's body images: The results of a national survey in the U.S.A. *Sex Roles: A Journal of Research, 33,* 19–28.

Chickering, A. W., & Reisser, L. (1993). *Education and identity* (2nd ed.). San Francisco: Jossey-Bass.

Derlene, L. M., & Bragowicz, A. A. (1990). Student healthcare needs, attitudes, and behaviors: Marketing implications for college health centers. *Journal of American College Health, 38,* 157–164.

Evans, N. J., Forney, D. S., & Guido-DiBrito, F. (1998). *Student development in college: Theory, research, and practice.* San Francisco: Jossey-Bass.

Feingold, A., & Mazzella, R. (1998). Gender differences in body image are increasing. *Psychological Science, 9*(3), 190–196.

Gilligan, C. (1982). *In a different voice.* Cambridge: Harvard University Press.

Hart, K., & Kenny, M. E. (1997). Adherence to the superwoman ideal and eating disorder symptoms among college women. *Sex Roles: A Journal of Research, 36*(7), 461–479.

Hesse-Biber, S., Marino, M., & Watts-Roy, D. (1999). A longitudinal study of eating disorders among college women: Factors that influence recovery. *Gender and Society, 13*(3), 385–387.

Josselson, R. (1987). *Finding herself: Pathways to identity development in women.* San Francisco: Jossey-Bass.

Kaminski, P. L., & McNamara, K. (1996). A treatment for college women at risk for bulimia: A controlled evaluation. *Journal of Counseling and Development, 74*(3), 288–295.

Kano, S. (1989). *Making peace with food: Freeing yourself from the diet obsession.* New York: Harper & Row.

Keil, K. L. (1998). An intimate profile of generation X. *The American Enterprise, 9*(1), 49–53.

Koszewski, W. M., Newell, G. K., & Higgins, J. J. (1990). Effect of a nutrition education program on eating attitudes and behaviors of college women. *Journal of College Student Development, 31*, 201–210.

Lake, A. J., Staiger, P. K., & Glowinski, H. (2000). Effect of Western culture on women's attitudes to eating and perceptions of body shape. *International Journal of Eating Disorders, 27*, 83–89.

Lee, R. M. (1989). Anorexia nervosa and bulimia nervosa. In P. A. Grayson & K. Cauley (Eds.) *College psychotherapy* (pp. 274–297). New York: Guilford Press.

Lenihan, G., & Kirk, W. G. (1990). Using paraprofessionals in the treatment of eating disorders. *Journal of Counseling and Development, 68*, 332–335.

Lester, R., & Petrie, T. A. (1998). Physical, psychological, and societal correlates of bulimic symptomatology among African-American college women. *Journal of Counseling Psychology, 45*(3), 315–321.

Lindner, M. A., Ryckman, R. M., Gold, J. A., & Stone, W. F. (1995). Traditional vs. nontraditional women and men's perceptions of the personalities and physiques of ideal women and men. *Sex Roles: A Journal of Research, 32*(9), 675–691.

Ludwig, M. R., & Brownell, K. D. (1999). Lesbians, bisexual women, and body image: An investigation of gender roles and social group affiliation. *International Journal of Eating Disorders, 25*, 89–97.

Masterson, J. F. (1988). *The search for the real self.* San Francisco: Free Press.

College-age women unaware of harm of advertising stereotypes. (1999). *Media Report to Women, 27*(2), 1–2.

Meyer, D. F., & Russell, R. K. (1998). Caretaking, separation from parents, and the development of eating disorders. *Journal of Counseling and Development, 76*(2), 166–173.

Mintz, L. B., & Betz, N. E. (1988). Prevalence and correlates of eating disordered behaviors among undergraduate women. *Journal of Counseling Psychology, 35*(4), 463–471.

Molloy, B. L., & Herzberger, S. D. (1998). Body image and self-esteem: A comparison of African-American and Caucasian women. *Sex Roles: A Journal of Research, 38*(7), 631–644.

Mukai, T., Kambara, A., & Sasaki, Y. (1998). Body dissatisfaction, need for social approval, and eating disturbances among Japanese and American college women. *Sex Roles: A Journal of Research, 39*(9), 751–781.

Muth, J. L., & Cash, T. F. (1997). Body image attitudes: What difference does gender make? *Journal of Applied Social Psychology, 27*(16), 1438–1452.

Polivy, J., & Herman, C. (1987). Diagnosis and treatment of abnormal eating. *Journal of Consulting and Clinical Psychology, 21*, 635–644.

Rodin, J., Silberstein, L. R., & Streigel-Moore, R. H. (1985). Women and weight: A normative discontent. In T. B. Sonderegger (Ed.) *Psychology and gender: Nebraska Symposium on Motivation* (pp. 267–307). Lincoln: University of Nebraska Press.

Schulken, E. D., Pinciaro, P. J., Sawyer, R. G., Jensen, J. G., & Hoban, M. T. (1997). Sorority women's body size perceptions and their weight-related attitudes and behaviors. *Journal of American College Health, 46*(2), 69.

Schwitzer, A. M., Bergholz, K., Dore, T., & Salimi, L. (1998). Eating disorders among college women: Prevention, education, and treatment responses. *Journal of American College Health, 46*(5), 199–208.

Showers, C. J., & Larson, B. E. (1999). Looking at body image: The organization of self-knowledge about physical appearance and its relation to disordered eating. *Journal of Personality, 67*(4), 659–664.

Siever, M. D. (1994). Sexual orientation and gender as factors in socioculturally acquired vulnerability to body dissatisfaction and eating disorders. *Journal of Consulting and Clinical Psychology, 62*(2), 252–260.

Smith, D. E., Thompson, J. K., Raczynski, J. M., & Hilner, J. E. (1999). Body image among men and women in a biracial cohort: The CARDIA study. *International Journal of Eating Disorders, 25*, 71–82.

Spann, L., & Fischer, J. L. (1990). Identifying co-dependency. *The Counselor, 8*, 27.

Springer, E. A., Winzelberg, A. J., Perkins, R., & Barr-Taylor, C. (1999). Effects of a body image curriculum for college students on improved body image. *International Journal of Eating Disorders, 26*, 12–20.

Steiner-Adair, C. (1986). The body politic: Normal female adolescent development and the development of eating disorders. *Journal of the American Academy of Psychoanalysis, 14*, 95–114.

Streigel-Moore, R. H., Silberstein, L. R., & Rodin, J. (1986). Toward an understanding of risk factors for bulimia. *American Psychologist, 42*, 247–263.

Thombs, D. L., Rosenberg, J. M., Mahoney, C. A., & Daniel, E. L. (1996). Weight-loss expectancies, relative weight, and symptoms of bulimia in young women. *Journal of College Student Development, 37*(4), 405–413.

Turner, S. L., Hamilton, H., Jacobs, M., Angood, L. M., & Dwyer, D. H. (1997). The influence of fashion magazines on the body image satisfaction of college women: An exploratory analysis. *Adolescence, 32*(127), 603–615.

Weiderman, M. W., & Pryor, T. L. (2000). Body dissatisfaction, bulimia, and depression among women: The mediating role of drive for thinness. *International Journal of Eating Disorders, 27*, 90–95.

Wiseman, C. V., Gray, J. J., Mosimann, J. E., & Ahrens, A. H. (1992). Cultural expectations for thinness in women: An update. *International Journal of Eating Disorders, 11*, 85–89.

Wolf, N. (1991). *The beauty myth*. New York: William Morrow.

Worobey, J. (1999). Temperament and loving-styles in college women: Associations with eating attitudes. *Psychological Reports, 84*, 305–311.

4

The Gender of Violence on Campus

William F. Pinar

Violence sublimates same-sex desire and reinforces paranoid distances between men. At the same time, it terrorizes and subjugates women who are necessary to establish the heterosexuality of the masculine order.

—Scott S. Derrick, *Mounumental Anxieties*

[A]n understanding of virtually any aspect of modern Western culture must be, not merely incomplete, but damaged in its central substance to the degree that it does not incorporate a critical analysis of modern homo/ heterosexual definition.

—Eve Kosofsky Sedgwick, *Epistemology of the Closet*

A single event sometimes expresses something telling about the gender of violence on college campuses. The gender of that violence is, in a fundamental sense, masculine, and more specifically, heterosexual, at least as this sexual "preference" is made "compulsory" (Rich, 1980, p. 637) in the current and hegemonic sex/gender system (Butler, 1990). That event, and others I will report momentarily, require those of us committed to higher education as a social democratic and not a narrowly vocational project, to press for the inclusion of women's and gender studies in general education requirements for all undergraduates, as I will suggest in the final paragraphs of this chapter.

The single event to which I refer occurred on December 6, 1989. On that day one Marc Lepine mounted a well-planned aggressive armed assault at the School of Engineering (Ecole Polytechnique) at the University of Montreal. Expressing his rage against women, he killed or injured 14 people with a rifle. After one wounded victim screamed for help, Lepine pulled out his knife and stabbed her repeatedly in the chest until she was dead. Finally he put the muzzle of the rifle against his head, said "Oh shit," and shot himself. It was the worst mass murder and hate crime against women in Canadian history. Lepine left a suicide note that said:

Please note that if I kill myself today 12/06/89 it is not for economic
reasons (because I waited until I used up all my financial means even
refusing jobs) but for political reasons. Because I decide to send Ad
Patres [meaning gathered to the fathers, or simply, dead] the feminists
who have always ruined my life. For seven years my life has brought
me no joy, and, being utterly weary of the world, I have decided to
stop those shrews dead in their tracks. (quoted in Simon, 1996, p. 248)

Six months later, Lepine claimed his last victim. Sarto Blais, an engineer who
had been at the same school and who could not rid himself of his memories of
the killings of his classmates and friends, hanged himself. Seeing no reason to
go on living, his parents then committed suicide as well (Simon, 1996).

While spectacular, the event is not entirely unique. Violence on campus
is not uncommon. In 1993, for instance, students and faculty on American
college campuses were victims of 1,353 robberies, 3,224 aggravated assaults,
7,350 motor vehicle thefts, 21,478 burglaries, 466 rapes, and 17 murders.
This violence was gendered, much of it directed toward women and sexual
minorities. For example, 21% of lesbian and gay students, compared to 5 percent of the total student body, report having been physically attacked (Comstock, 1991).

Life on college campuses is not, of course, insulated from life in the nation,
including developments in American youth culture. One of the most disturbing developments is the seemingly increasing and often unpredictable violence
of young men. In Olivehurst, California, Eric Huston returned to his old high
school and killed four people to take revenge on those he held responsible for
preparing him for such a "lousy job" with Hewlett-Packard, from which he had
just been fired (quoted in Simon, 1996, p. 249). But alumni have not been the
main players in this crying game. Students murdered other students and teachers in 1997 in Pearl, Mississippi and West Paducah, Kentucky, in 1998 in
Arkansas and Oregon, and in 1999 in Littleton, Colorado and Conyers, Georgia. During 1993, 39% of urban school districts reported a shooting or a knif-
ing, 23% had a drive-by shooting, and 15% reported at least one rape. Most
violence in the workplace is committed by white men (Simon, 1996). If the
shootings mentioned are any indication, it appears most violence in schools is
committed by young men—young white men.

Gender differences show up in statistics about handguns and other
weapons. Approximately 40% of the boys (and 12% of the girls) in South Carolina's public schools, for instance, reported carrying a weapon to school in the
preceding 30 days; knives were the weapon carried most frequently, except by
black males who were more likely to have carried guns (Valois, Vincent, Mc-
Keown, Garrison, & Kirby, 1993). College students are only slightly less likely
to carry guns or other weapons. Approximately 14% of male college students
carry a weapon on campus; 5% carry a gun (Douglas, et al., 1997).

Many young men we see on university campuses attempt to sublimate these gendered tendencies toward violence into institutionally organized activities, such as sports. Many characterize their favorite activities as "rough sports," probably the most popular of these being football. One young male respondent reported he likes "mauling people, and hurting 'em so they're afraid to come again." (Of course, in an athletic context by "people" he means other young men.) That is important, the respondent continued, because "I want others to know about me. . . . If you hurt someone, or shoot an animal in hunting, you know you are somebody. . . . The pain on the face of the adversary or the lifeless carcass are witness to your awful power" (quoted in Comstock, 1991, p. 104). Many college men substitute identification for actual athletic activity, and from the stands and local bars cheer on other young men during football games each fall.

This apparently innocent and media-hyped preoccupation of millions of American college students, especially college men, may well be implicated in the violence on campus. Such organized violence—sport—allows young men to "toughen up," to become "men," that is, competitive, aggressive, masculine versions of "men." Such hegemonic masculinity seems to guarantee greater tendencies toward violence, especially sexualized violence toward women. As we will see momentarily, college athletes are more likely than nonathletes to engage in sexual aggression, including rape. While many—especially older men— see such activity as "boys being boys," there is nothing inevitable about such violence. It is a predictable consequence of a sex/gender system in which masculinity sublimates homosexual desire into homosocial violence and heterosexual aggression (Pinar, 1998).

Given this view of hegemonic masculinity, it is not surprising that football and other team sports fail to excite many gay men, as Mark Simpson (1994) points out. Why? "It might be argued," he suggests, "that with their homosexuality completely (or mostly) desublimated they have no need for them; for gay men team sports are experienced not as sexualized aggression, just aggression" (Simpson, 1994, p. 90). As Oscar Wilde once quipped: "Football is all very well as a game for rough girls, but it is hardly suitable for delicate boys" (quoted in Simpson, 1994, p. 90).

If men are engaged with each other sexually, the sublimated homoerotics of sport are superfluous. Simpson (1994) argues that it is the very brutality of football that makes permissible moments of homoerotic intimacy for the players and those who watch them: the hugs, the slaps on the butt, boys piling on top of boys, disguised versions of sex in uniform. "In this masculine universe," Simpson (1994) observes, "there can be no loveliness without horror; pleasure is circumscribed by pain, gain by loss, love by hate; each goal scored and game won, each and every joy attained, is wrung from the despair of other men" (p. 71). It is violence that makes the experience of homoeroticism permissible as it occurs in the context of "manly" aggression. Given the pervasive homophobia in the current sex/gender system, all such desire must be sublimated and focused on the game. Simpson (1994) understands exactly: "[I]nterest in men is permitted, indeed encouraged, but must always be expressed through the game. A man's love for football is a love of and for manhood, composed of a condensation of introjected (turned inwards) homoerotic desire" (p. 73).

If straight men, by definition, are repressed homosexuals (and exclusively homosexual men are repressed heterosexuals), one would not be surprised to find homosexual desire converted to heterosexual currency in a homphobic homosocial economy. That is exactly what Gayle Rubin (1975) and others have observed, namely that many straight men have sex with women to solidify their standing with other men. In such an economy, straight men sleep with women in part to impress their male buddies. Appreciating, then, that "macho" masculinity contains within it repressed homosexual desire re-expressed as an aggressive heterosexuality in which women are objectified as commodities in a homosocial economy, one might expect all-male preserves such as athletic teams or fraternities to be characterized by high levels of (homo)sexual tension.

Indeed, the research suggests that straight men who live together in groups do seem to experience aggravated levels of sexual tension. Even those "straight" men who do not live in all-male houses or dormitories but whose primary social affiliation is with other men also tend to exhibit greater (hetero)sexual aggressivity specifically, and exaggerated conformity to traditional male norms generally. The primary examples of such "fraternal" settings are predictable: campus fraternities (Hirsch, 1990; Martin & Hummer, 1989; O'Sullivan, 1991; O'Sullivan, 1993; Sanday, 1990; Sandler & Ehrhart, 1985); intercollegiate and professional athletic teams, primarily football, basketball, lacrosse and ice hockey, which are considered high-contact sports (Crosset & McDonald, 1995; Eskenazi, 1991; Messner, 1992; Sanday, 1990); and military combat units, especially in times of war (Brownmiller, 1975; Herman, 1989; O'Sullivan, 1992; Pope, 1993). Like fraternities and athletic teams, sectors of the U.S. military are typified by a culture of gendered violence, as well, illustrated by the famous Tailhook incident in September 1991 (Pope, 1993).

Because heterosexually-identified male groups such as fraternities, intercollegiate athletic teams, and soldiers tend to be involved in a disproportionate number of gang rape incidents, Chris O'Sullivan (1993) opposes campus fraternities and athletic teams. (What to do about the military remains a puzzle, apparently.) Studies have shown that members of fraternities and team sports are not only more likely to commit sexual assaults as a group, but they show that group members are more likely to perpetrate individual acts such as acquaintance rapes. O'Sullivan (1993) is clear that "combined with male socialization in our society and the connotations of masculinity in our culture, fraternal cultures at schools and colleges breed a propensity to abuse women sexually, along a continuum of behaviors" (p. 25). They also abuse gay men

(Comstock, 1991). O'Sullivan's views are visible in my curricular recommendations outlined at the end of this chapter.

Compared to sexual assault, much less data is available on domestic, or courtship, violence on the college campuses. We do know that even going out on dates can be risky for young women, and that date rape is only one kind of acquaintance rape that occurs (Schwartz & DeKeseredy, 1997). Women might also keep in mind when they accept that date that one-third of college men report that they would rape if they were sure they would not get caught. Approximately fifteen percent (15.4 to be exact) of college women report having been raped (Candib & Schmitt, 1996).

That figure may be too low. A study on campus rape sponsored by the National Institute of Mental Heath suggests so. In one study, quantitative descriptive data regarding assaults, victims, and the social context of date rape were obtained from surveys administered to a nationally representative sample of 3,187 women and 2,972 men at undergraduate institutions across the United States. Among the key findings were that 25% of women surveyed had an experience that met the legal definition of rape or attempted rape, and that 84% of those raped knew their attacker. Moreover, one in 12 college males surveyed confessed to having committed acts that met the legal definition of rape or attempted rape (Koss, Gidycz & Wisniewski, 1987).

The "Greeks"

If rape is understood to be at the end of a continuum of sexually aggressive behaviors, then one understands that the event is not, in a sense, exceptional. The potential for rape may always be present among heterosexually identified men. (Is it superfluous to remind readers that gay men do not rape women? Significantly, it is also straight men who rape other men, specifically gay men [Scarce, 1997].) For instance, of 261 undergraduate psychology and business students interviewed at Auburn, 17% reported having committed both sexually and physically aggressive acts against their partners (Hannan & Burkhart, 1993). Rapes tend to occur in social settings—such as fraternities—that promote rape-supportive beliefs and that condition men to accept them. Male assumptions regarding masculine sex roles (i.e., the behavioral content of heterosexual manhood) were the most reliable predictors of college men's acceptance, even endorsement, of rape myths (Good, Hepper, Hillenbrand-Gunn, & Wang, 1995).

The homosexual content of much heterosexual aggression becomes clearer in group rape. The FBI defines *group rape* as rape committed by three or more offenders. Twenty percent of all rapes are group or "multiple" rapes (Simon, 1996). Is gang rape a growing fad, not only among street gangs, but in fraternity houses as well? Ten men rape an unconscious woman surrounded by their male friends. Some of the terms that have been used to describe these rapes include "beaching"—the woman being likened to a "beached whale"—and "spectoring," to emphasize how integral a role those who watch play (Bordo, 1993, p. 275).

Gang rapes committed by college males—in particular, by members of fraternities—typically follow a "script." The victim is selected by one of the fraternity brothers before the party or soon after she arrives. She is then "seduced" by that fraternity brother and led to a room where the other fraternity brothers are waiting. She is assaulted upon entering the room. Typically, alcohol is plentiful at fraternity social events, alcohol that can render the victims helpless, sometimes unconscious (Hirsch, 1990). Clearly, this event is not only about her. It is also about them.

The culture of rape is reflected in fraternity culture, especially in its language and its rituals. In such a culture, gang rapes function as bonding rituals for fraternity members, confirming their "macho masculinity." Because fraternities often attract men who tend to be insecure about their manhood, the brotherhood of the fraternity becomes a compensatory and thus powerful influence. Fraternities demand conformity and solidarity. Conformity is created by men bonding together against women (Hirsch, 1990). And against gay men.

The sexual objectification of women remains a primary element of fraternity life; it is sometimes evident in fraternity serenades. In 1992, the UCLA-based feminist magazine *Together* (now called *FEM*) received an anonymous copy of the Phi Kappa Psi songbook in which one song—"S&M Man"—contained lyrics depicting female genital mutilation. At Cornell University, four male undergraduates posted on the Internet the "Top 75 reasons why women (bitches) should not have freedom of speech." Reason #20: "This is my dick. I'm gonna fuck you. No more stupid questions" (quoted in Jensen, 1998, p. 99).

After prisons and military bases, the U.S. Bureau of Justice reports that more rapes occur within the property lines of Greek-letter houses than any other community location. The initiation rites of young men into fraternities are notorious for symbolic and literal (homo)sexual assault. A researcher of prison rape, Anthony M. Scacco, Jr. (1975) reported that "one such fraternity makes the pledges strip naked, then bend over after having greased a nail which is handed to a senior member of the fraternity standing behind them. Although the nail is never delivered to the buttocks, the pledge gets the idea that he has subjected himself to another male in this manner" (p. 85). Here the homosocial aggressivity of fraternity members nearly dissolves into homosexual rape.

There are many examples of such (homo)sexualized aggression disguised as hazing. For instance, a University of Minnesota fraternity allegedly forced two Kappa Sigma pledges to strip. Their "brothers" then taped them together while fraternity members photographed the unhappy couple. The Delta Kappa Epsilon fraternity at Tulane University was banished from campus in 1984 after a series of hazing incidents. Neighbors of the DKE house reported that pledges had cords tied to their genitals and bricks tied to the other end. In 1988 two fraternity pledges at the University of Colorado were forced to spread their legs while their drunken fraternity brothers threw darts near their genitals. In 1990 the Sigma Nu chapter at the University of Texas was expelled from campus for hazing that allegedly included sexual abuse. At the University of Florida, one-fourth of the fraternities faced disciplinary action in 1992 for alcohol abuse and hazing. Illustrative of hazing activities was Kappa Sigma, whose members forced pledges to ride around campus nude while chained to a pickup truck. During another hazing episode a pledge of Delta Tau Delta lost a testicle (Scarce, 1997).

Nineteen-year-old Gavin Fugate, a 1996 pledge to Sigma Alpha Epsilon at Louisiana State University, reports he was beaten, then forced "to scoot across the floor covered with broken glass" (Varney, 1997, p. 1). The result was "severely lacerated elbows and butt." However, Fugate reports, "one brother was nice enough to treat the cuts with a traditional Louisiana topping, Tabasco sauce" (p. 17). Fugate recounted how fraternity brothers tried to sodomize him with a bar of soap, beat him, all the while forcing him to drink liquor until he vomited blood. When his parents visited one weekend, "the Fugates saw their son muddy and nearly naked, his body bruised and his spirit broken" (p. 17).

At one fraternity at a large midwestern university, hazing resembled the verbal harassment evident in many prisons. Rush participants were called "little women," "girls," and "wusses," during a week of intense hazing. During this time they were compelled to act out in exaggerated female stereotypes. Finally, they were directed to "do to women what we did to you to get your manhood back" (Funk, 1994, p. 17; quoted in Scarce, 1997, p. 54). Comparing fraternities and prisons—both homosocial settings structured by masculinist assertions of power—Scacco (1975) remarked: "The inmate in prison, chosen as the victim, is not so lucky. The attacker not only makes sure he completes the act of sodomy, but usually invites his friends to share his punk, thereby making the act even more humiliating and 'demaling' for the victim" (Scacco, 1975, p. 85).

Hazing is not limited to white or predominantly white fraternities, if we can take film as "data." In the conflict between the frat boys and the "fellas" in Spike Lee's *School Daze*, verbal "fag-bashing" becomes the tactic of preference in the competition for male domination: "When I say Gamma, you say Fag. Gamma. Fag. Gamma. Fag." As black gay artist Marlon Riggs (1991) complained, Lee's movie not only reflects homophobia among black men, it "glorifies it" (quoted phrases, p. 257).

Since 1978, 36 states have passed laws prohibiting hazing. A study commissioned by the president of Rutgers University concluded that "fraternities 'demean human dignity' and are hostile toward women, minority-group members and homosexuals" (quoted in Comstock, 1991, p. 108). Since the early

1990s, prestigious colleges such as Trinity, Middlebury and Bowdoin Colleges have abolished the Greek system (Twardowski, 1997). As I recommend in the conclusion, all universities would be well-advised to follow their lead.

FEMINIST MEN ON CAMPUS?

There are a few signs that some college males are unwilling to participate in the misogynistic and homophobic performances so common to fraternity members and athletes. A Duke University student organization called Men Acting for Change (MAC) and Men Against Violence organized at Louisiana State University (Hong, 1998) are two of several such men's groups at colleges and universities across the United States and Canada. Besides meeting regularly to talk among themselves, these groups present programs to fraternities and other campus groups on gender and sexuality, focusing on heterosexual violence and homophobia. MAC members were interviewed regarding pornography on the ABC newsmagazine program *20/20*. On January 28, 1993, these college men described the negative effects of pornography on their (hetero)sex lives and their relationships with women (Stoltenberg, 1998). Unfortunately, these organizations represent a tiny fraction of college and university students.

Recently there have been articulations of a black male feminist position, expressed perhaps most prominently by literary theorist Michael Awkward (1995, 1996), and in terms of teaching by Gary Lemons (1998). Drawing on Alice Walker's notion of "womanist" as "a black feminist or feminist of color . . . committed to survival and wholeness of entire people, male *and* female" and bell hooks' call for "reconstructing black masculinity," Lemons (1998) connects sexism and racism, insisting that black men must come to appreciate that the struggle for civil rights in the United States has for too long been focused on black men. He is not alone; he points to the efforts of black male undergraduates at Morehouse College who founded the organization Black Men for the Eradication of Sexism. He recalls that during the weekend of September 28 and 29, 1996, a year after the Million Man March, "they (we) made history" (quoted passages, p. 43). At the conference entitled "Black, Male and Feminist/Womanist," devoted to the subject of black men's relation to feminism/womanism, African American men organized this group to make a public declaration of their commitment to the eradication of sexism. In their mission statement they proclaimed:

> We believe that sexism is a global form of oppression of no less importance than any other form of oppression. All forms of oppression, including sexism, racism, classism, homophobia are interconnected and support each other. *For too long the struggle for the liberation of African people in the united states [sic] has been centered on the liberation*

of black men. This male-centered analysis inhibits us from fully confronting the oppression we constantly face and perpetuate within and without the black community. The struggle against sexism must become an issue of primary importance if we are to advance as a people. (quoted in Lemons, 1998, p. 44, emphasis Lemons')

The establishment of Black Men for the Eradication of Sexism suggests to Lemons the possibility for the organization of a broader movement of anti-sexist black men. Acknowledging the necessity of a critique of black sexism, BMES declared:

We believe that sexist oppression against women pervades every aspect of our communities and must be eradicated. . . . Although it has often been said that black women are held in high regard by the black community, the reality is that black women are either denigrated as whores and enemies or placed on a confining pedestal as superwoman. The humanity of our sisters is lost in these classifications which only succeed in further dividing our people and preventing us from dealing with other forms of oppression. Sexism is a radical problem that requires a radical solution. . . . We support feminism/womanism and all efforts to eradicate sexist oppression. We ultimately demand a complete and revolutionary change that eradicates oppression based on sex, race, class, and sexual orientation, both within and without. (quoted in Lemons, 1998, pp. 44–45)

Such a "womanist" declaration, Lemons (1998) acknowledges, "goes against the grain of the racist and sexist mythology of black manhood and masculinity in the United States." Such "mythology" is, he suggests, historically grounded in white supremacist patriarchal ideology, but still communicates the idea "that we pose a racial and sexual threat to American society such that our bodies exist to be feared, brutalized, imprisoned, annihilated—made invisible" (Lemons, 1998, p. 46).

It is important to point out that some men do not always sharply distinguish rape from "normal" heterosexual relations. Like John Stoltenberg (1990), Dianne F. Herman (1989) suggests that "the [very] image of heterosexual intercourse is based on a rape model of sexuality" (p. 22). This dangerous mix of violence and lovemaking in the sexed subject position of the heterosexually-identified man is suggested by the fact that many rapists do not regard their actions as rape. Many report they imagine themselves as terrific lovers (Simon, 1996).

Consistent with this "sociocultural" interpretation of rape, men who rape tend to exhibit "normal" personality characteristics, physical appearances, intelligence, and social behavior. They cannot easily be construed as deviants in a broad social sense; indeed, they see themselves as conforming to the traditional, mainstream ideal of manhood. Understood in this way, rape is one means for a heterosexual man to prove this masculinity (Herman, 1989). Some straight guys seem to have to prove it over and over again. Take athletes, for instance.

SPORTS BUILD CHARACTER?

A star tailback on the nationally ranked LSU football team, Cecil Collins was arrested on June 25, 1998 on a felony charge of unauthorized entry and sexual battery. Two Oregon State football players, Jason Dandridge and Calvin Carlyle, were arrested the same day as Collins and charged with sexual assault and sodomy and unlawful sexual penetration. Sometimes these young men get lucky: a Queens, New York jury acquitted three members of the St. John's University lacrosse team, Andrew Draghi, Walter Gabrinowitz, and Matthew Grandinetti. The three men were accused of plying a woman with alcohol and making her perform oral sex on them; the teammates alternately used force and took advantage of her intoxicated state. Although the defendants were acquitted, St. John's University did the right thing: it expelled the three men on the grounds that each of them was guilty of "conduct adversely affecting his suitability as a member of the academic community of St. John's" (quoted in Bohmer & Parrot, 1993, p. 30).

These were not isolated cases. A recent report by ESPN SportsZone indicated 145 college athletes were arrested in 1998 for 134 alleged crimes. Other studies suggest the same. For instance, using information from 30 NCAA Division I schools, a study conducted between 1990 and 1993 by Northeastern University and the University of Massachusetts showed that of the reports received by campus administrators, male athletes were connected to 19% of sexual assaults (Thompson, 1998). Another report, based on information from an FBI survey, indicated that police had 38% more complaints of sexual assault by basketball and football players at NCAA colleges than the average for the combined amount of males on college campuses (Bohmer & Parrot, 1993). Another study suggests that male student—athletes are six times as likely as their nonathlete peers to be reported for sexual assault to campus judicial affairs offices (Crosset & McDonald, 1995). Is there something in "male team sport culture [that] somehow *encourages* this sort of behavior" (Katz, 1995, p. 173)?

The National Survey of Initiation Rites and Athletics, a yearlong study performed by Alfred (N.Y.) University in cooperation with the NCAA, found almost 80% of the 10,000 student—athletes at various Division I to Division III colleges and universities had been hazed. Sixty percent of the athletes who responded said they had engaged in criminal, dangerous and/or alcohol-related hazing. The study also found that men were more at risk than women, and that the sports most associated with hazing are swimming and diving, lacrosse, soccer, football and ice hockey. Hazing was also more likely in the East or South, and on rural or residential campuses. Sports with significantly fewer reports of hazing were track, fencing and golf (White, 1999). Among the milder activities typifying the practice was being forced to wear "embarrassing" clothes (Duncan, 1999, p. D-6). This male–male sadomasochism is not limited to nonprofessional sports. In 1998 New Orleans tight end Cam Cleeland was injured in a well-publicized hazing incident at training camp (Duncan, 1999).

Nor is hazing limited to college men. In 1992 a junior teammate of the Johnson Creek High School wrestling team in Wisconsin filed a lawsuit alleging that his fellow wrestlers had beaten then raped him by shoving a mop handle into his rectum. He was punished for missing practice, his teammates said. The athletic director of the high school found the young man blindfolded and naked on an exercise mat. His legs, hands, and head were bound with tape. During the resulting trial a teammate testified that other school athletes had also been threatened with "getting the mop." Those accused were acquitted of the rape charges due to insufficient evidence. Because the young man had been blindfolded he was unable to identity who had assaulted him, although he knew that at least six of his teammates had held him down while he was taped. The assistant wrestling coach testified that "taping" was not uncommon among wrestling teams, particularly in college athletics (Scarce, 1997).

Five students at a Waynesville High School in Ohio were suspended in 1988 for allegedly staging a locker room hazing event. Freshmen players were forced to masturbate and fondle each other's genitals. A similar incident occurred a year later at a high school football training camp in Pennsylvania. There a high school sophomore was allegedly forced to insert his finger into the anus of another sophomore while 20 to 30 teammates watched. In 1990 the *Boston Globe* reported that eight new members of the local Brockton High School track team had been hazed:

> According to one anonymous student, the eight new team members were stripped to their underwear and pushed halfway out the back door of the [school] bus. Some of them had their underwear ripped off them, and some were made to choose between eating pubic hair and being beaten up. Some were forced to rub their genitals. (Bloom, 1990, p. 22; quoted in Scarce, 1997, p. 50)

The town of Smithfield, a small Utah farming community, blamed the victim when in 1993 a member of the local high school football team was taken naked from the shower by 10 of his teammates, then bound by his genitals with tape to a towel rack. Approximately 20 of his male and female schoolmates watched. High school sports were so popular in the community that when the victim reported this event, *he* received telephone threats. The national media reported the story; later the young man appeared on the television talk show *Phil Donahue*. From his point of view, "The humiliation I suffered was tons worse than the physical injury" (Plummer & Johnson, 1993, p. 52; quoted in Scarce, 1997, p. 51).

If some team sports represent organized and sublimated forms of homosexual aggression, then "hazing" can be decoded as a mangled, disguised form of homosexual rape. Sometimes it is not so disguised. In January 1997, Sheldon Kennedy, a hockey player with the Boston Bruins of the National Hockey League, alleged that a former coach had sexually assaulted him more than 300 times over the course of 11 years. Kennedy was 14 when the coach first approached him; he was 26 when the "relationship" ended. The events included forced oral sex and masturbation. The coach was found guilty on two counts of sexual assault against Kennedy and another unnamed man, who alleged he had been assaulted approximately 50 times in four years. The coach was sentenced to three and one-half years in jail. Kennedy reported in a newspaper interview with the *Toronto Star* that the coach had used a variety of tactics to maintain control over him, from verbal abuse to a shotgun. On January 17, Reuters newswire reported that "Mick Mitrovic, president of the eastern region of the Canadian Professional Hockey School, said he was not surprised when he heard about the conviction because there had been cases and rumors about problems with players and coaches before" (Blinch, 1997; quoted in Scarce, 1997, p. 51). If "sport" is sublimated sex, should we be shocked if on occasion desublimation occurs?

CONCLUSION

In the preceding I have, of course, only hinted at the complexity of the current sex/gender system, a system that leaves women, children, and other marginalized persons such as gay men at risk. Although long-term solutions are certainly needed, what can be done in the short term to intervene in this violence against women and vulnerable "others" on campus? There are three obvious steps colleges and universities can take now. First, all social fraternities should be closed immediately. Over and over again, these all-male groups have proven that they are dangerous not only to women but to their own pledges as well. They are an antiquated, anti-democratic, elitist homosocial form that supports and often intensifies misogyny, homophobia, and heterosexism. Fraternities' roles in the reproduction of social elitism, class privilege, and racism cannot be overlooked either. It is too late for speak of reform: simply close them. Of course, this will not be easy. Members of boards of trustees are often old fraternity brothers; influential donors and, for state-supported institutions, politicians, often maintain ties to fraternities or, given their gender politics, have sympathy for current members. Faculty, administration and students will have to work together if any progress is to be achieved, and we know that the odds are against us even on campus.

Second, for the sake of women, gay men and exploited racial minorities (see, for instance, Edwards 1973), big-time college sports should be sharply restricted if not ended altogether. The model of athletics supported by colleges and universities should shift from highly competitive, media-sensationalized institutionally associated teams to an intramural model in which students may elect to enjoy "sport" under careful supervision that emphasizes not winning but movement and exercise. Informal, intramural sport—while hardly free of masculinist aggression—does decrease the dangers associated with media-hyped gladiator sports now dominant. In addition, alumni enthusiasm for their alma maters needs to be focused on academic, not athletic, accomplishments.

Third, during the past thirty years there has emerged a discipline expressly committed to understanding that system in all its complexities and significance; I am referring, of course, to women's and gender studies. Drawing on research and scholarship in the various disciplines, this important multidisciplinary area becomes key in thinking about what can be done to address the gender of violence on campus. What I portrayed impressionistically in this chapter makes clear that it is more urgent than ever for colleges and universities to move to curricular center stage women's and gender studies (as well as African American and other so-called "ethnic" studies). At the very least, basic courses in women's and gender studies must be added to general education requirements for all undergraduates. Degree programs in women's and gender studies at all levels—B.A., M.A., Ph.D.—must be approved and generously supported. Departmental status would be helpful. Regular campus-wide conferences on topics associated with women's and gender studies would underscore the centrality of these subjects in the education of young men and women in America today. The inclusion of women's and gender studies in secondary school curricula is long overdue.

Such curricular reconfigurations will happen no time soon, of course, in part because faculty in the politically powerful disciplines continue to ensure high enrollment in their introductory courses (and significant portions of the university budget pie) by insisting their disciplines constitute the "core" of "general education." For those pioneers in women's and gender studies, this is an old story. Still, the struggle must go on. While we continue to labor to persuade patriarchal administrators of the urgency of our discipline, the violence on campus continues. Straight women are raped, straight men are hazed, lesbians and gay men are harassed and assaulted.

The gender of violence on college campuses is embedded in a sex/gender system that makes heterosexuality "compulsory," and in so doing produces a hegemonic masculinity tending toward homosocial competition, heterosexual aggression, and violent homophobic suppression of a pandemic homosexual desire. We cannot expect our students to understand the relations among these complex gendered phenomena without at least an introduction to the discipline that has taken scholarly examination of the sex/gender system as its professional vocation. It is long past time for all of us, regardless of scholarly expertise, to join in support of a general education that is explicitly gendered, a general education with women's and gender studies included, if not at its curricular center.

REFERENCES

Awkward, M. (1995). *Negotiating difference: Race, gender, and the politics of positionality*. Chicago: University of Chicago Press.

Awkward, M. (1996). A black man's place(s) in black feminist criticism. In M. Blount & G. P. Cunningham (Eds.) *Representing black man* (pp. 3–26). New York: Routledge.

Blinch, R. (1997, January 6). Canadian hockey in shock over sexual assaults by coach. Reuters Newswire.

Bloom, J. (1990, April 6). Brockton officials may seek charges in hazing. *Boston Globe*, Metro section, p. 22.

Bohmer, C., & Parrot, A. (1993). *Sexual assault on campus: The problem and the solution*. New York: Lexington Books.

Bordo, S. (1993). *Unbearable weight: Feminism, Western culture, and the body*. Berkeley & Los Angeles: University of California Press.

Brownmiller, S. (1975). *Against our will: Men, women, and rape*. New York: Fawcett Columbine. (Republished 1993)

Butler, J. (1990). *Gender trouble*. New York: Routledge.

Candib, L., & Schmitt, R. (1996). About losing it: The fear of impotence. In L. May, R. Strikwerda & P. D. Hopkins (Eds.) *Rethinking masculinity: Philosophical explorations in light of feminism* (pp. 211–234). Lanham, MD: Rowman & Littlefield.

Comstock, G. D. (1991). *Violence against lesbians and gay men*. New York: Columbia University Press.

Cott, N. F. (1990). On men's history and women's history. In M. C. Carnes & C. Griffen (Eds.) *Meanings for manhood: Constructions of masculinity in victorian America* (pp. 205–211). Chicago: University of Chicago Press.

Crosset, T. J. B., & McDonald, M. (1995). Male student athletes reported for sexual assault: A survey of campus police departments and judicial affairs offices. *Journal of Sports and Social Issues, 19*(2), 126–140.

Derrick, S. S. (1997). *Monumental anxieties: Homoerotic desire and feminine influence in 19th-century U.S. literature*. New Brunswick, NJ: Rutgers University Press.

Douglas, K. A., Collins, J. L., Warren, C., Kann, L., Gold, R., Clayton, S., Ross, J. G. & Kolbe, L. J. (1997). Results from the 1995 National College Health Risk Behavior Survey. *Journal of the American College Health Association 46*, 55–66.

Duncan, J. (1999, September 11). Hazing apparently in the past at LSU, Tulane. New Orleans, LA: *Times-Picayune*, p. D-6.

Edwards, H. (1973, November). The black athlete: 20th century gladiators for white America. *Psychology Today*, 7, 43–47, 50, 52.

Eskenazi, G. (1991, February). Male athletes and sexual assault. *Cosmopolitan*, 220–223.

Funk, R. E. (1994). *Stopping rape: A challenge for men*. Philadelphia: New Society Publishers.

Good, G. E., Hepper, M. J., Hillenbrand-Gunn, T., & Wang, L. (1995). Sexual and psychological violence: An exploratory study of predictors in college men. *Journal of Men's Studies*, 4(1), 59–71.

Goyer, P. F., & Eddleman, H. C. (1984). Same-sex rape of nonincarcerated men. *American Journal of Psychiatry*, 141(4), 576–579.

Hannan, K. E., & Burkhart, B. (1993). The topography of violence in college men: Frequency and co-morbidity of sexual and physical aggression. *Journal of College Student Psychotherapy*, 8(3), 219–237.

Hemphill, E. (1991). Introduction. In E. Hemphill (Ed.) *Brother to brother: Collected writings by black gay men* (pp. xv–xxxi). [Conceived by Joseph Beam. Project managed by Dorothy Beam.] Los Angeles: Alyson Books.

Herman, D. F. (1978). The rape culture. In J. Freeman (Ed.) *Women: A feminist perspective* (pp. 41–63). (2d ed.). Mountain View, CA: Mayfield.

Hirsch, K. (1990, September/October). Fraternities of fear: Gang rape, male bonding, and the silencing of women. *Ms.*, 52–56.

Hong, L. (1998). *Redefining babes, booze, and brawls: Men against violence—a new masculinity*. Unpublished Ph.D. dissertation. Baton Rouge, LA: Louisiana State University, Department of Educational Leadership, Research and Counseling.

Hopkins, P. D. (1996). Gender treachery: Homophobia, masculinity, and threatened identities. In L. May, R. Strikwerda, & P. D. Hopkins (Eds.) *Rethinking masculinity: Philosophical explorations in light of feminism* (pp. 95–115). Lanham, MD: Rowman & Littlefield.

Jensen, R. (1998) Patriarchal sex. In S. P. Schacht & D. W. Ewing (Eds.) *Feminism and men: Reconstructing gender relations* (pp. 99–118). New York: New York University Press.

Julien, I., & Mercer, K. (1991). True confessions: A discourse on images of black male sexuality. In E. Hemphill (Ed.) *Brother to brother: Collected writings by black gay men* (pp. 167–173). [Conceived by Joseph Beam. Project managed by Dorothy Beam.] Los Angeles: Alyson Books.

Katz, J. (1995). Reconstructing masculinity in the locker room. The mentors in violence prevention project. *Harvard Educational Review*, 65(2), 163–174.

Koss, M. P., Gidycz, C. A., & Wisniewski, N. (1987). The scope of rape: Incidence and prevalence of sexual aggression and victimization in a national sample of higher-education students. *Journal of Consulting and Clinical and Clinical Psychology*, 55, 162–170.

Lemons, G. (1998). To be black, male, feminist: Making womanist space for black men on the eve of a new millennium. In S. P. Schacht & D. W. Ewing (Eds.) *Feminism and men: Reconstructing gender relations* (pp. 43–66). New York: New York University Press.

Loh, E. (1995, June 22). N. O. jury convicts Graves. Baton Rouge: Louisiana State University, *Daily Reveille*, p. 6.

Martin, P. Y., & Hummer, R. A. (1989). Fraternities and rape on campus. *Gender and Society 3*, 457–473.

Messner, M. A. (1992). *Power at play: Sports and problem of masculinity*. Boston: Beacon Press.

O'Sullivan, C. S. (1991). Acquaintance gang rape on campus. In A. Parrot & L. Bechhofer (Eds.) *Acquaintance rape: The hidden crime* (pp. 140–156). New York: John Wiley & Sons.

O'Sullivan, C. S. (1992, August 10). Navy resembles a fraternity in its sexism. *New York Times*, letter to the editor, A-16, col. 2.

O'Sullivan, C. S. (1993). Fraternities and the rape culture. In E. Buchwald, P. R. Fletcher & M. Roth (Eds.) *Transforming a Rape Culture* (pp. 23–30). Minneapolis: Milkweed Editions.

Pinar, W. F. (1994). *Autobiography, politics, and sexuality: Essays in curriculum theory 1972–1992*. New York: Peter Lang.

Pinar, W. F. (Ed.). (1998). *Queer theory in education*. Mahwah, NJ: Lawrence Erlbaum.

Pinar, W. F. (2001). *The gender of racial politics and violence in America: Lynching, prison rape, and the crisis of masculinity*. New York: Peter Lang.

Plummer, W., & Johnson, J. (1993, December 13). Fit to be tied: The hazing humiliation of a high school athlete has a Utah town in a snit. *Time*, p. 52.

Pope, B. S. (1993). In the wake of Tailhook: A new order for the Navy. In E. Buchwald, P. R. Fletcher, & M. Roth (Eds.) *Transforming a rape culture* (pp. 301–309). Minneapolis: Milkweed Editions.

Rich, A. (1980, Summer). Compulsory heterosexuality and lesbian existence. *Signs, 5*, 631–660.

Riggs, M. (1991). Black macho revisited: Reflections of a SNAP! queen. In E. Hemphill (Ed.) *Brother to brother: Collected writings by black gay men* (253–257). [Conceived by Joseph Beam. Project managed by Dorothy Beam.] Los Angeles: Alyson Books.

Rotundo, E. A. (1990). Boy culture: Middle-class boyhood in nineteenth-century America. In M. C. Carnes & C. Griffen (Eds.) *Meanings for manhood: Constructions of masculinity in victorian America* (pp. 16–36). Chicago: University of Chicago Press.

Rubenstein, W. (1997). Foreword. To Michael Scarce's *Male on male rape* (pp. vii–xi). New York: Insight Books/Plenum.

Rubin, G. (1975). The traffic in women: Notes on the "political economy" of sex. In R. Reiter (Ed.) *Toward an anthropology of women* (pp. 157–210). New York: Monthly Review Press.

Sanday, P. R. (1990). *Fraternity gang rape: Sex, brotherhood, and privilege on campus.* New York: New York University Press.

Sandler, B. R., & Ehrhart, J. K. (1985). *Campus gang rape: Party games?* Washington, DC: Project on the Status and Education of Women, Association of American Colleges.

Scacco, Jr., A. M. (1975). *Rape in prison.* Springfield, IL: Charles C. Thomas.

Scarce, M. (1997). *Male on male rape.* New York: Insight Books/Plenum.

Schwartz, M. D., & DeKeseredy, W. S. (Eds.). (1997). *Sexual assault on the college campus.* Thousand Oaks, CA: Sage.

Sedgwick, E. K. (1990). *Epistemology of the closet.* Berkeley & Los Angeles: University of California Press.

Simon, R. I. (1996). *Bad men do what good men dream: A forensic psychiatrist illuminates the darker side of human behavior.* Washington, DC & London: American Psychiatric Press.

Simpson, M. (1994). *Male impersonators: Men performing masculinity.* New York: Routledge.

Stoltenberg, J. (1998). "I am not a rapist!" Why college guys are confronting sexual violence. In S. P. Schacht & D. W. Ewing (Eds.) *Feminism and men: Reconstructing gender relations* (pp. 89–98). New York: New York University Press.

Stoltenberg, J. (1990). *Refusing to be a man.* Portland, OR: Breitenbush Books. (Original work published 1989)

Thompson, T. (1998, July 20). Warped by criminal activity, college athletics tries to regain perspective. Baton Rouge: Louisiana State University, *Daily Reveille,* pp. 1, 6–8.

Trelease, A. W. (1971). *White terror: The Ku Klux Klan conspiracy and the Southern reconstruction.* Baton Rouge: Louisiana State University.

Twardowski, L. (1997, September). Greek mythology. *U: The National College Magazine, 28,* 16–17

20/20. (1999, April). *Sorority hazing.* New York: ABC News.

Valois, R. F., Vincent, M. L., McKeown, R. E., Garrison, C. Z., & Kirby, S. D. (1993). Adolescent risk behaviors and the potential for violence: A look at what's coming to campus. *Journal of the American College Health Association, 41,* 141–147.

Varney, J. (1997, August 30). Hazing was brutal, former pledge says. New Orleans: *Times-Picayune,* pp. A1, A17.

White, J. (1999, August 31). Study says 80 percent of college athletes hazed. Baton Rouge: Louisiana State University, *Reveille,* p. 13.

Yang, J. S. (1991, August 18–25). Article on Paul Broussard. *Gay Community News, 19*(6), p. 1.

Part III

Deconstructing the Present

Faculty Lives

5

Women Faculty and Part-Time Employment

The Impact of Public Policy

Judith Glazer-Raymo

Policy studies of women's participation in higher education as students and faculty have focused attention on their underrepresentation and underutilization, and the corrective measures that have been employed in demonstrating good faith efforts to reach equity goals (Glazer-Raymo, 1999; Marshall, 1997). This process has varied considerably among disciplines, departments, and institutions, calling attention to disparities in women's status since the advent of protective legislation in the 1970s. In their ongoing research, feminist scholars have raised questions about the gendered nature of policy development and the impact of protective laws and regulations on their professional careers. Recurring themes in this literature have been the difficulties inherent in overcoming the public–private dichotomies of purportedly gender-neutral policies in higher education institutions, the unintended consequences of policymaking in a political context, and the external factors that influence academic policy. Two sets of policies, in particular, exemplify the capricious nature of the policy process and its dynamic impact on women in the professoriate. I refer to the growth of the part-time workforce and the decline in commitment to affirmative action.

In reviewing the data on women's overall progress in the academy, it is evident that in three decades, they have become the majority of students and have made important advances as faculty in several fields. Feminist scholarship has transformed disciplines, challenging traditional assumptions and reconceptualizing theories, methodologies, data collection, and outcomes. As Hawkesworth (1994) outlines in her overview of feminist contributions to policy studies, feminist policy scholars have not only critiqued the dominant approaches to policy analysis, they have proposed alternatives for setting agendas, implementing and evaluating policies and a range of methodological techniques to inform the field. In investigating the growth of part-time employment in higher education, I do so within the context of affirmative action policy, demonstrating how temporary remedies inevitably become entrenched policies in an unstable political and economic environment. That this should be the case in higher education, which has attempted to insulate itself from external influences, warrants consideration in any discussion of "gendered futures."

GENDER EQUITY AS PUBLIC POLICY

Throughout the 1970s, the liberal feminist critique of public policy focused on sex discrimination, anti-bias legislation, and the goals of access and sex equity. Women became a protected group under the law following enactment of Title IX of the Education Amendments in 1972, outlawing sex bias in all educational institutions receiving federal grants and contracts, and the extension of Title VII of the Civil Rights Act of 1964 and the Equal Pay Act of 1963 to higher education, prohibiting discrimination based on race, sex, religion, color, and national origin. Presidential executive orders required that affirmative action be taken to devise goals and timetables and make good faith efforts for the recruitment of women and minorities in all institutions receiving federal grants and contracts and employing 50 or more persons (see Glazer-Raymo, 1999 for a full discussion of the implementation of these laws and orders). Using strategies adapted from the civil rights and anti-war movements in which women played active roles, neophyte organizations such as the Women's Equity Action League, the National Women's Political Caucus, and the National Organization of Women lobbied, picketed, sued, and campaigned actively for passage and enforcement of these laws. In higher education, colleges and universities responded by adopting affirmative action plans, appointing officers to monitor campus progress, eliminating nepotism and in loco parentis rules, and in single-sex colleges and universities, moving toward coeducation.

By the 1980s, economic and cultural shifts in American society increased the likelihood that both married women of childbearing age and single women who were heads of households would remain in the workforce, raising the stakes for salary equity, pension and health benefits, and subsidized child care. Being a protected group had its downside, and charges of affirmative discrimination, racial preferences, and other more colorful phrases became part of the vocabulary of neoconservatives who gained political power in the 1980s as key domestic and foreign policy advisors in the Reagan–Bush administrations. The withdrawal of resources from the Office of Women's Educational Equity, the Office of Civil Rights, and the Equal Employment Opportunity Commission seriously weakened the oversight powers of these agencies in protecting women and minorities from discriminatory practices. Failure to win ratification of the Equal Rights Amendment in 1982 denied women constitutional protection against sex discrimination, reducing the defense of their legal status to "a handful of federal statutes and Supreme Court cases, dating from the mid-1960s to the late 1970s, now under serious attack" (Jarvis, 1998, p. 175).

In the 1990s, ideological and generational differences became apparent in the rise of gender studies, cultural studies, gay and lesbian studies, and ethnic studies as identity politics played a larger role in the curriculum. This fragmentation has meant that feminists no longer share a commitment to the goals that provided the foundations for the women's movement, and has made it more difficult for women to unite around critical policy problems. Now, in 2002, one year into the Bush–Cheney administration, a conservative strategy is once more evident, initially in terminating the women's liaison office in the White House, and since then, in proposals to privatize public services and enact a states-rights agenda, replacing affirmative action policies with meritocratic standards, elevating conservative judges to the federal courts, withdrawing resources from social programs, and directing them to further military buildups and corporate dominance. Feminism and multiculturalism are rejected as divisive and irrelevant, and as a result, little support can be expected for universal childcare, health insurance, school construction, and environmental protection. Women's gains may slowly erode as a result.

WOMEN'S STATUS IN THE NEW CENTURY

Women are now the majority of part-time students, part-time faculty, and part-time professional staff. Of the 14.5 million students now enrolled in higher education, over eight million, or 56% are women; 44.7% of these attend part-time. Also by 1995, almost two-thirds of undergraduates in public institutions and 44% of those in private institutions were older than 30 years. The growth of part-time enrollments dates from 1970 when colleges and universities, faced with the task of compliance with federal affirmative action guidelines for the admission of women and people of color, determined that part-time programs would provide an important mechanism for recruiting individuals commonly referred to as "nontraditional students." As a consequence, the traditional student of the post–World War II generation, 18 to 22 years of age, predominantly male and middle-class, attending full-time, and earning a bachelor's degree in four years, is no longer the norm. Neither is it the norm to be taught mainly by white male faculty, many of whom had been encouraged to complete their graduate degrees with support from the federal GI Bill. This pattern of male dominance changed after passage of anti-bias and student aid legislation, the growth of the community colleges and conversion of single-sex colleges and universities to co-education. Much of the impetus for these changes came about as the result of affirmative action and equal opportunity policies with consequent increases in the recruitment of minority and women students in liberal arts, professional, and graduate schools. With the acquiescence of professional accrediting associations and state boards, universities eased admission and residency requirements, inaugurated off-campus extension programs, and launched nontraditional degrees. Faced with class-action bias suits, federal, state, and institutional fellowships and scholarships were initiated to prepare women and minority candidates as college faculty. By 1984, women surpassed men as the majority of students at both the undergraduate and graduate levels as well as in full-time and part-time programs. Minority enrollments also increased to 27% by 1998, and women of color are now 16% of all women students.

A more recent debate arose as a consequence of increases in part-time enrollments—it not only takes longer for undergraduate and graduate students to earn their degrees, but also underserved and underrepresented students frequently require additional services and financial aid support. Women now earn almost 56% of all academic degrees; the only two degree levels in which they are not yet the majority—but are gaining rapidly—are first professional and doctoral degrees. Because many of these women are also heads of household, health and social services, financial aid, child care, and counseling must all be factored into the cost of their education.

The impact on the professional workforce is significant; by 1997, 90% of women with Ph.D.s were in the workforce, and 65% of these were in academia. On the downward side, however, by 1999, the Survey of Earned Doctorates revealed that fewer women and men expected to assume full-time tenure-track appointments following receipt of their doctorates—41% percent of women and 30 percent of men (Sanderson, Dugoni, Hoffer, & Myers, 2000). Why is this the case? What is driving newly minted Ph.D.s out of the academy into other fields?

GENDER EQUITY AND THE PROFESSORIATE

Three sets of policies account for the transformation of the academic profession: (1) the decline in tenure-track positions; (2) the growth of part-time, adjunct, and nontenure-track hiring; and (3) the widening gap in faculty compensation.

Tenure

Higher education is a big business; by 1998, it employed 2.7 million people in its 4,070 colleges and universities: 1.8 million professional (45% women) and .9 million nonprofessional (64% women). The number of faculty included 569,000 full-time and 421,000 part-time, mainly adjuncts and teaching assistants. Of the full-time instructional faculty, 36% were women and 13.2% minorities (Snyder & Hoffman, 2001). The proportion of faculty enjoying tenure status has changed little in the past two decades. The same is true of the sizable disparities between tenure rates for men and women. By 1998–99, the National Center for Education Statistics (NCES) reported that 64% of all full-time instructional faculty had tenure status regardless of rank. However, when disaggregated by gender, 71% of all male full-time faculty enjoyed tenure compared to only 52% of their female colleagues, a 19% gap (Snyder & Hoffman, 2001, p. 285). Although the percentage of women has increased at every rank, they still compromise only 18% of full professors and 30% of associate professors, but 42% of assistant professors and more than 50% of all instructors and lecturers.

Tenure is one of the most contentious topics in academia, with the American Association of University Professors (AAUP), the American Federation of Teachers, and the National Education Association taking leadership roles in actively defending the continuation of tenure and academic freedom as public policies. They argue rather vehemently that faculty autonomy and participation in institutional governance are being eroded through attacks on tenure that, in effect, undermine the professionalism of faculty as pedagogues and scholars. In the corporate university, fiscal accountability, worker productivity, and flexible employment policies take precedence as presidents and trustees place increased emphasis on external sources of funding, whether through student enrollments, philanthropic donations, industrial or federal research contracts, or state aid. As contingent hiring and post-tenure review policies become the norm, incentives also diminish for faculty to undertake long-term research projects or public service on behalf of their institutions. The outcome of the debate over tenure will have serious implications for all academic institutions, particularly as they attempt to remain competitive in an uncertain economic environment.

In high-prestige fields, such as academic medicine, in which women are now achieving gender parity in enrollments, the commensurate status of women faculty is even more problematic than in feminized fields such as education and nursing. Enrollments of women medical students now exceed men's (AAMC, 1999). However, on average, women account for only 19 full professors per medical school (unchanged since 1997) compared to 160 male full professors per school, up from 159 in 1997. Even more discouraging, the mean number of women department chairs per medical school is one; and only seven women serve as deans of medicine, three of them being interim appointments. At the Massachusetts Institute of Technology (MIT), a study by senior women scientists documented pervasive gender bias in tenure, grants, laboratory assignments, and perks for women in science and engineering compared to their male colleagues. The fallout from this report prompted MIT's president to undertake immediate action on behalf of women scientists at his institution, forming a Council on Faculty Diversity, and convening a meeting of presidents, chancellors, and 25 women professors of nine research universities to discuss equitable treatment of women faculty in science and engineering. In their joint statement following this meeting, they agreed to analyze salaries and other resources provided to women faculty, to work toward faculty diversity more reflective of their students, and to share specific initiatives in achieving those objectives (Campbell & Halber, 2001). At Harvard University, tenure may be granted only at the rank of full professor, diminishing opportunities to increase the numbers of women in its prestigious departments.

Salaries

Faculty compensation plays a major role in this scenario as women with doctorates also seek quality of life incentives for themselves and their families. It is no longer the case, if it ever was, that women can rely on their partners as primary wage earners. In its 2000–2001 report on the economic status of the professoriate, the AAUP ruefully observes a widening gap of 25 to 30% between faculty salaries and those of comparable, highly educated professionals. It also notes a similar trend in salaries earned by faculty in elite and nonelite institutions where compensation is used to lure "the most talented faculty", and in higher- and lower-paying disciplines (Committee Z, 2001, p.4). Linda Bell, the AAUP's chief economist, attributes this pattern of widening pay gaps by field to "relative demand-and-supply shifts outside the university as well as demands for talent within" and to the "rising inequality in the distribution of incomes generally," which she sees reflected in "the growing inequality within our ranks" (p. 6). In comparing salary differences between the highest- and lowest-paying disciplines as reported in the Oklahoma State University Faculty Salary Survey, she points out that salaries in the top-paying disciplines increased three times as rapidly when compared to lower-paying disciplines in the nineties as in the eighties, resulting in a roughly 35% pay gap by 1999 (p. 5). Although these data are not broken down by gender or race, the most remunerative fields are dominated by men, for example, law, business, and health professions, computer and information sciences, engineering, physical sciences, and mathematics. In contrast, the lower-paying fields include such feminized specialties as visual and performing arts, library science, English composition, education, home economics, and communications.

Part-Time and Nontenure-Track Employment

According to the AAUP, which has been monitoring nontenure-track and part-time employment patterns for two decades, the policy of hiring part-time faculty began as a temporary measure between 1972 and 1977, a period of fiscal stress and "increased institutional interest in alternatives to the tenure system"

(Committee A, 2001, p. 77). It interprets its continued implementation as an administrative claim for budgetary discretion, flexibility in controlling faculty size, and "to buffer the strain between fluctuating student demand and funding constraints for hiring permanent faculty." Ironically, when I traced the sequence of events leading to the adoption of part-time employment of faculty in higher education in 1972, I found that laws and regulations designed to protect women and minorities now served to inhibit their prospects for permanent employment.

Albeit with good intentions, among those who played a significant role in the policy process were private foundations, which joined with women's groups to propose part-time hiring as a strategy for implementing affirmative action. The Carnegie Council on Policy Studies (1975), in its report on "making affirmative action work in higher education," observed the lack of provision for part-time faculty appointments except in lecturer or other nonladder faculty positions or for administrators doing part-time teaching. Spurred on by women's groups, it urged the adoption of policies to permit part-time faculty appointments for women "and sometimes for men" with family responsibilities. The Council's survey of universities indicated that in 1972, only 38% of institutions permitted part-time faculty appointments in regular or ladder ranks, 22% permitted part-timers to be eligible for promotion to tenure, but in most cases, "part-time appointments in regular faculty ranks could not be on less than 50% of a full-time basis" (p. 88). They recommended that part-time appointments be permitted in regular faculty ranks for persons whose sole employment is to the college or university, and not elsewhere. "Under appropriate conditions, these appointments may lead to tenure on a part-time basis" and beyond that, promotion policies should allow for extensions to those who have been employed part-time because of family responsibilities. To its credit, it did recommend that lecturers who were qualified for regular faculty positions should be reclassified and covered by fringe benefits on a prorated basis if they are part-time.

Patricia Graham, who was later appointed the first woman dean of the Harvard Graduate School of Education, wrote in *Science* in 1970 that part-time professorial appointments with full perquisites should be considered for women scholars "particularly those who are married [and] might welcome the opportunity to teach on a part-time basis with full professional recognition" (p. 1287). Observing that the only options for most women in that category were to teach full-time or be "consigned to the ranks of lecturers and instructors," she recommended that universities consider staffing their departments with "persons of diverse interests and specialties whom they could not afford to employ on a full-time basis." She warned (with good justification, as it turned out) that unless provisions were made for part-timers to shift to full-time status at a mutually agreed-on time, departments would risk creating a category of second-class citizens. Other proposals that surfaced during those early years related to the need for campus child care, an end to nepotism rules, and more liberal maternity leave policies.

Three decades following the implementation of these policies to bring women and minorities into the professoriate in greater numbers, it is evident that part-time employment policies have been subverted from temporary to permanent status. The "invisible faculty" of Gappa and Leslie's (1993) study of part-time and adjunct faculty has become increasingly militant in the last decade. The Women's Research and Education Institute recently observed that thirty years after the enactment of equal employment legislation, workplace reforms occur at a "glacial pace" and women in all occupations remain caught between the workplace and their family responsibilities. It recommends the redefinition of work "through such measures as flextime, shared or *part-time* jobs (italics added) with full benefits, parental leave, and on-site child care" (Evans, 2001, p. 100). In this construct, the family-values argument weighs in very strongly. In higher education, the unintended consequences of part-time employment as acceptable public policy make it an attractive and low-cost alternative to full-time tenure-track commitments. Until universal child care becomes the norm, the trade-offs inherent in the part-time/full-time construct will remain a women's issue in American society.

Part-time and nontenure-track contracts have become entrenched policies in all accredited colleges and universities. In medical, law, and dental schools, clinical appointments have long been the norm, permitting doctors, lawyers, and dentists, and other fee-for-service professionals to provide their professional expertise, gain prestige and status from their affiliations, but also maintain full-time private practices. In their survey of clinical faculty in schools of education, Hearn and Anderson (2001) identify several models for clinical or nontenure-track, practitioner-oriented faculty in counseling, business, law, social work, and the health professions. They provide useful recommendations for schools of education that opt for clinical appointments, including more rigorous job descriptions that also acknowledge the political and professional concerns of full-time faculty and the need for gender and race diversity in appointments. The risk is that the clinical category might be used to ghettoize underrepresented groups. Hearn and Anderson (2001) express concern that the part-time nature of clinical contracts may put at risk the benefits of established tenure systems, reifying hierarchical systems of faculty work—some teach, some do research, and some supervise student fieldwork—diminishing student exposure to tenured faculty, and making units more vulnerable to institutional retrenchment (p. 134).

Further proof of the entrenched nature of part-time faculty positions occurs in the for-profit universities, the major growth area in higher education today with 750 campuses, 305,000 students, and 26,000 full-time, nontenure-track faculty (Ruch, 2001). This sector epitomizes the commodification of the university, paying faculty competitive salaries, offering them 401k retirement plans and "stock options in the form of bonuses and rewards for outstanding performance," and requiring no scholarship or community service (Ruch, 2001,

p. 100). At the University of Phoenix, the largest for-profit system, two-thirds of the 100,000 students are women, only 150 of the 5,000 instructors are full-time, and classes are held on 137 campuses across the United States. Faculty, who are paid per course, may be reimbursed for travel to and from their campuses, earn stipends for attendance at faculty meetings, and complete twenty hours of training prior to entry into the classroom.

In 1997, eight scholarly associations and the AAUP issued a statement on the use of part-time and adjunct faculty, deploring their low pay, lack of benefits, and heavy teaching loads. They recommended equitable salaries indexed to those of full-time, tenure-track faculty. Speaking at the Modern Language Association meeting in 1998, doctoral students in the humanities also admonished faculty and deans to abandon their heavy reliance on part-timers and adjuncts and cease their rhetoric regarding nonacademic jobs (Kelley, Pannapacker, & Wiltse, 1998). There is little evidence that this has happened, and as part-time and nontenure-track appointments become more acceptable, academic jobs for the growing numbers of women doctorates may diminish even further.

At public and private institutions, the growing use of part-time, nontenure-track faculty has resulted in a resurgence of union activism. The United Automobile Workers and the American Federation of Teachers are two of the unions now seeking to capitalize on unrest among faculty who may carry full-time teaching loads at two or three institutions. Rarely do they qualify for employer-sponsored pension plans, health benefits, office space, or other such taken-for-granted perks of full-time faculty. Further evidence of the scope of the problem can be seen in the unionization of graduate and teaching assistants at public and private universities in the past five years, including at the University of California, New York University, Temple University, and the University of Washington. In his study of unionized faculty and the restructuring of the professoriate, Rhoades (1998) observes that, on the one hand, unionized faculty have attempted to keep part-time faculty at the margins, but that ironically, "it is the full-time faculty who are being marginalized in American higher education as managers hire greater numbers and percentages of part-time faculty" (p. 264). Once again, he states, women bear a disproportionate share of this burden because they are "most highly concentrated in the ranks of part-time faculty, and in the lower-status institutions and fields that have the highest percentage of part-time faculty" (Rhoades, 1998).

RECOMMENDATIONS FOR CHANGE

In focusing attention on part-time employment as an unintended consequence of affirmative action policy, my objective has been to illustrate the importance of conducting policy analyses that consider gender as an analytic category rather than a demographic variable to be weighed in considering the costs and benefits of higher education policies and practices. I would also emphasize the significance of reflecting on the political, economic, and cultural ideologies that inform agenda-setting, issue-definition, and policy choices. Affirmative action is a case in point. The retreat from support of affirmative action has signaled a reversal in public policy based on the myth of meritocracy—that the university is insulated from the social problems of an increasingly diverse society. Eroding support for affirmative action is exemplified in Proposition 209 in California, Proposition 200 in Washington State, and in legislative and court actions in Florida, Georgia, Texas, and Michigan. Much attention has been given to undergraduate or professional school admission policies. On the other hand, the implications for women and minorities in employment and contracting policies are rarely touched on by the media or the affected institutions. As a result of legal maneuvers related to affirmative action, higher education is embroiled in a policy debate of colossal proportions, particularly for public institutions that are dependent on states for their resources. What exactly does it mean for policies related to the hiring and promotion of women and people of color? In focusing attention only on racial preferences, a gender-neutral stance lulls those in positions of power into thinking that, as far as women are concerned (including women of color), the problems have been solved. Looking beyond short-term managerial decisions, it is difficult to predict the long-range impact on professional schools generally if good faith efforts to bring about equity and diversity are replaced by laissez faire attitudes of meritocracy, race- and gender-neutral standards, and general attacks on advocates for women and people of color. Each adverse decision about affirmative action gets full media treatment, heightening public ambivalence, and ultimately lulling institutions into renewed acceptance of the status quo.

I am wary of attempting to forecast the future, gendered or otherwise, and mindful of Toni Morrison's admonition to graduates of (my alma mater) Smith College's class of 2001:

> I am not certain, nor should you be, that somehow a burgeoning ménage à trois of political interests, corporate interests, [and] military interests will not prevail and literally annihilate an inhabitable humane future. . . . We can no longer rely on the separation of powers to keep this country invulnerable to that possibility while finite humans in the flux of time make decisions of permanent damage. (2001, p. B6)

Is it possible to anticipate that women will find an enlightened feminist future in a society that is so divided politically, economically, and culturally? On an intellectual level, our institutions espouse values of free and unfettered inquiry in the pursuit of knowledge. However, on an economic level, they adhere to values that reflect the realities of operating costly enterprises and competing in a globalized society. Colleges and universities that advertise themselves as "equal opportunity employers" find it necessary at times to engage in less lofty and more short-term goals, restructuring departments, downsizing staff, and engaging in entrepreneurial activities of questionable academic value. Meanwhile, ideals of shared governance, collegiality, and diversity become lower priorities. Evidence of increased activism on the part of multisystem governing boards to increase faculty accountability, eliminate remedial programs, and legislate core curricula provide depressing evidence that the quest for equity and social justice in the academy can indeed be elusive. In this context, I offer three recommendations to advance a feminist policy agenda during this decade.

Women must become agents of social change and advocates for women's concerns. In my research, I have learned a great deal about the important role of women's commissions from the many dedicated, courageous, and articulate women who have taken on pro bono leadership roles. Ironically, when we view commissions as a strategy for social and economic change, it is evident that we have come full circle (Glazer-Raymo, 1999). Originating as early as 1970 as an instrumental response to federal demands that good-faith efforts be undertaken in designing and implementing affirmative action plans, the difficult task for commissions and task forces alike has been how to negotiate the boundary between their advisory and advocacy roles, and to avoid the risk of becoming adversarial. Women who have sought to work within their systems to gain equity and power for their peers have found that, in many cases, the boundaries within organizational structures are impermeable and limit their collaboration. The experience of senior women scientists at MIT indicates that issue definition at the highest levels frequently begins when prestigious institutions are confronted by evidence of inequities from ad hoc groups that demand immediate and positive action on the part of those in positions of authority. The challenge for feminists in other institutions is to let grassroots activism inform feminist theory rather than the other way around. We need to become more proactive problem solvers at a time when social backlash extends beyond affirmative action in law school admissions and the size of science laboratories at elite institutions to ad hominem attacks on universal childcare, public education, family planning, and environmental protection.

Women should be encouraged to serve on boards of trustees and other such positions of power and influence. Women's participation on boards is much too low, only 27% on independent college and university boards and 30% on public boards. The selection of public-sector trustees has a demonstrable political dimension that should not be overlooked, that is, election by popular vote or appointment by governors or legislatures presents opportunities for women interested in public service. The official and unofficial discourses of governing boards reflect institutional values of various stakeholder groups as well as executive, legislative, and judicial interventions. Given the interrelationship between trustees and their inattentiveness to issues of gender, race, social class, and sexual orientation, increased representation of women, including women of color, is essential. Until women are perceived as decision makers who speak out on matters of diversity and social justice, boards will continue to adhere to the corporate model—white, male, affluent, and focused on the bottom line.

Women should be encouraged to seek positions as deans, department and division chairs, changing the rules of the game and becoming advocates as well as mentors of other women. Women should assume leadership roles in policy formation and evaluation, opening up the dialogue to include those who are now on the margins. Part-time and clinical faculty should be partners in this discourse, analyzing more critically the reasons for the erosion of full-time, tenure-track faculty positions at a time when women and people of color are entering the professoriate in greater numbers than men. Ways and means must also be found to balance fiscal and educational demands if we are to preserve the academic integrity of our institutions. Higher education will face difficult issues in this decade as information technology transforms our colleges and universities, fosters global networks, and continues to blur the lines between nonprofit and for-profit institutions. We can no longer afford to be diverted from our goals. Undoubtedly, women are a formidable intellectual resource and a critical source of institutional and community vitality. However, there is much evidence that even now, their unrealized potential remains to be fully understood and cultivated.

REFERENCES

Association of American Medical Colleges (AAMC). (1999, February). Women faculty still hitting the wall on the tenure track. *AAMC Reporter, 8*(5), 1, 2.

Campbell, K. D., & Halber, D. (January 31, 2001). Universities issue statement on equity for women faculty. *Tech Talk.* <http://web/mit.edu/newsoffice/tt/2001/jan31/gender.html>

Carnegie Council on Policy Studies in Higher Education. (1975). *Making affirmative action work in higher education: An analysis of institutional and federal policies and recommendations.* San Francisco: Jossey-Bass.

Committee A on Academic Freedom and Tenure. (2001). The status of nontenure-track faculty. In *Policy documents and reports.* Washington, DC: American Association of University Professors.

Committee Z on the Economic Status of the Profession. (March–April, 2001). Uncertain times: The annual report on the economic status of the profession, 2000–2001. *Academe,* 1–8. <http://www.aaup.org.htm>

Evans, S. M. (2001). American women at the millennium. In C. B. Costello, S. Miles, & A. J. Stone (Eds.) *The American woman: A century of change—What's next?* (pp. 45–101). New York: Norton.

Gappa, J., & Leslie, D. W. (1993). *The invisible faculty: Improving the status of part-timers in higher education.* San Francisco: Jossey-Bass.

Glazer-Raymo, J. (1999). *Shattering the myths: Women in academe.* Baltimore: Johns Hopkins University Press.

Graham, P. A. (1970, September). Women in academe. *Science,* 169, 1284–1290.

Hawkesworth, M. (1994). Policy studies within a feminist frame. *Policy Sciences,* 7, 97–118.

Hearn, J. C., & Anderson, M. S. (2001). Clinical faculty in schools of education: Using staff differentiation to address disparate goals. In W. G. Tierney (Ed.) *Faculty work in schools of education: Rethinking roles and rewards for the twenty-first century* (pp. 125–150). Albany: State University of New York Press.

Jarvis, S. J. (1998). Women and the law: Learning from the past to protect the future. In C. B. Costello, S. Miles, & A. J. Stone (Eds.) *The American woman: A century of change—What's next?* (pp. 151–175). New York: Norton.

Kelley, M. R., Pannapacker, W., & Wiltse, E. (December 18, 1998). Scholarly associations must face the true causes of the academic job crisis. *Chronicle of Higher Education,* B4, 5.

Marshall, C. (1997). *Feminist critical policy analysis: A perspective from post-secondary education.* London & Washington, DC: Falmer Press.

Morrison, T. (2001, May 28). At college graduation, wit and wisdom for the price of airfare. *New York Times,* p. B6.

Rhoades, G. (1998). *Managed professionals: Unionized faculty and restructuring academic labor.* Albany: State University of New York Press.

Ruch, R. S. (2001). *Higher ed inc.: The rise of the for-profit university.* Baltimore: Johns Hopkins University Press.

Sanderson, A. R., Dugoni, B. L., Hoffer, T. B., & Myers, S. I. (2000). *Doctorate recipients from United States universities: Summary report 1999.* Chicago, IL: National Opinion Research Center.

Snyder, T., & Hoffman, C. (2001). *Digest of educational statistics 2000.* Washington, DC: Department of Education, Office of Educational Research and Improvement.

6

Future Prospects for Women Faculty

Negotiating Work and Family

Lisa Wolf-Wendel and Kelly Ward

The increase in the number of women in the labor force is the single most important development in the labor market in the last half of the twentieth century (Gunderson, 1989; Lazear, 1989). In 1940, 28% of American women were in the labor force, a percentage that has increased to nearly 60% by 1997 (Smith & Bachu, 1999). Similarly, the proportion of women in the labor force has increased from 25% in 1940 to approximately 50% by 1997 (Smith & Bachu, 1999). These labor market changes are gradually occurring in higher education as well. Women make up an increasing share of new tenure-track faculty hires. This is particularly significant because the academic labor market is in a period of expansion, and new faculty members (defined as being hired 1 to 7 years ago) now constitute 33.5% of all faculty (Finkelstein, Seal, & Schuster, 1998).

Women represent 41% of this new cohort—an unprecedented rate for women in the academic profession. More specifically, independent of race or ethnic background, even though men continue to appreciably outnumber women in academic positions, women increased their numbers more than men between 1980 and 1993 (Aguirre, 2000). This portrait varies by race, with White women faculty making greater progress than their peers from minority groups. In some institutions, incoming cohorts of full-time tenure-track faculty are equally composed of men and women for the first time in history (Finkelstein, Seal, & Schuster, 1998). It is important to note that this progress is not equal by institutional type: women have made more progress in less prestigious institutions than in more prestigious settings and have made more progress among the ranks of adjunct and part-time faculty than they have among the ranks of full-time, tenure-track faculty (Finkelstein, Seal, & Schuster, 1998; Glazer-Raymo, 1999).

Indeed, more detailed examination of data related to the aggregate representation of women in academe demonstrates that although change is occurring, questions about the equitable representation within the faculty ranks remain. Women's promotion in the academy significantly lags behind their entrance into the academy, meaning that although more women are entering higher education at every level (i.e., as students and as faculty), they progress at different rates than their male peers. At the associate level, for example, women comprise about 30% of positions and at the full professor level, less than 20% (Aguirre, 2000). As one moves up the academic hierarchy into positions of power, women lose ground to men at every rank (Glazer-Raymo, 1999). This is particularly true as one moves up the academic hierarchy into institutions perceived as more prestigious (i.e., research universities). Indeed, despite recent progress, women still remain concentrated in lower ranks, in positions of relatively little power (i.e., untenured, adjuncts, instructors, part-time), and in less prestigious institutions, and make less money than their male counterparts (Allen, 1998; Bellas & Toutkoushian, 1999; Finkelstein, Seal, & Schuster, 1998; Glazer-Raymo, 1999; Perna, 2001).

There are many possible explanations of this lagging progress, including a chilly and patriarchal climate that stymies women in their quest for promotion in the academy (Aisenberg & Harrington, 1988; Caplan, 1993; Hall & Sandler, 1984), socialization experiences in graduate school and in the early career that fail to situate women to accumulate the advantages necessary to advance in an academic career (Clark & Corcoran, 1986; Fox, 1991; Spalter-Roth & Merola, 2001; Tierney & Bensimon, 1996; Ward & Bensimon, in press), and the presence of work and family issues that can inhibit women from advancement in academic careers (Finkel, Olswang, & She, 1994; Finkel & Olswang, 1996; Hensel, 1991; Perna, 2001; Williams, 1999). It is this last concern that is our focus here. Perusal through the *Chronicle of Higher Education* in the past three years shows that issues related to work and family are on the mind and conscience of academicians. Included are stories of dual-career couples, how they make it work, and the backlash they face (Wilson, 2001); women faculty and how they plan children for the academic year schedule (Wilson, 1999); and how different disciplines are responding to work and family issues (Mangan, 2000). It is on these issues that we focus in this chapter.

WORK, FAMILY, AND THE FACULTY CAREER: GENDERED AND THEORETICAL PERSPECTIVES

An existing body of literature related to work and family focuses largely on a critique of normative academic structures and how they have not served women well. This literature, in general, is grounded in personal experience and feminist ideology and seeks to critique higher education structures that have excluded women faculty in general and especially women faculty as mothers and wives. This literature suggests that while men and women as professionals, partners and parents struggle with the delicate balance work and family life can require, the challenge for women is even greater given the simple logistics of age, the biological clock, the tenure clock, the physical demands of pregnancy and childbirth, the gendered expectations of family obligations, and the ongoing disparity with which women take on the "second shift" through maintenance of children and home (Drago & Williams, 2000; Hochschild, 1989; Spalter-Roth & Merola, 2001; Varner, 2000). Further, the history and tradition of academic life as one that is male and childless has continued to pose barriers for women as they seek to gain entry and advancement in the academy. In the academic profession, the "ideal worker" is one who, in essence, is "married" to his work, leaving little time for bearing and raising children (Williams, 2000). This might explain why pioneering academic women who gained access to the faculty ranks often did so after having made the decision to remain single and/or childless (Solomon, 1985).

As a career that is very tied to a ladder of advancement, the professorate presumes a singularity of purpose that parenthood and partnership does not always allow (i.e., tenure) (Williams, 2000). As more women enter the academic profession, many of the norms that have precluded their participation are giving way to more open systems; however, the structures that exist to promote faculty are still largely focused on a normative and male model. The "clockwork of this career is distinctly male. That is, it is built upon men's normative paths and assumes freedom from competing responsibilities, such as family, that generally affect women more than men. In such a system, women with families are cumulatively disadvantaged" (Grant, Kennelly, & Ward, 2000, p. 66). For example, the tenure system is one that is very much based on "male clockwork," dictated by the dominant career and life-span development models that were based largely on research about men (Erikson, 1968; Levinson, 1978). At the same time, when the average age of earning the Ph.D. is 34, and with a typical tenure clock of six years, the doctoral education and tenure processes occur simultaneously with women's prime childbearing years (Hochschild, 1975; Rosen, 1999).

The idealized trajectory of a faculty career (i.e., from graduate school to assistant, associate, and full professor, in direct succession) may not describe the actual or expected career of an academic woman. For some women, the balance between work and family or personal life can disrupt the standard timetable for the ideal career trajectory. In the interest of spouses, children, or personal commitments, women may extend or suspend their graduate school careers, wait to join the professoriate, or attempt to stop or slow the tenure clock. A faculty member seeking to establish her career in the face of conflicting time demands between workplace and home may not be able to follow the traditional trajectory of faculty advancement (Ward & Bensimon, 2002).

Who Cares?:
Why Work and Family Issues are Important

The concerns of academic women in general and of their personal needs specifically should be of importance to higher education administrators and policymakers from an equity perspective. Women as professors will continue to lag in their progress in higher education if academic administrators fail to consider how certain structures can advantage some professors and disadvantage others. There are also more "selfish" reasons that institutions ought to be concerned about the external pulls faced by many of their faculty members. Specifically, if not addressed, these issues could translate into faculty retention problems—a prospect with serious financial implications for institutions (Boice, 1992). Further, if these issues are addressed proactively, then institutions stand to benefit from improved faculty loyalty, satisfaction, and productivity. Ultimately, this will lead to improvements in the quality of higher education itself. In addition, although labor market projections are notoriously inaccurate, experts project that the academic labor market will expand in the foreseeable future as many senior faculty members retire (Finkelstein, Seal, & Schuster, 1998). Although many of these openings are not filled by tenure-track faculty (for discussion of this significant issue, see Glazer-Raymo, this volume), many fields stand to benefit from this expansion of the academic labor market (Finkelstein, Seal, & Schuster, 1998; Hensel, 1991). As more tenure-track openings are created, institutions of higher education should see themselves change from that of a "buyer" to that of a "seller." This means that if academic institutions are to fill their faculty openings with the best and brightest available faculty members for tenure-track positions, they must be responsive to the needs of those seeking academic positions—a consideration not of concern in times of more qualified applicants than jobs.

The remainder of this chapter is focused on a review of the research and policy literature as it pertains to dual-career-couple issues and combining parenthood with the professoriate. In particular, we examine how these issues affect women in their quest for employment and advancement in academic professions. The chapter concludes with a discussion of the gendered future of faculty and how work–family issues play a part in that future.

Work, Family, and the Faculty Careers:
Research and Policy Perspectives

Need Two Jobs, Will Travel . . .

A review of the literature reveals that a significant proportion of today's current and aspiring academics are in dual-career partnerships. It is interesting to note, however, that women faculty are more likely than men faculty to be single—15 percent compared to eight percent (Ferber & Loeb, 1997). One survey indicated that 80% of faculty members had spouses or partners who were working professionals (Didion, 1996). Based on data from a national faculty survey, Astin and Milem (1997) report that 35% of male faculty and 40% of female faculty are partnered with other academics. This means that for both men and women in academe, the decision to take a job, especially if the position requires relocation, brings the partnership issue to the forefront for both the candidates and the hiring unit. Addressing this problem is particularly difficult in geographical areas where the population base is small and employment opportunities for partners may be especially restricted. While these are issues for dual-career couples both within and outside of academia, the primary focus of the following literature review is on dual-career academic couples (i.e., when both members of the pair are trained academics).

Even when both members of a partnership are professionals, there is a historical tendency for the woman's career to be considered after her husband's (Williams, 2001). This may lead to the woman limiting her job search geographically, taking a less than ideal position, or once hired in a faculty position, deciding not to pursue other employment opportunities (a factor associated with higher compensation) (Bielby & Bielby, 1992; Ferber & Kordick, 1978). While there is some evidence that women are more likely to sacrifice their careers to their partners' needs, it is also true that both members of a dual-career couple face concerns about finding rewarding work in geographic proximity to one another. Recent research, for example, indicates that fears of finding work for both members of a dual-career academic couple is sufficient to scare some doctoral students enough that they decide to pursue career paths outside the academy (Golde & Dore, 2001; Rice, Sorcinelli, & Austin, 2000). The weight of this evidence suggests that academic institutions serious about attracting and retaining the best faculty members need to take dual-career-couple needs seriously.

Aside from the worries and stress that dual-career academic couples face in finding work in close geographic proximity to one another, the recent research literature suggests that for academics, being married to an academic is typically associated with greater research productivity than being single or being married to a nonacademic. These results seem to hold true for both men and women (Astin & Davis, 1985; Astin & Milem, 1997; Bellas, 1992; Bellas & Toutkoushian, 1999; Long, 1990; Ward & Grant, 1996). These studies of faculty productivity center on publications, since it is publication, that is the primary predictor of success as a faculty member (Jarvis, 1992). (Although publication tends to be more important at research universities than at other types of institutions, Fairweather [1996] found that faculty are disproportionately rewarded for research regardless of institutional type.) It is important to note that research comparing the scholarly productivity of men and women, without regard to marital or family status, finds that women are less productive than their male counterparts (Astin & Davis, 1985; Creamer, 1998; Finkelstein, 1984; Fox, 1995; Moore & Sagaria, 1991; Zuckerman, 1987). Marital and family status exacerbates the gender differences in research productivity—with women producing less research than men (Astin & Davis, 1985; Astin & Milem, 1997; Bellas, 1992; Bellas & Toutkoushian, 1999; Long, 1990; Ward & Grant, 1996).

Research on the productivity effects of being married to an academic, however, implies that as long as both members of a couple find work, they may be productive members of the academic community. These results are in opposition to the widespread belief that hiring a "trailing" spouse means that an institution has abandoned its quest for hiring the most qualified faculty member available. Although this is a possibility, research suggests that when institutions employ rigorous hiring procedures in considering an accompanying partner, only very qualified partners will be granted tenure-track positions (Wolf-Wendel, Twombly, & Rice, 2000a). This is to say that institutions that try to accommodate the needs of dual-career couples are not necessarily "selling their souls to the devil," but instead are using responsive hiring practices in an effort to maintain qualified faculties.

Although there are anecdotal accounts of the lives of dual-career academics and comparisons between partnered academics and their single counterparts (e.g., Wilson, 2001), there is relatively little policy research on dual-career couples. Raabe's (1997) survey of chief academic officers indicated that 44% of academic institutions provided some form of job assistance for spouses. An additional 12% of institutions indicated that they were planning on implementing a job-assistance policy for spouses. Similarly, Wolf-Wendel, Twombly, and Rice (2000a) surveyed the chief academic officers of institutions belonging to the American Association of Colleges and Universities (AACU) and found that only 24% of respondents said that they have a dual-career-couple hiring policy. However, only 15% of respondents stated that they would "do nothing" to assist spouses or partners to find employment. The majority of respondents indicated that they would help the spouse or partners of an initial hire on an informal, ad hoc basis. The studies by Raabe (1997) and Wolf-Wendel, Twombly, and Rice (2000a) both concluded that research universities are the most likely of institutional types to have a dual-career-couple policy. Responses to the surveys suggest that compared to many smaller institutions, research universities are more likely to help dual-career couples because they have more resources and more flexibility in creating positions, both academic and administrative.

The research by Wolf-Wendel, Twombly, and Rice (2000a) also concluded that 80% of chief academic officers indicated that spousal or partner accommodation is an important issue facing colleges and universities. Further, over 42% of respondents believe that demand for spousal or partner accommodations has increased, while 54% state that demand has remained constant. These findings are in line with other studies that demonstrate that this is an increasingly important issue facing institutions of higher education (Association of Governing Boards, 1995; Burke, 1988). The stated goal of such policies is to recruit and retain the "best" faculty. More specifically, respondents indicated that they are most likely to activate their policies to assist in hiring people of color, full professors, and women (as the initial hire), in that order (Wolf-Wendel, Twombly, & Rice, 2000a).

Follow-up, qualitative case studies of five institutions with different types of dual-career couple hiring policies yielded the following results:

- All the case study sites, whether they had a written policy or not, recognized that "family friendly" policies yield institutional benefits in terms of faculty productivity and satisfaction with the institution. There is a benefit in trying to accommodate dual-career couples, even if the outcome is not what individual faculty members might have hoped for.
- The institutions studied minimized the problems associated with dual-career couples and, instead, focused on the possibilities.
- Many of the solutions to the dual-career-couple hiring dilemma, even at places with more formal polices, rely on luck, serendipity, timing and flexibility.
- Not every couple can be accommodated as they might like. The needs of the couple must be weighed in light of maintaining institutional quality, strategic planning and faculty rights. Institutions that strive to accommodate dual-career couples constantly work to balance the needs of the institution with the needs of the individual (Wolf-Wendel, Twombly, & Rice, 2000b).

Further, the case study research by Wolf-Wendel, Twombly, and Rice (2000b) described four avenues used by academic institutions to assist dual-career couples: (1) relocation services; (2) shared positions; (3) temporary, non-tenure-track and adjunct faculty positions; and (4) tenure-track positions. Relocation services are designed to assist couples who are new to a community in finding their way around their new surroundings and to help the accompanying partner find career opportunities both within and outside the university. In relocation services, a dual-career couple coordinator, often a position filled by a person with a background in career or personal counseling, works with partners to make inquiries about potential jobs and career interests, distributes resumes to potential employers, and occasionally arranges for interviews. In general, the coordinator serves as a resource to the partner looking for work. A big part of a dual-career coordinator's job involves establishing ongoing relationships with local business and agencies that could serve as potential employers for situations when academic jobs are not available or appropriate (Wolf-Wendel, Twombly, & Rice, 2000b).

Some institutions rely on creating shared positions as a means to accommodate the needs of dual-career academic couples. A case study of a small liberal arts college that utilized shared positions demonstrates how this arrangement might work. In a shared position arrangement, each partner receives one-half of a single salary, but both partners are able to apply in their own right for the college's professional development fund and for research support. In addition, both partners receive full benefits. For the purposes of tenure and promotion, each partner is treated separately; it is conceivable that one partner could receive tenure while the other would not. Under this arrangement, each partner may receive half of a regular salary, but this is not always the case in practice. Usually one or both partners will have opportunities to teach extra courses or to fill some other institutional need, and they are paid above their regular half-time faculty salary for such services. The basic requirements of this kind of policy are that both partners are qualified for a position, teach in the same discipline, and are willing to share a single job and a single salary (Wolf-Wendel, Twombly, & Rice, 2000b).

Hiring accompanying spouses or partners into nontenure-track or adjunct positions is quite common and is approached via formal as well as informal policies. A formal example of this approach includes a program that creates one-year temporary positions for academic couples. Under this policy, the dean of the primary hire's college informally contacts the dean of the college housing the department where the accompanying spouse/partner might fit. This program provides one-year (in most cases) appointments in teaching, research or administration, office space, and some benefits for spouses/partners. In this arrangement, the "trailing spouse" receives a one-time stipend that is funded by central administration. The temporary position is intended to be a bridge to or a place from which the individual can look for a full-time position either at the university or at other institutions in the area. Under this policy, it is possible for a department to extend the trailing spouse/partner's contract beyond the one year without the financial assistance from central administration (Wolf-Wendel, Twombly, & Rice, 2000b).

The most elusive positions for dual-career couples are tenure-track positions for both members of the pair. This is a rare accommodation, both in terms of the number of institutions that will attempt such an endeavor but also in terms of the number of couples that get accommodated by any one institution. The process followed will vary by institution and by search; however, the typical process involves a department deciding that they want to hire someone so much that they would be willing to ask another department to consider hiring their partner. If the partner's qualifications look promising and the partner meets a departmental need, then the partner will be invited to campus and will go through a complete interview. Typically the hiring department will vote to hire the partner, just as they would with any new hire. In some institutions there is a financial arrangement that exists to make the hiring of a partner more palatable to all involved. This often involves having the initial hiring department donate one-third of the salary of the partner, the provost's office contributes one-third of the salary, and the accompanying partner's department donates the remaining one-third. Getting departments to agree to hire an accompanying partner is no simple matter (Wolf-Wendel, Twombly, & Rice, 2000b).

Policies and practices to accommodate dual-career couples are generally positive for those being accommodated. However, they raise interesting questions or tensions. Some of these dilemmas are practical, whereas some arise from seemingly incompatible institutional and individual commitments. Consideration of these sticky issues is essential if we are to move toward satisfactory solutions to the growing phenomenon of dual-career academic couples. We consider these dilemmas in the close of the chapter. We now turn to a review of the literature as it relates to faculty and how they manage another aspect of work–family—parenthood.

Have Child, Need Tenure . . .

The numbers of women with children in the work force has steadily increased throughout the past 40 years. In 1960, only 19% of mothers with small children (under age six) were in the work force. By 1990, this number had increased to 56% and data from 1999 indicate that 64% of women with children under age six work outside the home (Department of Labor, 2000; Swiss & Walker, 1993). What trends exist with regard to women faculty as mothers? The most recent data analyzed by gender and available from the National Survey of Postsecondary Faculty show that only 31% of women faculty have children (Perna, 2001). Further, research comparing women faculty to women in other professions (i.e., medicine and law) shows that women faculty are more likely to be childless (Cooney & Uhlenburg, 1989).

Although many faculty women have chosen not to have children, the increasing numbers of women faculty entering the profession, many of whom are of childbearing age, dictate that they understand the personal and institutional dynamics that affect how women faculty decide whether or not to have children. Further, for those women faculty who opt to have children while on the tenure track, it would be useful to understand how women attempt to juggle the often conflicting demands of small children and the tenure track. Indeed, for women faculty who want to have children, the tenure clock often ticks simultaneously with the biological clock, requiring them, and their institutions, to find ways to make being a professor and a mother a reality (Varner, 2000; Varner & Drago, 2001). These kinds of accommodations were previously unnecessary when a majority of academic professionals were men with stay-at-home wives (Finkel & Olswang, 1996; Tierney & Bensimon, 1996; Williams, 2000). Although women faculty themselves bear significant responsibility for achieving their own sense of balance, institutions also need to understand the barriers and challenges these women face, and work to make the academic environment conducive to the success of all who participate. These personal and institutional accommodations will affect who enters academia, as well as faculty productivity and satisfaction, faculty retention, and ultimately the overall quality of higher education.

The purpose of this part of the chapter is to examine the dynamics present for women faculty and, in particular, for junior women faculty related to work and family concerns. To accomplish this end, two literatures are reviewed: (1) research that examines the effects of work and family on different aspects of faculty life, and (2) the policy arena as it relates to work and family in academe.

Although the literature is replete with personal accounts of how children compromise research productivity (e.g., David, Davies, Edwards, Reay, & Standing, 1996; Munn-Giddings, 1998), research on the topic is thin and ambiguous regarding what effect having children has on publication rates (Creamer, 1998). Bellas and Toutkoushian (1999) found that number of dependents did not affect time devoted to research activities. They also found that faculty with children had higher levels of research productivity than those without. This is somewhat paradoxical to the finding from the same study that indicates that women faculty produced less than men in terms of research. The juxtaposition of these findings may be the result of the greater proportion of men in the sample whose productivity overshadows the negative effects of dependents on research (Bellas & Toutkoushian, 1999). Several researchers have found having children did not generally affect faculty research productivity (Cole & Zuckerman, 1987; Fox, 1995; Hamovich & Morgenstern, 1977; Zuckerman, 1987). Still, other research has found that the presence of children has a negative effect on the productivity of women faculty (Hargens, McCann & Reskin, 1978; Sonnert & Holton, 1995).

Some of the variability in these research findings can be attributed to the samples used in the research studies, stages in careers, disciplinary differences, institutional type, and also to the variability in what women bring to their academic careers, which supports the research about socialization and accumulative advantage (Clark & Corcoran, 1986; Tierney & Bensimon, 1996). The variability in this research may also be attributed to the location of women in the academy, with women being more likely to be found in lower-rank positions and institutions that typically have higher teaching loads and less support for research (Fox, 1991).

Salary is another variable of interest with regard to work and family. Recent studies conducted on basic wage differences between men and women all show that the gendered wage gap still exists, with men making more than women in comparable faculty positions (Nettles, Perna, Bradburn, & Zimbler, 2000; Perna, 2000; Toutkoushian, 1998). With regard to how family plays into this difference, the research findings are again, as with productivity, mixed.

Research conducted in 1974 found that number of children and marital status influenced labor force participation and that number of children and time out of the labor force was negatively related to earnings (Johnson & Stafford, 1974, cited in Perna, 2001). Another study found that having children had a positive effect on male faculty salaries, but a negative effect on the salaries of female faculty (Barbezat, 1988).

Employment status is another outcome variable to consider when looking at the effect having children has on women's careers. Women's representation on the faculty is greatest in least secure positions (i.e., adjuncts, instructors) and in institutions perceived as least prestigious (i.e., community colleges) (Dwyer, Flynn, & Inman, 1991; Glazer-Raymo, 1999). What role does family status play in women "choosing" these career paths? Although some have suggested that part-time, adjunct, and nontenure-track positions work well for women with children because they afford women flexible scheduling and limited institutional and research obligations and thus more time with their family (Wilson, 1998), there has been limited research on the subject. Some of the literature also suggests that some women leave the tenure track in the interest of wanting to have children. These women opt to revolve out of full-time and tenure-track positions in higher education in anticipation of conflicts between work and family (Dwyer, Flynn, & Inman, 1991; Hensel, 1990). In a recent empirical study looking at connections between family responsibilities and employment status, Perna (2001) found that the employment of women in non-tenure-track positions is attributable in part to their marital and parental status. Perna's findings suggest that the effects of family responsibilities are more problematic for women than for men.

In addition to the research examined thus far, other research literature looks more generally at the dynamics of academic work and motherhood. Recognizing the limits of outcomes research, what these studies focus on is how motherhood affects the faculty career as a whole. This research tends to be more in-depth, is contextually based and is focused on the totality of women's experience. In general, this research shows that significant tension exists for women faculty who combine work and family.

For example, Armenti (2000), in a qualitative study of how women academics blend private and public lives, found that the structure of academic careers "silences" women's personal lives and creates "taboos" related to being a parent and a female faculty member. Armenti also found those faculty members who were childless were worried about the effect children might have on their careers, a finding that has been reported elsewhere (Aisenberg & Harrington, 1988). Similarly, Grant, Kennelly, and Ward (2000) found that for faculty in scientific disciplines, considerable conflict exists between scientific careers and family life for both men and women, but especially for women. The institutions of family and science are both "greedy," leaving women at odds when trying to combine a career as a science faculty member with the demands of parenthood.

From a more holistic standpoint, Ropers-Huilman (2000) found that even though women faculty were given mixed messages about having children, many sought coherence between the various aspects of their lives and "spoke of the ways they envisioned their family and work experiences as complementing each other" (p. 26).

Finkel and Olswang (1996), in a survey of women faculty at a research university, found that women perceive that time required by children poses a serious threat to tenure. Further, this study found that almost half the participants were childless as a result of their careers and that 34% of those who delayed children did so because of their careers. Sorcinelli and Near (1989) found that for faculty, balancing the needs of professional responsibilities and family life was a significant source of stress. They also found that for junior faculty, "negative spillover"—that is work negatively "spilling over" into personal lives—was a source of stress and dissatisfaction with an academic career.

The research on women faculty with regard to work and family offers mixed messages about what effect family status has on different aspects of the career (e.g., salary, employment status, productivity). More context-based studies that focus more generally on the career, however, are clear that balancing work and family is no easy task. Although many women faculty opt not to take on this challenge, those who do attempt to balance parenthood with faculty life find that academic work, although intrinsically satisfying, is also consuming and can therefore "spill over" in negative ways into personal life. What we see in this research is that while some women combine work and family and do it well, they also pay a cost. We now turn to the literature that analyzes policy perspectives to see what institutions of higher education are doing to support the connections between work and family.

Traditional views of work and family view these as separate spheres to be maintained through gendered patterns (Gappa & MacDermid, 1997). With changes in the workplace, traditional views are no longer suitable and effectively functioning institutions are examining policies and practices in an effort to make their work environments more "family friendly." As we have argued throughout this chapter, work and family concerns are increasingly of concern to individual faculty and to the institutions where they work. If institutions want to stay competitive and vie for the best talent in times of shifting labor markets, then they must pay attention to work and family issues. If these same institutions want to offer quality programs with qualified and talented faculty (many of whom have small children), "family friendly" policies must be established. A review of the current literature on faculty, work–family issues, and institutional policy is heartening in that it reveals the ways that institutions are starting to deal more forthrightly with work and family issues. However, the extent to which these policies are used deserves further exploration.

At the most general level, to support faculty, and in particular women, institutions need to continue addressing inequities that exist for women with regard to hiring, promotion, tenure, and salary (Hensel, 1991). In spite of progress, women faculty are still "frozen in time" (West, 1995), continuing to lag in achieving positions of power in top-tier institutions. If institutions are to press for workplaces that meet the needs of women as parents, they must start by simply looking at numbers. There is a tendency to think the "woman problem" in higher education is solved because a majority of undergraduates are women and the number of women faculty in some units and at some institutions has surpassed 50% (Glazer-Raymo, 1999). Although increasing numbers is a start, Adrienne Rich (1979) reminds us that equal rights is just the beginning of creating a "woman-centered university." True equality is not just representation in terms of numbers; it also means equality of economic, political, and social power that continues to elude many women in higher education (Glazer-Raymo, 1999). One way that institutions can affect shifts in power is through policy implementation that supports faculty, both men and women, in their efforts to combine work and family. The policy literature has two general foci: an examination of policies that have been implemented, the effect they have, and the extent to which they are used; and prescriptions for policies needed to create work–family synergy in higher education.

A survey of chief academic officers at research universities reveals that 84% of institutions provide unpaid maternity leave, while 74% provide paid maternity leaves (some institutions offer both options). Forty-seven percent of research universities have on-campus child-care facilities; 21% offer financial assistance for child care; 36% offer accommodative scheduling to meet family needs, and 29% offer expansion of time for tenure if faculty are faced with family-related issues. This research indicates that the personal lives of academics are garnering the attention of institutional policymakers (Raabe, 1997). Unfortunately, research also demonstrates that such policies are typically underutilized by faculty (Finkel, Olswang, & She, 1994; Hochschild, 1997; Raabe, 1997).

In a study of faculty members' attitudes about leave policies for childbirth and infant care, Finkel, Olswang, and She (1994) found that an overwhelming majority of faculty, regardless of gender, rank, and family status, supported paid leave for women faculty for childbirth and newborn care, and unpaid leave for ongoing infant care. A majority of faculty also supported stopping the tenure clock. Interestingly enough, however, these same faculty reported that taking leave would hurt them professionally and, as a consequence, of those surveyed who had children (almost 50%), only a small percentage took all of the allowable leave. What these findings suggest is that the presence of a policy is not enough and that policy needs to be backed by a climate that unequivocally supports utilizing such policies (Hochschild, 1997).

The remaining policy literature is focused on directions and actions universities can take as they strive to be more integrative of work and family issues. Friedman, Rimsky, and Johnson (1996) provide the most comprehensive suggestions to institutions regarding work/family support. They base their suggestions on a survey of over 3,000 colleges and universities to see what campuses do to support family-friendly environments. Generally what they found (as summarized by Gappa and MacDermid, 1997, p. 11) is that "leadership" campuses in the area of work–family programs tend to have:

- Larger operating budgets, student enrollments, and number of employees;
- Doctoral programs;
- Human resource managers familiar with the family demographics of employees and focused on strategic planning and change management;
- Targeted diversity efforts;
- Connections between work–family efforts and strategic issues of morale, recruitment, and retention;
- Commitment of top administrators and faculty to work–family initiatives with department chairs playing a critical role in the success of work–family efforts;
- Completed needs assessment; and,
- Campus-wide task forces.

In terms of specific policies, the literature abounds with suggestions for making higher education more "family friendly" including but not limited to the following:

- Creating "designer" tenure clocks for academic careers (Boxer, 1996) that include *centralized* (as opposed to departmental based) stop-clock policies or extended tenure clocks;
- Training department chairs about leave policies and when their use is warranted (Gappa & MacDermid, 1997);
- Offering paid family leave for birth or adoption of up to 12 weeks for both men and women (Kolodny, 1998);
- Coordinating family leave with allowable delays in the tenure clock (Boxer, 1996; Kolodny, 1998; Norrell & Norrell, 1996);
- Avoiding the scheduling of meetings for extreme early morning, evening, and weekends (Kolodny, 1998);
- Maintaining affordable and accessible child care on campus and/or providing on-campus referral for child care and elder care services (Kolodny, 1998);
- Allowing accommodative scheduling for the short term (e.g., classes) and the long term (e.g., the tenure clock) (Boxer, 1996; Gappa & MacDermid, 1997; Williams, 2000).

The literature also makes more general policy recommendations to improve the family-friendly nature of academia. In particular, the literature recommends that institutions tap into existing networks (e.g., College and University Personnel Association, College and University Family Work Association) to find solutions to deal with specific family–work-related situations (Benedict & Taylor, 1995; Gappa & MacDermid, 1997). Maintaining campus dialogue about work–family issues is also recommended in the creation of both formal and informal policies (Kolodny, 1998). These dialogues, according to Hensel (1991), should "consider the needs of diverse individuals, including the feminine perspective in expectations for family" (p. v). A recent prescription for campuses in creating work–family policies is to utilize an "integrative model." Such a model is said to recognize the way people work (Benedict & Taylor, 1995) and support the coherence faculty want with regard to work and home (Ropers-Huilman, 2000).

PROSPECTS FOR THE FUTURE: FACING THE DILEMMAS OF ENGENDERING FACULTY, WORK, AND FAMILY

How should academic institutions go from here to there? The literature reveals many challenges with regard to how higher education might move toward dealing more forthrightly with work–family issues. What we see in the literature reviewed throughout this chapter is a series of dilemmas that need to be addressed. We close this chapter by posing these dilemmas as a way to move forward. If we can begin to address these dilemmas, or to at least recognize them as problems to be faced, faculty and administrators can keep work–family issues on the policy agenda and continue to improve the quality of life for its faculty members.

Dual-Career Couple Dilemmas

Balancing Competing Needs. Typically, policies and practices concerning dual-career couples in higher education are couched in terms of "needs." For example, institutions usually justify the creation of these policies and practices in terms of meeting certain needs, such as the need to attract and retain academic stars, women, or minorities. Couples often view hiring accommodations as necessary to their success and happiness as a couple. Further, the department making a hiring offer to one member of a dual-career academic couple might argue that this individual meets an important need. At the same time, the department asked to hire the accompanying partner might well argue that such a hire would divert them from pursuing more pressing hiring needs. The identification and prioritizing of these often competing needs is not a value-neutral act. Who is allowed to participate in this process, for instance, will have a profound effect on what is seen as a need. Similarly, different parties will arrive at different conclusions about how particular needs can best be satisfied. Institutions attempting to meet the needs of dual-career couples will have to consider the sometimes conflicting needs of others in deciding what to do in any particular case (Wolf-Wendel, Twombly, & Rice, 2000b). The dilemma departments face is how to best meet their own needs and how to accommodate university and personal needs for dual-career-couple hiring.

Finding the Best: Redefining the Meaning of Quality and How We Find It. No issue is more central to spousal/partner hires than that of quality. Because quality is typically determined by disciplinary faculty, it is inseparable both from the processes used to find quality faculty members and from the question of who holds power in the hiring process. The traditional means of hiring faculty has been regularized and widely known: a searching department places an ad in relevant scholarly outlets, seeks candidates, narrows the pool, identifies three candidates to bring to campus and from among those three hires the "best." This practice falls into what Rosenbaum (1979) calls "tournament mobility." The practice has been reinforced by Affirmative Action regulations. Faculty often say that they must engage in this competitive practice to find the "best" candidate. To identify a faculty colleague through other means, which is what spousal/partner accommodation policies for faculty often do, gives rise to the fear that equally good or even better candidates will be overlooked. Indeed, one of the most serious criticisms of spousal/partner accommodation policies is that they will result in inferior faculty being hired because they circumvent the open-contest nature of searches (Wolf-Wendel, Twombly, & Rice, 2000b).

At the same time, however, research on faculty search and selection processes demonstrates that the notion of an "open contest," so valued by academic faculty, is in large part a myth. This research shows that the concept of sponsored mobility better describes faculty hiring, especially at research universities. This model argues that, despite the open and democratic nature of searches and a commitment to merit, ascriptive criteria inevitably enter into the search and selection process because scholarly performance (at least in junior faculty) is hard to define and predict with certainty (Lewis, 1975; Burke, 1988). Ascriptive criteria include gender, race/ethnicity, prestige of doctoral granting institution, reputation of faculty mentor and what others think of the candidate (Lewis, 1975; Burke, 1988). Thus, despite attempts to regularize search processes, searches have never been the open contests in which winners are chosen on merit alone that faculty claim so strongly. There is nowhere that this belief gets expressed more strongly than when spousal/partner hires are hired. Nonetheless, institutions wishing to implement a spousal/partner hiring policy will have to face the dilemmas presented by the perceived threat to traditional definitions of quality and determine if there is a need for new definitions of quality (Wolf-Wendel, Twombly, & Rice, 2000b).

Affirmative Action/Equal Opportunity and Spousal/Partner Accommodation: Conflicting Goals? Although diversifying the faculty is a primary stated goal in accommodating dual career couples, the purpose of the policies and practices serves the more generic goal of recruitment and retention of faculty regardless of race, ethnicity or gender. The role of Affirmative Action in relationship to dual-career-couple accommodations is complex because it requires the institution to authorize a hire without going through the formal, regularized practice mandated. Indeed, the hiring of the accompanying spouse/partner is typically accomplished in lieu of a national, open search. Academic institutions that choose to make an exception to this open hiring process, regardless of whether it is for a spousal hire or for some other purpose, would be wise to ensure that their decision-making process could be deemed "reasonable" by an outside body, including the courts and federal regulatory agencies. Because what is "reasonable" is not codified, the institution might consider asking the following questions: How will this search affect Affirmative Action goals at the department level and at the institutional level? How scarce are resources at this institution—if we make this hire, will this slow our progress in meeting departmental Affirmative Action goals in the foreseeable future? Looking at the situation holistically, are we better off having the initial hire, even if hiring the spouse doesn't help us to achieve our goals? An example of this last scenario might include a case in which an institution hires a woman in engineering as an initial hire, but she will come only if her partner, a White man and a chemist, is also hired. The question to be asked from an Affirmative Action stance might be—does the plus of hiring the woman in engineering outweigh the potential minus of hiring a White man in chemistry? What is clear from this preliminary analysis of how dual-career-couple hiring intersects with affirmative action and equal opportunity hiring is that it is a complicated dilemma that will keep higher education administrators and their lawyers busy for years to come (Wolf-Wendel, Twombly, & Rice, 2000b).

Faculty and Family Dilemmas

What Good is a Policy if People Don't Use it? A major finding from the literature is that the mere presence of a policy does not mean people will use it. Stopping tenure clocks, taking paternity or maternity leave for the birth of a child, or taking leave to care for a sick child are all policies that are available (to greater or lesser degrees) at most institutions. The research, however, shows that these policies are underutilized, because people perceive it may not be professionally prudent to use such policies (Finkel, Olswang, & She, 1994; Friedman, Rimsky, & Johnson, 1996; Gappa & MacDermid, 1997). Campuses playing a leadership role in work–family issues report that employees use flextime and leave for dependent care moderately and rarely use job-sharing, stop-clock, or eldercare referral services. Use is dependent on the extent to which faculty perceive a program to have a negative impact on their careers (Gappa & MacDermid,

1997). This suggests that colleges and universities need to continue to work on centralized policies that apply for all faculty, thereby fostering a climate that attempts to integrate work and family. This must be coupled with the education of people in positions of power (e.g., department chairs, promotion and tenure committees) about the use of the policies, and the illustration of how people have used policies while continuing to be successful in their work. The dilemma that administrators need to address is how to create workplace cultures that support the utilization of policy.

Tenure Clocks and Biological Clocks: Can They Co-Exist? Throughout this chapter we have discussed how tenure, as a normative academic structure, is a step in a career progression that was and is fashioned after a male career trajectory. Because men do not have the same issues with biological clocks as women, and because men have been socialized to different expectations with regard to work and family, only recently have concerns with work and family come into full view as issues to be addressed. Tenure is a safeguard for both men and women and is crucial to women gaining equal access to social and political power in academe. We do not advocate for the abolition of tenure as a way to reconcile tensions between work and family or as a way to reconcile differences between male and female "clocks." What we do advocate is a tenure clock that, if necessary, can offer flexibility—not an attribute for which tenure tracks have been known. Given the coincidence of the tenure clock and the biological clock, many women are left with difficult decisions of when to have a baby in relation to tenure—before (graduate students are busy and notoriously poor), during (tenure expectations can be consuming), or after tenure (it might be too late for fertility). Although individuals need to make difficult choices about life decisions, higher education needs to examine its conscience about policies that make life-enduring decisions (such as children and jobs) seemingly mutually exclusive (Varner & Drago, 2001). The dilemma institutions face here is with regard to how to have a tenure policy that is flexible and "family friendly" while maintaining the integrity of tenure.

Not Just a Woman's Problem. Policy needs to be implemented that seeks to integrate work and family for men *and* women. Throughout this chapter we have focused on how the tenure track can challenge women in their decisions regarding bearing and rearing children. Although we have articulated how this is a "woman's" issue given the physical demands of having a child and caring for a newborn, the intent is not to exclude or alienate men from policy. Instead, institutional policy should be universally applied in an effort to bring men more fully into the fold of childbirth and care in an effort to make women less responsible for the "second shift." If we have equitable families, we could have more equitable workplaces as well. The dilemma that needs to be addressed is how to make policies more woman-centered and, at the same time, framed in a way that makes them male-inclusive. Policies need to be available and utilized by both sexes (Gappa & MacDermid, 1997).

CONCLUSION

As we move into the future, faculty and administrators need to consider the research, policies, and dilemmas involved with work–family issues. Although it is easy to think of combining work and family as a private problem, one that belongs primarily to women, it is important to consider the research done on women faculty and family issues in an effort to understand how the phenomenon affects the entire higher education community. As higher education moves into a new century, work–family issues need to be on policy and research agendas.

REFERENCES

Aguirre, A. (2000). *Women and minority faculty in the academic workplace: Recruitment, retention and academic culture*. ASHE-ERIC Higher Education Report, Vol. 27, no. 6. San Francisco: Jossey-Bass.

Aisenberg, N., & Harrington, M. (1988). *Women of academe: Outsiders in the sacred grove*. Amherst: University of Massachusetts Press.

Allen, H. L. (1998). Faculty workload and productivity: Ethnic and gender disparities. *NEA 1998 Almanac of Higher Education* (pp. 19–24). Washington, DC: National Education Association.

Armenti, C. (2000). *Women academics blending private and personal lives*. Unpublished dissertation. Ontario Institute for Studies in Education.

Association of Governing Boards of Colleges and Universities. (1995). Ten public policy issues for higher education in 1995. AGB Public Policy Series 95-1. Washington, DC: Author.

Astin, H. S., & Davis, D. E. (1985). Research productivity across the life and career cycles: Facilitators and barriers for women. In M. F. Fox (Ed.) *Scholarly writing and publishing: Issues, problems, and solutions* (pp. 147–160). Boulder, CO: Westview Press.

Astin, H. S., & Milem, J. F. (1997). The status of academic couples in U.S. institutions. In M. A. Ferber, & J. W. Loeb (Eds.) *Academic couples: Problems and promises* (pp. 128–155). Urbana: University of Illinois Press.

Barbezat, D. (1988). Gender differences in the academic reward system. In D. W. Breneman & T. I. Youn (Eds.) *Academic labor markets and careers* (pp. 138–164). New York: Falmer Press.

Bellas, M. (1992). The effects of marital status and wives' employment on the salaries of faculty men: The (house) wife bonus. *Gender and Society, 6*(4), 609–622.

Bellas, M. L., & Toutkoushian, R. K. (1999). Faculty time allocations and research productivity: Gender, race, and family effects. *Review of Higher Education, 22*, 367–390.

Benedict, R., & Taylor, C.A. (1995). Managing the overlap of work and family: A shared responsibility. *CUPA Journal, 46*, 1–10.

Bielby, D., & Bielby, W.T. (1992). I will follow him: Family ties, gender role belief and reluctance to relocate for a better job. *Journal of Sociology, 97,* 1247–1267.

Boice, R. (1992). *The new faculty member: Supporting and fostering professional development.* San Francisco: Jossey-Bass.

Boxer, M. (1996). Designer clocks for academic careers. *The History Teacher, 29,* 471–481.

Burke, D. (1988). *A new academic marketplace.* New York: Greenwood Press.

Caplan, P. J. (1993). *Lifting a ton of feathers: A women's guide to surviving the academic world.* Toronto: University of Toronto Press.

Clark, S. M. & Corcoran, M. (1986). Perspectives on the professional socialization of women faculty: A case of accumulative disadvantage. *Journal of Higher Education, 57,* 20–43.

Cole, J. R., & Zuckerman, H. (1987). Marriage, motherhood, and research performance in science. *Scientific American, 256*(2), 119–125.

Cooney, T. M., & Uhlenberg, P. (1989). Family-building patterns of professional women: A comparison of lawyers, physicians, and postsecondary teachers. *Journal of Marriage and the Family, 51,* 749–758.

Creamer, E. (1998). *Assessing faculty publication productivity: Issues in equity.* ASHE-ERIC Higher Education Report, No. 26. Washington, DC: ASHE-ERIC/George Washington University, Graduate School of Education and Human Development.

David, M., Davies, J., Edwards, R., Reay, D., & Standing, K. (1996). Mothering and education: Reflexivity and feminist methodology. In L. Morley & V. Walsh (Eds.) *Breaking boundaries: Women in higher education.* London: Taylor and Francis.

Department of Labor. (2000). *Facts on working women.* Washington, DC: Department of Labor.

Didion, C. J. (1996). Dual careers and shared positions: Adjusting university policy to accommodate academic couples. *Journal of College Science Teaching, 26*(2), 123–124.

Drago, R., & Williams, J. (2000). A half-time tenure track proposal. *Change, 32,* 46–51.

Dwyer, M. M., Flynn, A. A., & Inman, P. (1991). Differential progress of women faculty: Status 1980–1990. In J. Smart (Ed.) *Handbook of theory and research,* Vol. 7 (pp. 173–222). New York: Agathon.

Erikson, E. H. (1968). *Identity: Youth and crisis.* New York: Norton.

Fairweather, J. S. (1996). *Faculty work and public trust: Restoring the value of teaching and public service in American academic life.* Boston: Allyn & Bacon.

Ferber, M. A., & Kordick, B. (1978). Sex differentials in the earnings of Ph.D.s. *Industrial and Labor Relations Review, 31,* 227–238.

Ferber, M. A., & Loeb, J. W. (1997). *Academic couples: Problems and promises.* Urbana: University of Illinois.

Finkel, S. K., & Olswang, S. G. (1996). Child rearing as a career impediment to women assistant professors. *The Review of Higher Education, 19*(2), 123–139.

Finkel, S. K., Olswang, S., & She, N. (1994). Childbirth, tenure, and promotion for women faculty. *The Review of Higher Education, 17*(3), 259–270.

Finkelstein, M. J. (1984). *The American academic profession*. Columbus: Ohio State University Press.

Finkelstein, M. J., Seal, R. K., & Schuster, J. H. (1998). *The new academic generation: A profession in transformation*. Baltimore: Johns Hopkins University Press.

Fox, M. F. (1991). Gender, environmental milieu, and productivity in science. In H. Zuckerman, J. R. Cole, & J. T. Bruer (Eds.) *The outer circle: Women in the scientific community* (pp. 188–204). New Haven, CT: Yale University Press.

Fox, M. F. (1995). Women in scientific careers. In S. Jasanoff, G. E. Markle, J. C. Petersen, & T. Pinch (Eds.) *Handbook of Science and Technology Studies* (pp. 205–223). Thousand Oaks, CA: Sage.

Friedman, D. E., Rimsky, C., & Johnson, A. A. (1996). *College and university reference guide to work–family programs: Report on a collaborative study*. New York: Families and Work Institute.

Gappa, J. M., & MacDermid, S. M. (1997). *Work, family, and the faculty career*. Washington, DC: American Association for Higher Education.

Glazer-Raymo, J. (1999). *Shattering the myths: Women in academe*. Baltimore: Johns Hopkins University Press.

Golde, C. M., & Dore, T. M. (2001.) *At cross purposes: What the experiences of today's doctoral students reveal about doctoral education*. Retrieved from the Web January 2001 <http://www.wcer.wisc.edu/phd-survey/golde.html>

Grant, L., Kennelly, I., & Ward, K. B. (2000). Revisiting the gender, marriage, and parenthood puzzle in scientific careers. *Women's Studies Quarterly, 1&2*, 62–85.

Gunderson, M. (1989). Male–female wage differentials and policy responses. *Journal of Economic Literature, 27*(1), 46–72.

Hall, R. M., & Sandler, B. (1984). *Out of the classroom: A chilly classroom climate for women*. Washington, DC: Project on the Status and Education of Women, Association of American Colleges.

Hamovich, W., & Morgenstern, R. D. (1977). Children and the productivity of academic women. *Journal of Higher Education, 48*, 633–645.

Hargens, L. L., McCann, J. C., & Reskin, B. F. (1978). Productivity and reproductivity: Fertility and professional achievement among research scientists. *Social Forces, 57*(1), 154–163.

Hensel, N. (1990). Maternity, promotion and tenure: Are they compatible? In L. Welsh (Ed.) *Women in higher education: Changes and challenges* (pp. 3–11). New York: Praeger.

Hensel, N. (1991). *Realizing gender equality in higher education: The need to integrate work/family issues*. ASHE-ERIC Higher Education Report No. 2. Washington, DC: George Washington University, School of Education and Human Development.

Hochschild, A. R. (1975). Inside the clockwork of male careers. In E. Howe (Ed.) *Women and the power to change* (pp. 470–480). New York: McGraw-Hill.

Hochschild, A. (1989). *The second shift: Working parents and the revolution at home*. New York: Viking Press.

Hochschild, A. R. (1997). *The time bind: When work becomes home and home becomes work*. New York: Metropolitan Books.

Jarvis, D. K. (1992). Improving junior faculty scholarship. In M. D. Sorcinelli & A. E. Austin (Eds.) *Developing new and junior faculty* (pp. 63–72). San Francisco: Jossey-Bass.

Kolodny, A. (1998). *Failing the future: A dean looks at higher education in the twenty-first century*. Durham, NC: Duke University Press.

Lazear, E. P. (1989). Symposium on women in the labor market. *Journal of Economic Perspectives, 3*(1), 3–7.

Levinson, D. J. (1978). *The seasons of a man's life*. New York: Knopf.

Lewis, L. S. (1975). *Scaling the ivory tower: Merits and its limits in academic careers*. Baltimore: Johns Hopkins University Press.

Long, J. S. (1990). The origins of sex differences in science. *Social Forces, 71,* 159–178.

Mangan, K. S. (2000, March 3). Female professors said to lag at medical schools. *Chronicle of Higher Education, 46.* Retrieved March 3, 2000 from the World Wide Web: <http://chronicle.com/weekly/v46/i26/26a01802.htm>

Moore, K. M., & Sagaria, M. A. D. (1991). The situation of women in research universities in the United States: Within the inner circles of academic power. In G. P. Kelly & S. Slaughter (Eds.) *Women's higher education in comparative perspective* (pp. 185–200). Netherlands: Kluwer.

Munn-Giddings, C. (1998). Mixing motherhood and academia—a lethal cocktail. In D. Malina & S. Maslin-Prothero (Eds.) *Surviving the academy: Feminist perspectives.* (pp. 56–68). Philadelphia: Falmer Press.

Nettles, M., Perna, L. W., Bradburn, E. M., Zimbler, L. (2000). Salary, promotion, and tenure status of minority and women faculty in U.S. colleges and universities. Washington, DC: U.S. Department of Education (NCES 2000-173).

Norrell, J. E., & Norrell, T. H. (1996). Faculty and family policies in higher education. *Journal of Family Issues, 17,* 204–226.

Perna, L. W. (2000). *Sex differences in faculty salaries: A cohort analysis.* Paper presented at the annual meeting of the American Educational Research Association, New Orleans, LA.

Perna, L. W. (2001). The relationship between family responsibilities and employment status. *Journal of Higher Education, 72*(5), 584–611.

Raabe, P. H. (1997). Work–family policies for faculty: How "career- and family-friendly" is academe? In M. A. Ferber & J. W. Loeb (Eds.) *Academic couples: Problems and promises* (pp. 208–225). Urbana: University of Illinois Press.

Rice, R. E., Sorcinelli, M. D., & Austin, A. (2000). *Heeding new voices: Academic careers for a new generation.* Washington, DC: American Association for Higher Education.

Rich, A. (1979). Toward a woman-centered university. In *On lies, secrets, and silence: Selected prose, 1966–1978* (pp. 126–155). New York: Norton.

Ropers-Huilman, B. (2000). Aren't you satisfied yet?: Women faculty member's interpretations of their academic work. In L. S. Hagedorn (Ed.) *What contributes to job satisfaction among faculty and staff.* Series: *New Directions for Institutional Research, 27*(1), 21–32.

Rosen, R. (1999). Secrets of the second sex in scholarly life. *Chronicle of Higher Education, 45*(46), A48.

Rosenbaum, J. (1979). Tournament mobility: Career patterns in a corporation. *Administrative Science Quarterly, 24,* 220–241.

Smith, K. E., & Bachu, A. (1999). Women's labor force attachment patterns and maternity leave: A review of the literature. U.S. Census Bureau, Population Division Working Paper, #32. <http://www.census.gov/population/www/documentation/twps0032/twps0032.html>

Solomon, B. (1985). *In the company of educated women: A history of women in higher education in America.* New Haven, CT: Yale University Press.

Sonnert, G., & Holton, G. (1995). *Gender differences in science careers: The project access study.* New Brunswick, NJ: Rutgers University Press.

Sorcinelli, M. D., & Near, J. P. (1989). Relations between work and life away from work among university faculty. *Journal of Higher Education, 60*(1), 59–82.

Spalter-Roth, R., & Merola, S. (2001). *Early career pathways: Differences among moms and dads, childless men, and childless women in sociology.* Paper presented at the Annual Meeting of the American Sociological Association, Anaheim, CA.

Swiss, D. J., & Walker, J. P. (1993). *Women and the work/family dilemma.* New York: John Wiley & Sons.

Tierney, W. G., & Bensimon, E. M. (1996). *Promotion and tenure: Community and socialization in academe.* Albany: State University of New York Press.

Toutkoushian, R. K. (1998). Sex matters less for younger faculty: Evidence of disaggregate pay disparities from the 1988 and 1993 NCES Surveys. *Economics of Education Review, 17*(1), 55–71

Varner, A. (2000). *The consequences of delaying attempted childbirth for women faculty.* Penn State Work–Family Initiative. Retrieved on August 6, 2002, from <http://lsir.la.psu.edu/workfam/delaykids.pdf>

Varner, A., & Drago, R. (2001). *Fertility and work in the United States: A policy perspective. Penn State Work–family Initiative.* Retrieved on August 6, 2002, from <http://lsir.la.psu.edu/workfam/fertilityreport.pdf>

Ward, K., & Bensimon, E. M. (2002). Engendering socialization. In K. Renn & A. Martinez Aleman (Eds.) *Women in higher education: An encyclopedia.* Santa Barbara, CA: ABC-CLIO.

Ward, K. B., & Grant, L. (1996). Gender and academic publishing. In J. C. Smart (Ed.) *Higher education: Handbook of theory and research. (Vol.11).* (pp. 172–212). New York: Agathon.

West, M. S. (1995). Women faculty: Frozen in time. *Academe, 81*(4), 26–29.

Williams, J. (1999). *Unbending gender: Why work and family conflict and what to do about it.* New York: Oxford University Press.

Williams, J. (2000, October 27). How the tenure track discriminates against women. *Chronicle of Higher Education,* B10.

Williams, W. M. (2001, July 20). Women in academe, and the men who derail them. *The Chronicle of Higher Education,* B20.

Wilson, R. (1998, April 17). When office mates are also roommates. *Chronicle of Higher Education,* A12–13.

Wilson, R. (1999, June 25). Timing is everything: Academe's annual baby boom. *Chronicle of Higher Education,* A14–15.

Wilson, R. (2001, April 13). The backlash against hiring. *The Chronicle of Higher Education,* A16.

Wolf-Wendel, L. E., Twombly, S., & Rice, S. (2000a). Dual-career couples: Keeping them together. *Journal of Higher Education,* 71(3), 291–321.

Wolf-Wendel, L. E., Twombly, S., & Rice, S. (2000b). *Dual-career couple accommodation policies in higher education: Dilemmas of balancing institutional and individual needs.* Paper presented at the Association for the Study of Higher Education Annual Meeting, Sacramento, CA, November, 2000.

Zuckerman, H. (1987). Persistence and change in the careers of men and women scientists and engineers. In L. Dix (Ed.) *Women: Their underrepresentation and career differentials in science and engineering* (pp. 127–156). Washington, DC: National Academy of Sciences, National Academy Press.

7

Negotiating Identities and Making Change

Feminist Faculty in Higher Education

Becky Ropers-Huilman and Monisa Shackelford

Over the past several decades, scholarship on higher education has expanded to include analyses of the ways that feminists in academic environments experience and construct their work (Dickens & Sagaria, 1997; Griffin, 1992; Middleton, 1993; Neumann & Peterson, 1997; Richardson, 1997; Ropers-Huilman, 1998). A focus on feminist faculty is important to the changing landscape of higher education for several reasons. First, feminist faculty as a group produce vast amounts of scholarship in a wide variety of disciplines (Kramarae & Spender, 1992; Minnich, O'Barr, & Rosenfeld, 1988). Their efforts contribute to a reconstruction of the knowledge that shapes our understanding of the gendered aspects of society. Knowledge by, for, and about women is used in college classrooms and contributes to teaching and learning experiences. Second, many feminist faculty use innovative, less hierarchical teaching practices (Fisher, 2001; Lewis, 1993; Maher & Tetreault, 1994; Middleton, 1993; Ropers-Huilman, 1998). Through their pedagogy and research, feminists have examined the principles of "good teaching" for their effects on the diverse participants in higher education classrooms. Third, feminist faculty serve as leaders on college campuses. Beyond suggesting alternative leadership, they serve on formal commissions and committees that monitor the "climate" for women on their campuses (Glazer-Raymo, 1999; Kolodny, 1998). This presence is important to ensure that women students—who now constitute more than half of the undergraduate student population in this country—can find educational experiences that foster their growth.

The importance of the contributions made by feminist and female faculty suggests the need to ensure that rather than feeling marginalized, they feel supported and valued on college campuses. Unfortunately, the literature is not optimistic in this regard. In one example of this marginality, an entire book was recently dedicated to the topic of *Anti-Feminist Harassment in the Academy* (Clark, Garner, Higonnet, & Katrak, 1996). The essays in this book discuss harassment as "the demeaning or devaluing of feminist work and of feminists in terms of their academic progress and their professional lives" (p. xii) and document occurrences in teaching, scholarly publishing, and interactions with students, colleagues, and administrators. As Jane Roland Martin (2000) writes, "Right now, to be a feminist scholar in the academy is to experience stress and strain on a daily basis" (p. xxv).

The strain of which Martin speaks is perhaps compounded as feminist faculty, most often women, have a multitude of complex and sometimes even contradictory identities. In today's society, in today's academy, what does it mean to be a woman, a professor, a scholar, an activist, a researcher, a teacher, a community member, a "server," a citizen, a mother, a partner, a colleague, a feminist?

In this chapter, we focus on the ways in which feminist faculty members construct their identities within the social structures present in the academy. Using Goffman's (1959) emphasis on social interaction as performance, we consider how feminist faculty members, as social actors, are both shaped by their involvement in their academic contexts, and serve as change agents to shape those same contexts. We first present our methodology, and then introduce our theoretical frame. Then, we move on to discuss data from qualitative interviews with feminist faculty about how they construct their roles as researchers and teachers, while also considering how they understand their roles as feminists and change agents within the academy. Finally, we analyze what might be learned from them about how academic environments could be changed to better support the efforts of all participants.

METHODOLOGY

Data were gathered during 1999 and 2000 using semistructured, open-ended interviews with fifteen feminist faculty at a Research I university in the South. We began interviewing faculty members who we believed, because of their involvement in campus organizations or events, would identify themselves as feminist. Throughout the process we found additional respondents "opportunistically" (Honigmann, 1982), by asking those we interviewed to refer others who might be interested in being interviewed. In this way, we identified feminist faculty who represented a wide range of disciplinary affiliations. All participants were Caucasian and three were men. They ranged in age from 29 to 58. Eight are married, and seven report having children of varying ages. Two self-report that they are "queer."

INTERVIEW AND ANALYSIS PROCEDURES

The interviews lasted from 45 to 90 minutes. Interviews were tape recorded and fully transcribed. Case numbers and pseudonyms were assigned to ensure participant anonymity. Prior to or at the time of their interview, participants were also asked for copies of their vitae, to fill out a demographics form, and to sign a consent form. The participants were told that the purpose of the research was to investigate feminist action in higher education.

Through the use of semistructured, open-ended questions, we were able to maintain the direction of the interview while allowing participants to respond in as open-ended a manner as possible. As the interviews proceeded, modification to the interview protocol was necessary to allow participants to tell us of their experiences in their own words (Glaser, 1992; Strauss, 1987).

Following the completion of the interviews, we began the analysis by reviewing the transcripts several times and making notes of emerging themes as well as significant incidents described by the respondents. As certain common themes were noted, we then returned to the transcripts to clarify, confirm, and understand the complexities of the evidence that was gathered. Following this process, we focused both on the themes that we identified as prevalent among our participants and on themes that were suggested by the literature on feminist faculty.

THEORETICAL FRAMEWORK

Erving Goffman (1959) suggests that we create our social world by acting the part we wish to be exhibited in any particular situation and by controlling the impression given to others. We do not show all that makes up our presentation, hiding what we do not wish to show in a given situation or social structure. This is a fluid, dialectical process between the actor and others. It is necessary for others to collaborate with the actor by upholding the impression that she or he is bringing to the fore and thus reinforcing the social structure to which the individual was reacting initially (Brissett & Edgley, 1990; Goffman, 1959; Schwalbe, 1993; Stryker, 1980). In this way, identities are shaped within the context of specific "social worlds" and, in turn, shape those worlds.

In this chapter, we used this emphasis on performance and social structure to examine the ways feminist faculty believed their performances were shaped by the academic contexts in which they do their work. Specifically, we asked faculty to tell us about how they were able to enact feminism in their research and teaching. Our interviews included questions such as, "In your experience, what facilitates feminist action in the academy?" "How does that feminist action relate to the three primary responsibilities of faculty member: teaching, research, service?" "In what ways are you able to—and unable to—integrate your identity as a feminist into all aspects of your academic life?" and "To what extent do you think feminism is possible in academic settings?" Through these questions, we entered into dialogues with feminist faculty in which we learned about the ways they constructed their performances in academic contexts.

PERFORMING PROFESSORIAL IDENTITIES: (HOW) CAN I BE A FEMINIST TOO?

By using the concept of performance, we are not suggesting that faculty are acting as something that they are not. Rather, identities are multiple and context-specific (Josselson, 1996; Stryker, 1980). Feminist faculty can, and often do, have many roles that they perform in their lives. For a person with many identities, switching between them is an ambitious task and in itself takes much energy. However, when one deals with a stigmatized identity on a daily basis, such as being a "feminist," management may become particularly cumbersome (Griffin, 1992; Martin, 2000; Middleton, 1993).

Some of the tensions between feminist faculty members' identities are more obvious than others. For example, feminism implies working toward positive social change. Yet, faculty who take on the responsibility of working for social change in the academy are seen as advocates of a cause, and thus not able to be objective in their scholarship. Traditionally, objectivity has been held as the gold standard for academic success and power. And yet, professorial power may not congeal with a caretaker identity that is often expected of a woman. Being a woman in our society still suggests being a caretaker of one's family and, in many cases, of students in one's academic unit (Park, 1996; Thorne & Hochschild, 1997). Gail Griffin (1992) aptly points out, "The woman professor's sense of her authority is a complicated phenomenon. It is not reinforced by the power structures of the extra-academic world, except to the extent that Mom is seen as a power" (p. 140). Yet, scholars (particularly at Research I institutions) must disentangle themselves from personal matters that might get in the way of producing unbiased scholarship. In this quagmire, feminist scholars question how (or if) they can craft coherent identities within the academy (Frye, 1980; Martin, 2000; Middleton, 1993).

Feminist faculty members in this study talked about the ways they experience conflicting expectations in all three roles typically associated with the professoriate: teaching, research, and service. Berger and Luckman (1966) suggest that roles are created by typification of one's own and others' performances. That is, if a certain type of actor "usually" plays a certain role, other actors will come to expect that role to be filled by only that type of actor. Unless this assumption is challenged by a group of actors over an extended period of time, it will perpetuate in an established system. One assistant professor told us that she sees part of her job as "providing a haven of sort for women" students. Yet, she elaborates: "I just see it as part of my work. . . . But there is the danger for the women in the faculty to become mommy. . . . It could hamper your career if your career means to you writing, publishing, rising up some sort of academic ladder." Thus, just as there is a societal expectation for the female role of "mother" in the family, the same role of "mother" to students is expected but not reward because it is not an established, traditional role for an "academic" to play.

While recognizing that her relationships with students might not be rewarded, a faculty member in this study goes on to describe how she feels "completely entitled" to be in the academy. She explains how that entitlement is complex, though, with the following words:

> I feel like my natural place is in the classroom and my natural gift is for teaching, so in that sense, I've never felt like I've never belonged here. As a feminist, I have to say that I find myself censoring my words, thinking twice about making statements, because I guess I'm so used to running into resistance that sometimes I just—I don't have the energy for it.

At the same time, she emphasizes that she nevertheless incorporates her feminism into her teaching, largely because it is simply who she is. She describes:

> Personally, I can't separate it from who I am and I couldn't live without it. It validates everything that I do for me. It's useful in the classroom because it's necessary in a number of ways I think for young women; even if they're going to resist the label of feminist, they are seeking a female role model, they are seeking words of empowerment.

This faculty member, who speaks perhaps most intensely about the integration of her feminist and teaching identities, acknowledges the struggles but also the necessities of merging these two identities. However, there are others who do not feel the freedom to bring their feminist identity into the classroom. Another participant, an assistant professor, describes how she has put her feminist teaching on hold. She states, "I have separated my feminist work into my research, and I haven't brought it as much into the classroom. And I think that is partly because I have a certain fear about being the only woman voice."

Feminist faculty members in our study discussed the ways they either waited to engage with feminist theory in a public way until after tenure, or felt pressured to keep feminist work "closeted" within their departments. One participant, a full professor, describes how the public representation of her feminist identity changed throughout her academic experience. In her words:

> I always thought I was a feminist. I thought I was a feminist since high school, but it was not until after I finished my Ph.D. and, in a

sense, established my male credentials that I started to be able to work toward bringing together my feminist identity and my identity as a scholar, a teacher, and a professor.

This same faculty member described how feminist colleagues in her generation felt that they needed to publish a mainstream book first to establish their "male credentials" (and often to receive tenure). Then, they could write their "feminist book." The fear or concern about utilizing feminist work in research directly relates to material effects (through the reward system) as well as to more informal "climate" issues. Another full professor told us, "If I were to do any kind of writing, publishing that reeked of feminist theory, it wouldn't even be counted."

In addition to their feminist work not being recognized for tenure and promotion, other faculty spoke of the outright sanctions applied if one were to dare use feminist teaching or contribute to feminist scholarship. One professor stated, "Lots of senior colleagues would advise the junior women to do that— to downplay their feminism until they get tenure . . . for the fear that it will be held against them." Another full professor pointed to the overt hostility in her department. She states:

> I think they're threatened as hell. I think that I was supposed to wait my turn [to go up for promotion], that I was not supposed to get promoted ahead of other people, and that I was supposed to fail. And, it was absolutely clear that my association with [a women's organization] was not to my advantage.

Relationships with colleagues affect the ways feminist faculty members feel that they integrate the various aspects of their identities. One person describes her strategy: "I do what I have to do in my discipline. I play the game, if you want to call it that, explore in my discipline. . . . But I am branching off to this more philosophical stuff, but I'll balance it and make sure I do what I need to do." This faculty member explains the context of her department with the following example: "I used to have that sign on my wall, the NOW [National Organization for Women] thing, 'Feminism is the radical notion that women are people.' My male colleagues would come in and look at it and call me a 'Feminazi.' It's not popular."

Even when departmental colleagues are open enough to consider the possibilities of feminist intellectual work, a comfortable work environment is not guaranteed. One faculty member reflected on an interchange she had with a senior colleague after he had publicly made a negative comment about feminism. She told us:

> When we talked about it, it was really very interesting, because what I realized was not that he was this raging anti-feminist, misogynist

person, but simply that it just didn't occur to him that anyone would question the connection of feminism and bitchiness. [This was] despite his having very good feelings about me as a scholar and as a colleague.

Some faculty members acknowledge the influence that negative sanctions have in their own self-censorship. This faculty member wrestles with how the context of her department intersects with self-censorship to silence her feminist work.

I think I'm very fortunate to be in a department that doesn't at least consciously suppress a feminist consciousness, or feminist action. So I don't feel like if I do take a stand, or I do step out there, I'm endangering my job. I think I'm too good at what I do for that to be an issue. I think what's intriguing to me is that some of it is self-censorship. . . . [If I construct myself as a feminist] what are the assumptions that are going to be made about me? And will I on some level as a teacher, lose credibility with my students? As a scholar, lose credibility with my colleagues? And I am at least partially responsible for that self-censorship. . . . Not so much in the classroom, actually, but more in faculty meetings, because I'm, I guess, afraid of being an outcast; of being 'oh, you're one of those people.' It's a wonderful silencing technique.

While some colleagues may have good intentions and simply be unaware of the ways in which their actions signal that feminist faculty members need to keep their identities hidden, other faculty members are less subtle in their attempts to silence their feminist colleagues. One faculty member described how she perceives the context of her department.

What if I'd listened to [my departmental colleagues]? What if I'd thrown myself into my teaching and abandoned my scholarship? They'd have screwed me anyway. Because it wasn't about that! It was about how they could screw me! . . . You have to meet the stated standards. You have to play it as if it's really true, because then you can call them on it. And it's like the difference between the state retirement system and TIAA-CREF. You can't take the retirement system with you. Your work is portable. Kissing ass isn't. You can't take it with you.

For the most part, the feminist faculty members in this study discussed how their aspirations and beliefs conflict in some ways with those expressed explicitly and, especially, implicitly by their colleagues. These tensions between their various roles caused conflicts and forced choices about the ways they were going to foreground or sublimate their various identities.

From Goffman we know that for a "performance" to be successful, it is imperative that all involved express mutual agreement about the meanings of the "performance" or situation. Building on Goffman, Stryker suggests that the social structure with which we interact directly influences the social interaction between actors. This social interaction, in turn, reinforces the established social structure. Reflecting this notion, one faculty member stated that, ". . . you can't look at [what's happened in my department] and say there is true gender bias going on. No, that's not the way bias happens. It's structural. And so this is the problem and this is what makes it so difficult." It is difficult because structural problems are hard to see and hard to change. Yet some feminists are using their roles as faculty members within academic institutions to create more fair and equitable teaching, learning, and leading opportunities.

CREATING CHANGE

Wanting to learn and teach in a more open, accepting environment, feminists in the academy have both demanded and worked for change. For example, although Women's Studies programs did not exist in the United States in the 1960s, today more than 800 campuses have such programs. Further, feminist scholarship has now contributed so much to so many disciplines that it is characterized as a "knowledge explosion" (Kramarae & Spender, 1992). In this section, we turn from the ways that feminist faculty crafted their professorial identities as traditionally defined to concentrate instead on what they believe about the potential of their roles as change agents in academic environments.

Feminist faculty become agents of change when they choose to perform their feminist identities within the traditional social structure of the university. By interacting with each other, with nonsupportive others, and with the university social structure, change toward a more egalitarian academic environment has the potential to slowly emerge. Throughout the interviews we heard evidence of this process. One associate professor discussed how important it is to continually dialogue on women's value in the academy. She stated:

> I think we are getting there, but it's taken a long time and we have to fight that battle all the time. We have to fight it everyday . . . that not everything can be measured by the male body, by the male brain, by the male standard, and particularly by the male notion of what's fair to him.

The entrenched nature of the male standard in academic settings suggests a substantial difficulty in creating change. Berger and Luckman (1966) point out that any type of change to an established social institution, such as the university, must be forced. Those in power will always support the status quo until challenged to do otherwise. This challenge must be supported by large groups of actors over an extended period of time to enact and establish an improved social structure.

And this change does not occur smoothly. Instead, often those who serve as change agents pay a price for their efforts. One participant spoke of the price of change from a faculty member's perspective. She stated, "There's a price. But I think that after, after you become somewhat established, then the price is lower." Because including women and work by, for, and about women has not historically been considered part of the established university social structure, there continues to be risk associated with initiating this type of change. Humans, being creatures of habit, repeat certain behaviors until they are, out of need for efficiency, considered "human nature." Any change to "human nature" or the established system, will be met with resistance (Berger & Luckman, 1966). What is important is the understanding of the need for reform and the tools to make it happen. Social structure and meaning in a situation must be mutually agreed on by the actors and acted in collaboration with each other. This collaboration is what feminist faculty are working both against in the established system and toward in the new vision of a more egalitarian system. One faculty member discussed how the system is changing and what is expected:

> And feminism, and feminist scholarship is something that has now come to inform my practice as an intellectual and the various ways in which I enact that in my roles as teacher, as scholar, as administrator, as member of the university community and, thus, through the university community to the community at large. So, that's the goal. That's the kind of new utopia . . . a gender-inflected utopia.

In thinking broadly about their own identities, two feminist faculty members describe their overall philosophies as related to change. While admitting that they don't always live out their philosophies in the ways they would like, they assert the importance of doing so to bring about reform in higher education. One junior faculty member told us:

> At some point, there's a test. And the test is: Will you be authentic in the world? Will you say and do what you truly feel is right? And it's easy for me to say, well, maybe not quite—or it had been. After a certain point, after a meeting [with feminist colleagues], you get help in that condition. You say, no, I need to say what I think. And if everybody starts doing that, then change happens.

Yet another faculty member conveys her philosophy about being a feminist in an academic setting:

It's almost that I think that activism is a cop-out. It's like we should be doing it in our practice. How then in our practice as teachers and scholars, and as members of the university community, how do we change the world in a feminist way? . . . What I like about this life is the way in which you have these various different things that you do and you allocate your time, but it all interacts and enriches the other parts so that [it's not like you wear] different hats. . . . No, I don't have different hats. . . . And feminism, and feminist scholarship is something that has now come to inform my practice as an intellectual and the various ways in which I enact that in my roles as teacher, as scholar, as administrator, as member of the university community and, thus, through the university community to the community at large.

Further pointing to the necessity of managing their identities and the impressions they present, another faculty member stated that feminist faculty must articulate their importance to the central goals of the university if they want to be valued. She told us:

We are central to the core mission of the university. . . . And that's what we have to claim. And that's what we have to get. And it's not going to be easy. Feminism is not a supplement. . . . It is the way in which we do our work.

If feminist faculty members are discouraged or even penalized for bringing an important aspect of their identities into their work, their willingness to remain active in academic communities may be compromised. Satisfaction with their work lives is related to faculty members' ability to craft some degree of coherency between the various parts of their identity within their particular academic contexts (Neumann & Peterson, 1997; Ropers-Huilman, 2000). As such, better understandings of what needs to happen to support the full integration of feminist faculty members' identities—to include their roles as change agents—is important for supporting feminist and, by extension, women's participation in academic environments.

Optimistic Imaginings

For a long time, academic feminists, like all feminists, are going to have to have to take personal risks—of confronting their own realities, of speaking their minds, of being fired or ignored when they do so, of becoming stereotyped as "manhaters" when they evince a primary loyalty to women (Rich, 1993, p. 132).

Over the past several decades, feminists have made great strides in higher education, contributing valuable and creative scholarship and pedagogy. And yet, the feminist faculty members in our study still struggled to shape identities that allowed them to be viewed both as competent and valuable researchers and teachers while also being acknowledged as feminists and change agents. In considering the ways feminist faculty shape their identities, then, it is important to ask how academic environments could support their efforts. What would university campuses look like if feminist faculty's contributions were more valued and better integrated into the mainstream university social structure? Judith Glazer-Raymo (1999) provides some direction:

> When viewed from a feminist policy analysis perspective, the underlying premise—that new policies will solve old problems—fails to recognize that basic attitudinal changes are needed to create female-friendly university systems. Rather than assert that women are more likely to work part-time than to earn tenure-track appointments, to teach more and publish less, to obtain their doctorates in the humanities rather than in the hard sciences, to remain single or childless, to leave rather than remain at the university, to be assistant or associate administrators rather than chief executive officers, it would be more appropriate to determine what makes institutional structures more compatible with men's lives. (p. 205)

And, more recently, Lisa Wolf-Wendel currently works to identify and articulate what coeducational institutions can learn from women's colleges—which often have a mission compatible with feminism—about how to foster better learning experiences for women (for example, see chapter 2 in this volume). Strategies and suggestions are not new. Over two decades ago, Adrienne Rich (1993) made many of the same critiques and suggestions that others are making today. Most directly, perhaps, she urged that both the content and hierarchical nature of universities be rethought such that we no longer have a situation in which "women's integrity is likely to be undermined by the process of university education" (p. 122).

The social structures in which identities are constructed exist because many individuals (usually those exercising power) agree that they serve an appropriate or useful function (Berger & Luckman, 1966; Stryker, 1980). In other words, because a certain social structure has been perpetuated by subsequent generations, it is stronger in its traditions and social norms. Feminists have critiqued the social structures found in or supported by academic environments, suggesting that they are largely traditional and patriarchal (Kolodny, 1998; Martin, 2000).

Social structures provide explicit and implicit guidelines for establishing and maintaining identities within certain contexts (Berger & Luckman,

1966; Stryker, 1980). It is within the context of academia that feminist faculty must work. Over the past twenty years there have been transformations of the academy, but the feminist scholars in our study show that continued change at the structural level is still needed to change the discrimination that continues against feminist and women faculty. This structural change should have as its goal the fostering of a climate that supports an increased range of performances by all its participants. This could ultimately prove to be higher education's greatest asset.

As evidenced by participants' experiences, "feminist bashing" certainly still exists, but actions that silence feminist intellectual work in more subtle ways are undoubtedly more present. Strategies for addressing the institutional relationships that make faculty members' work lives hard to integrate need to address that subtlety. If there is to be change toward a more egalitarian system, one that supports feminist faculty members' integration of their multiple identities, "we will have to rock the boat" (Martin, 2000, p. 168). We will have to allow all members of the academy to perform in ways that convey the various facets of their work and lives, while ensuring that all also respect the rights of others to do so as well. Collaboration and unification among feminist faculty and administrators, along with support from others, are absolute necessities if we are to realize the positive potential of gendered futures in higher education.

REFERENCES

Berger, P. L., & Luckman, T. (1966). *Social construction of reality: A treatise in the sociology of knowledge*. Garden City, NY: Doubleday.

Brissett, D., & Edgley, C. (1990). The dramaturgical perspective. In D. Brissett & C. Edgley (Eds.) *Life as theater: A dramaturgical sourcebook* (pp. 1–46). New York: Aldine de Gruyter.

Clark, V., Garner, S. N., Higonnet, M., & Katrak, K. H. (1996). *Anti-feminism in the academy*. New York: Routledge.

Dickens, C. S., & Sagaria, M. D. (1997). Feminists at work: Collaborative relationships among women faculty. *Review of Higher Education, 21*(1) 79–101.

Fisher, B. M. (2001). *No angel in the classroom: Teaching through feminist discourse*. Lanham, MD: Rowman & Littlefield.

Frye, M. (1980). On second thought. . . . *Radical Teacher, 17*, 37–38.

Glaser, B. (1992). *Basics of grounded theory analysis*. Mill Valley, CA: Sociology Press.

Glazer-Raymo, J. (1999). *Shattering the myths: Women in academe*. Baltimore: Johns Hopkins University Press.

Goffman, E. (1959). *The presentation of self in everyday life*. New York: Doubleday.

Griffin, G. B. (1992). *Calling: Essays on teaching in the mother tongue*. Pasadena, CA: Trilogy Books.

Honigmann, J. (1982). Sampling in ethnographic field work. In R. G. Burgess (Ed.) *Field research: A sourcebook and field manual.* Boston: George Allen & Unwin.

Josselson, R. (1996). *Revising herself: The story of women's identity from college to midlife.* New York: Oxford University Press.

Kolodny, A. (1998). *Failing the future: A dean looks at the 21st century.* Durham, NC: Duke University Press.

Kramarae, C., & Spender, D. (1992). *The knowledge explosion: Generations of feminist scholarship.* New York: Teachers College.

Lewis, M. G. (1993). *Without a word: Teaching beyond women's silence.* New York: Routledge.

Maher, F. A., & Tetreault, M. T. (1994). *The feminist classroom.* New York: Basic Books.

Martin, J. R. (2000). *Coming of age in academe: Rekindling women's hopes and reforming the academy.* New York: Routledge.

Middleton, S. (1993). *Educating feminists: Life histories and pedagogy.* New York: Teachers College.

Minnich, E., O'Barr, J. F., & Rosenfeld, R. A. (1988). *Reconstructing the academy: Women's education and women's studies.* Chicago: University of Chicago Press.

Neumann, A., & Peterson, P. (1997). *Learning from our lives: Women, research and autobiography in education.* New York: Teachers College.

Park, S. M. (1996). Research, teaching, and service: Why shouldn't women's work count? *Journal of Higher Education, 67*(1), 46–84.

Rich, A. (1993). Toward a woman-centered university. In J. S. Glazer, E. M. Bensimon, & B. K. Townsend (Eds.) *Women in higher education: A feminist perspective* (pp. 121–134). Needham Heights, MA: Ginn. Originally published in 1979.

Richardson, L. (1997). *Fields of play: Constructing an academic life.* New York: Routledge.

Ropers-Huilman, B. (1998). *Feminist teaching in theory and practice: Situating power and knowledge in poststructural classrooms.* New York: Teachers College.

Ropers-Huilman, B. (2000). Aren't you satisfied yet?: Women faculty members' interpretations of their academic work. In L. S. Hagedorn (Ed.) *What contributes to job satisfaction among faculty and staff.* Series: *New Directions for Institutional Research, 27*(1), 21–32.

Schwalbe, M. (1993). Goffman against postmodernism: Emotion and the reality of self. *Symbolic Interaction, 16,* 333–350.

Strauss, A. L. (1987). *Qualitative analysis for social scientists.* Cambridge: Cambridge University Press.

Stryker, S. (1980). *Symbolic interactionism: A social structural version.* Menlo Park, CA: Benjamin/Cummings.

Thorne, B., & Hochschild, A. R. (1997). Feeling at home at work: Life in academic departments. *Qualitative Sociology, 20*(4), 517–520.

Warren, C. A. B. (1977). Fieldwork in the gay world: Issues in phenomenological research. *Journal of Social Issues, 33*(4), 93–107.

Part IV

Re-Conceiving the Future

Advocacy Education

Teaching, Research, and Difference in Higher Education

Becky Ropers-Huilman and Denise Taliaferro

Recently, scholars and practitioners have generated urgent questions about how institutions of higher learning should encompass the diversity of participants and paradigms in academic settings. These questions have focused broadly on desired changes in institutional culture or climate (Chang, 2002; Hurtado, Milem, Clayton-Pederson, & Allen, 1998; Kezar & Eckel, 2002; Kolodny, 1996; Minnich, O'Barr, & Rosenfeld, 1988), the implications of reconfiguring disciplinary content and boundaries (Gumport & Snydman, 2002; Stanton & Stewart, 1995), and relationships among and between students, faculty, and administration (De La Luz Reyes & Halcon, 1988; Kraemer, 1997; Turner, Myers, & Creswell, 1997). Most scholarship insists, albeit in varying ways, that those in higher education need to embrace diversity and make teaching and learning environments both welcoming and educationally useful for all participants.

Although this literature has encompassed a broad range of perspectives, we continue to seek literature that both provides and questions strategies and rationales for those of us who are interested in serving as advocates to persons who have typically been marginalized as "diverse others" in our day-to-day academic environments. In this chapter, we want to add to literature on higher education theory and practice related to diversity by exploring the complexities of what we are calling "advocacy education." As faculty members in the field of education, we find that our research, teaching, and advocacy are inextricably linked. When we set out to do any of the three, the other two are implicated in various ways. As such, we use the term "advocacy education" throughout this chapter to convey that understanding. Our purpose in this work is to explore the ways scholars' positions in the academy influence their abilities to effectively act as advocates, teachers, and researchers in multicultural environments. We do this through close examination of our participation in a seminar entitled "Women of Color in College" on a predominantly White southern campus.

Setting the Stage

During the fall semester of 1996, Becky Ropers-Huilman and Stefanie Costner, a graduate student who had been assigned to work with Becky, initiated the development of a group to focus on women of color in college. As scholars of higher education and as persons who were interested in making educational environments more accepting of all participants, they decided that this project would mesh well with their convictions. Becky and Stefanie held an initial organizational meeting a few months before they intended to officially start meeting and decided to hold future discussions in the African American Cultural Center on campus. During the spring semester of 1997, those who chose to participate met about every other week for approximately three hours in the afternoon. This group originally consisted of Becky (a White assistant professor in Higher Education Leadership), ten graduate women (one Asian American and nine African American) in English, Higher Education Leadership, and Curriculum and Instruction, and two African American undergraduate women in English and General Sciences. Our ages spanned three decades, with our youngest member only eighteen years old. Denise Taliaferro was one of the graduate students who elected to participate.

We chose to ground our analysis of these experiences using various assumptions embedded in feminist, womanist, critical, and poststructural approaches to knowledge. These assumptions contradict and overlap each other in various ways, yet are united by their assertions that knowledge is partial, political, and related to the identities of its constructors and interpreters. Further assumptions assert the value of:

1. finding differences and sites of conflict rather than themes that can be generalized (Tierney, 1994);
2. telling previously silenced stories (Collins, 1991; Lorde, 1984; Reinharz, 1992);
3. recognizing that there is more than one way to measure the usefulness of research (Fine, 1994; Lather, 1986, 1991, 1994; Reinharz, 1992; Wolf, 1992);
4. suggesting that there is always more than one story that can be told of a given situation (Pagano, 1991; Tierney, 1994; Wolf, 1992).

Guided by these approaches, this section presents the context of the research, examines the theoretical (dis)junctures that informed this work, and considers the ways our positions influenced the questions that we were able to address and the understandings we were able to create.

Using this particular combination of theoretical tenets, we chose not to write this chapter as if we were telling one story. Although we agree on the importance of advocacy education, we often see and thus negotiate the emergent tensions differently. We believe that it is in between our differences that the potential for learning is greatest. In this vein, we attempt to offer a dialogic analysis of advocacy education from at least two perspectives. Becky writes from a White feminist paradigm while Denise writes from a Black womanist one. We are both guided by poststructural understandings that insist on the instability and fluidity of meanings and identities as well. What emerges are points of agreement and points of contention that do not allow us or our readers to come to a final answer about how to participate in advocacy education.

SITUATED BEINGS

The way things are for our life and body allows us only a partial view of things, not the kind of total view we might gain if we were godlike, looking down from the sky. But we can only know as situated beings. (Greene, 1995, p. 26)

Womanist, Scholar, Student

I, Denise, approached this collaborative work from my own peculiar disposition. I am an African American female who grew up in the predominately African American city of Detroit, where I was raised in a family committed to Black nationalist politics. During my freshman year of high school, I made the controversial decision to begin my sophomore year at a predominately White high school located in a middle-class suburb of Detroit. After graduating, I attended UCLA for my undergraduate studies and eventually went to Louisiana State University to complete my masters and doctorate degrees in secondary teaching and curriculum theory.

I say all of this to emphasize that the interaction I have had with White people in my lifetime has almost always been initiated in and mediated through educational settings, where White people—White women in particular—held positions of authority with respect to my education. Stretched between my nationalist background and my commitments to social justice for all, my feelings about the role White people have played in Black education are complicated and contradictory. How can I not respect the efforts of such women as Prudence Crandall and Margaret Walker, who defied the law and risked their lives to educate Black children prior to emancipation? Yet how can I not also be angry because the education they offered often reflected the unworthiness of Black history, culture, and experience? Yet they did not know any better. Did they? These were the tensions that most influenced my interest and participation in the group project and discussions organized by Becky and her graduate assistant, Stefanie.

At the time, I joined the group (as a student) for several reasons. First, I was simply intrigued by the idea of a group of intellectual women mostly of color coming together to share their knowledge and testimonials, laughing, talking, thinking and theorizing about who we are and where we are. I expected that our intellectual forays would be just as full of energy, contradiction, and contestation as they are in the kitchen, the beauty salon, or the front porch. There are few "safe" places, especially within the academy, where women of color engage in rigorous intellectual discussions on our own terms. Second, I wanted to contemplate this feminist–womanist relationship. Like Becky, I believe that it is imperative to engage and disrupt contradictions, instabilities and silences. Yet I did not come to the project with feminist eyes, so to speak. I came with womanist eyes, ones that cannot deny the salience of race in the construction of a gendered self. In fact, when I came to the group, I was grappling with the "other" side of Becky's dilemmas. I wanted to understand why many Black women, including myself, often downplayed the significance of gender in our processes of identifying as marginalized people. Finally, I thought a lot about this White feminist professor's attempt to position herself within a women-of-color student context. Who is she to advocate for us? How will this struggle for recognition and validation of identities play out of and into our conversations? What are the implications of race, gender and power in advocacy work?

Researcher, Teacher, Feminist

Previous study about and involvement in research, teaching and reading about education, and personal experiences had been insufficient to prepare me for my involvement in this group. What I mean by this is that I, Becky, committed to this project before I felt comfortable with the structure of my participation. Unlike what I had been taught in other research and teaching endeavors, I did not have a "problem statement" or a detailed syllabus dictating the terms of my relationships with other participants. Nor did I have a specific question I was trying to answer. I did not consciously know what I wanted or expected to happen. I did not know what my role was to be. I knew only that I wanted to help carve a space in the academy where a group of women of color could speak and have their speaking and experiences validated. I did not know what I wanted to hear or the precise methods through which this validation would take place.

This work was undoubtedly influenced by my move from Madison, Wisconsin to Baton Rouge, Louisiana to take my first assistant professor position at Louisiana State University. LSU has a rich history of serving some populations well while excluding others. Women were not admitted to LSU until 1906; African Americans (currently comprising roughly one-third of the state's population) were not admitted until 1953. Until recently, African American students were assessed a charge for the maintenance of the African American Cultural Center, regardless of their use, while Whites who attend programming at the Center did so free of charge.[1] Fraternities and sororities are largely segregated by race.

I expected to find, and was consciously seeking out, cultural differences in this move from the Midwest to the South. I had a fascination with, and a deep sense of ignorance about, the intense and historic racial tensions that I heard occurred in the "Deep South." I had learned about this region of the United States primarily through history books (that largely focused on war, in my recollection). My understandings of racial tensions came predominantly from educational theorists whose work drew attention to disparities in educational opportunity and experience between various groups of people.

My fascination with racial dynamics is articulated well in Steven Linstead's (1993) description of the motivation fueling any attempts to "know" others:

> The very existence of *another* is information which tells us that we are not *complete*, and the fundamental, intractable compulsion in social life is to reconcile this difference, to complete what is missing to being, to fill our own lack. (p. 61)

I admit that my need to see and understand individuals who have traditionally been characterized as "Others" in relation to me made my involvement in a project focusing on women of color very intriguing. I hoped to hear from these Others, perhaps in an effort to better understand myself and this new situation that I was living within.

My recognition of "incompleteness" developed poignantly during the first semester at LSU. I often heard stories of discrimination and disrespect that occurred in various places on campus—in classrooms, in the union, and at football games. Through my conversations and questionings with students, I began to learn that while parts of our backgrounds were similar, our life experiences were, in some ways, drastically, paradigmatically different. Christine Sleeter (1993) explains, "Spending most of their time with other white people, whites do not see much of the realities of the lives of Americans of color nor encounter their viewpoints in any depth. Nor do they really want to, since those viewpoints would challenge practices and beliefs that benefit white people" (p. 168). I knew I was missing a large part of the world.

I wanted, then, to use my newly acquired "strategic location" as a professor to learn about the experiences of women of color in college and university settings. Further, I wanted to provide a forum through which the students with whom I was working could be validated in an academic setting for forming and articulating theories based on their own experiences. Using my interpretations of feminism and poststructuralism, I wanted to focus on the "local" as a way to generate broader understandings and draw attention to the ways the personal is political. By offering course credit for this experience, I hoped to lend the academy's support to this type of intellectual engagement. My motives, I believed, were clearly set in my understandings of feminism, poststructuralism, and critical theory. Yet, as illustrated throughout the dialogue presented in this chapter, these motives were not simply defined or enacted.

WORLDVIEWS

With Womanist Eyes

> Black feminist thought consists of specialized knowledge created by African American women that clarifies a standpoint of and for Black women. In other words, Black feminist thought encompasses theoretical interpretations of Black women's reality by those who live it. (Collins, 1990, p. 581)

When I, Denise, use the expression "womanist eyes," I mean to acknowledge the reality that, because of my cultural and racial positioning, I do not, in fact cannot, interpret our project from a (White) feminist standpoint. In my view, I always understood the project to be a racially charged one, burdened by historical oppressions while struggling toward transcendence. Womanist eyes implicate both a way of thinking and a way of doing. In *Defining Black Feminist Thought*, Patricia Hill Collins (1990) contends that the interdependent relationship between experience and consciousness supports the idea of a Black feminist consciousness that is distinct from that of a White feminist one. She writes:

> Black women's work and family experiences and grounding in traditional African-American culture suggest that African-American women as a group experience a world different from that of those who are not Black and female. Moreover, these concrete experiences can stimulate a distinctive Black feminist consciousness concerning that material reality. Being Black and female may expose African-American women to certain common experiences, which in turn may predispose us to a distinctive group consciousness, but it in no way guarantees that such a consciousness will develop among all women or that it will be articulated as such by the group. (p. 584)

Collins goes on to argue that a Black feminist standpoint has several discernable characteristics. Some of the core themes include a legacy of struggle which has required a sense of independence and self-reliance, a tradition of activism, and attention to the interconnectedness of race, class, and gender oppression. Yet "womanist eyes" do not only recognize the racial and patriarchal roots of power relations; they also act from a cultural standpoint that has emerged from the downside of those relations. Specifically, Alice Walker (1983) coined the term "womanist," and defined it in this way:

> A black feminist, a feminist of color. From the black folk expression of mothers to female children, "You acting womanish," i.e., like a woman. Usually referring to outrageous, audacious, courageous or willful behavior. Wanting to know more and in greater depth than is considered "good" for one. Interested in grown-up doings. Acting grown up. Being grown up. Interchangeable with another black folk expression: "You trying to be grown." Responsible. In charge. Serious. (p. xi)

The vision Walker calls up is undeniably important to the way Black women have typically had to live their lives. This definition rejects the subservient image that has historically represented White womanhood. Granted, Black women have been physically subdued, yet we have always resisted for the sake of our own lives, cultivating a "grown up" attitude. Both Collins' and Walker's theories are relevant to my interpretations of advocacy education particularly in a multiracial context, and more specifically within the context of the collaborative efforts of Becky, the other group participants, and me. It is important that my use of the expression "womanist eyes" does not lie outside of, or in direct opposition to, the feminist purview. Womanism is in accordance with the primary goal of the feminist movement—"to end sexism, sexist exploitation and oppression" (hooks, 2000). Yet it engages this goal from a collective consciousness that is ontologically and epistemologically distinct from the mainstream White feminist perspective. Womanist eyes cannot but consider how sexism and sexist exploitation are informed by racial ideology. They see the different histories, cultures, and experiences of women of color, and they recognize the nonsynchronous nature of oppression (McCarthy, 1990).

Before I discuss the organization of my response, I want to acknowledge the participation of Luoluo Hong in our project. Luoluo as an Asian American woman was the only other non-African American woman involved in the group. Although I recognize Luoluo as a woman of color and a part of the womanist "vibe" I am constructing, I also want to point out that her experiences as an Asian American woman may at times fall outside of my analysis. Although the Asian female–White female relationship shares similarities with the

Black female–White female relationship, I am sure it has its own historical distinctiveness as well.

Unpacking Assumptions of White Feminist Praxis

Based on my emerging aspirations to participate in advocacy, teaching, and research for and with women of color, I, Becky, reflected on the theoretical bases that I commonly rely on in my living and thinking. The stage for this experience was partially set on the confluence of various theories. I am primarily compelled by approaches that label themselves critical, poststructural, or feminist. To my understanding, critical approaches suggest that power relations are uneven and, in part, based on our identity characteristics (Tierney & Rhoads, 1993). Further, power relations have the potential to be changed at local levels. Poststructural approaches suggest that power is fluid and shifting. Power is not an entity, but rather a strategic position (Foucault, 1978). As educators, we operate as the "throughput of discourses" (Hassard, 1993) and, as such, embody both power and resistance in the discourses in which we operate. Feminist approaches suggest that our identities affect our access to power in our society, and that women of all types are negatively affected, albeit differently, by the patriarchy that exists in Western society (Hurtado, 1989; Lerner, 1986). Feminism generally suggests that disrupting patriarchal institutions has the potential to change those negative relations.

I found that my understandings of these frameworks and their potential uses were shaken by this research. For example, why did many women of color resist the strategies and strengths that I thought feminism (through theory and political action) could offer them? Why did they often focus a skeptical eye on poststructuralism, wondering about its usefulness and the effects of its exclusive language? And why were several hesitant to embrace educators who attempted to act "critically" in teaching and learning environments?

While engaging with a book entitled *Critical Race Feminism* (Wing, 1997b), I began to piece together possible responses to several of my questions. Some of the authors of this collection recalled the failures of feminist and poststructural or postmodern approaches to address their needs. Angela Harris (1997) writes of how White feminist scholars broke their promises to the Black women whom the women's movement was courting when they chose to insult Black women by assuming that the experiences of White women would represent their concerns and identities. History indicates that this is a long-standing tension. For example, early in the twentieth century the White members of the National American Women's Suffrage Association (NAWSA) alienated Black women from their efforts to attain the right to vote (Rosenberg, 1992). Early and recent feminist actions have—either purposely or inadvertently—failed to take into consideration the interests of all women.

Postmodernism poses special challenges to interracial understandings as well. Celina Romany (1997) suggests that although postmodern approaches may decenter the essentialized concept of woman, thereby opening up rooms for difference in all of its forms, "This new entrance leads us into a meeting of discourses rather than to an encounter of those differences at the very concrete level of power differentials and unequal distribution of privileges" (p. 22). In a volume entitled *Learning From Our Lives: Women, Research, and Autobiography in Education,* Gloria Ladson-Billings (1997) contributes that Black feminist perspectives, research, and educational approaches need to be based on concrete experiences to be legitimized in various communities. Those experiences, in conjunction with theories, provide the context for rich and reliable work.

As I moved through my time with this group, I realized that advocacy education involves participants who are creating new theory together while testing, manipulating, and hearing challenges to our own "tried and true" perspectives. I needed to be open to the possibilities of re-creating a localized theory that worked for this specific group of people involved in this specific project. I also believed what we were creating might be useful in future experiences involving advocacy education.

REFLECTIONS

Motivations and Contradictions in Advocacy Education

I consider in this section what I, Becky, have learned about the motivations and contradictions involved in advocacy education, continually thinking about how to be an advocate, teacher, and researcher for and with persons who occupy an identity that is in some ways different from my own. Granted, the contradictions I present are no doubt included in this work because of what I have learned—how I am different from who I was when I started this project. Consequently, what I have chosen to present here—what stood out for me as I moved through this experience—tells as much about me as it does about the complexities within advocacy education. Yet, my identity is not unitary, and although racial dynamics undoubtedly influenced the thoughts I present here and group interactions throughout the semester, I am not sure how my "whiteness" shaped these dynamics. The varying parts of my identity are interwoven. Certainly my feminism, femaleness, northern upbringing, heterosexuality, and age (to name a few) shaped our interactions and my interpretations as well. Still, I offer my thoughts on advocacy education by interrogating the concepts of advocacy and difference, with the hope that they might be useful for others as they rethink the possibilities for advocacy in their own teaching, learning, and research.

Interrogating Advocacy

I believe that advocacy does not need to be limited to others with whom we readily identify based on apparent or assumed identity characteristics. Instead:

> The idea of difference provides an important reminder of the limi-
> tations of emancipatory political theory. Emancipation is not a
> likely prospect unless our political theories and practices stay open to
> other perspectives, take account of the diverse forms oppression can
> take, and remain consciously provisional and revisable. (Sypnowich,
> 1996, p. 288)

Buoyed by the cautious possibilities that Christine Sypnowich offers, one of my primary motivations in fostering this educational experience was to learn how to be an advocate for women of color in collegiate contexts, and then, in some sense, to enact that advocacy. Growing up in a small, White, rural, Midwestern community, my personal experiences with women of color throughout the majority of my life had been minimal. I had read about and engaged in heated dialogues about the importance of examining gendered and racialized relations in educational settings. Still, my knowledge was limited by my infrequent experience with women of color. I wanted to hear about personal experiences that would help me to grapple with and improve my understandings of the educational theory with which I regularly engaged. As Patricia Hill Collins (1991) suggests, "individuals who have lived through the experiences about which they claim to be experts are more believable and credible than those who have merely read or thought about such experiences" (p. 209). Perhaps because I am inclined to agree with Collins' statement, I hesitated to grant myself credibility to engage in this dialogue without first listening to those who were positioned both as subjects and objects therein.

I am well aware of one ironic twist to this belief—in trying to learn how to "do" advocacy, I needed to learn from, even use, members of the group for whom I wanted to serve as an advocate. Although I regularly worked to promote discussions about equity in my family and friend circles prior to this experience, I had consciously done so much less frequently in professional settings. I hoped to use my newly found power as a professor to push the boundaries of my localized experiences, to invoke change that would result in "better" education for, and understandings of, women of color. In moving from theory to practice, I wanted this group to inform my efforts.

As I looked around me in higher education settings, I was reminded of the dearth of women of color in the professorial ranks. Although literature would suggest such absences (Carter, Pearson, & Shavlik, 1996), my experiences at both the University of Wisconsin and Louisiana State University brought the related implications home. At the time, in neither place was there a woman of color at any rank of the professoriate in my department. What was worse was when I realized that it did not feel abnormal for this to be the case. Something was wrong when the absence of a certain identity group was normalized and no longer noticed by others. Seldom did the women in this group see anyone whom they might identify with as a person who shared similar race and gender backgrounds as well as occupational aspirations. The identities of those in various positions of higher education communities demonstrate the valuing of certain persons and the devaluing of others. I hoped the members of our group would learn from and teach each other how to crack the often normalized complacency of racism by preparing themselves for leadership positions in educational institutions or elsewhere.

Within this complicated terrain, I wanted to be an advocate for those who had often told me that their voices were not sought or even heard in most educational environments. Yet, putting myself in the role of advocating for or empowering traditionally marginalized persons was problematic. Empowerment implied that I had a power that I could share with them—something of which I was not yet certain (Ropers-Huilman, 1997; Ropers-Huilman, 1998). Further, it continued to focus the need for change on students, rather than looking to the ways that institutions could change to better accept, accommodate, and use their skills, abilities, and perspectives. As I perceived it, these women seemed quite "empowered"—indeed, they were intelligent and articulate—but they still were not being heard in the ways that they wanted to be within various academic settings. When understood in this context, empowerment again recasts women of color as those who need to change both themselves and the institution. They are the ones who are perceived to be in need of "fixing" and are simultaneously given the assignment to "fix" the institution of which they are a part.

When should we turn attention away from students, and instead focus on the institutional structures that preclude anyone from hearing their empowered speech or responding to their empowered actions? Does empowerment focus on personal agency at the expense of institutional change, and unwittingly perpetuate institutional racism and sexism? What does empowerment mean? Who gets to define it and act on those definitions? While several others and I have discussed some of these complexities elsewhere (Ellsworth, 1992; Lewis, 1993; Orner, 1992; Ropers-Huilman, 1998), the struggles with empowerment relate closely to my understandings about advocacy in teaching and research. Advocacy education must focus on self, students, institutions, and society. If empowerment is to be conceptualized as useful within this framework, it must be reframed to fit these terms. Clearly, though, each engagement demands different strategies to address the unique conditions of each setting.

Interrogating Difference

As another step in learning to advocate, I believed I needed to get to know those persons for whom I wanted to advocate. In my view, the negotiation of group members' wishes and aspirations with my own would eventually set the agenda for my advocacy. As is common with sentiments that seem too tidy and certain, my attempts to learn about difference in this setting were complicated by the realities of our engagements. In this section, I discuss the intersections of advocacy and difference through analysis of the concept of unitary difference, the implications of inclusive and exclusive practices, and the negotiation of voice and speech in advocacy education.

(De)constructing Unitary Difference

In some ways, my curiosity or longing to "know" led me dangerously close to wanting to conceptualize women of color as a unitary group, rather than as a group of individuals who sometimes share common experiences. That sense of "unitary difference" quickly dissipated, though, as our conversations drew out multiple standpoints, beliefs, and experiences. For example, one group member had started college at 15; another had been the only Black student in her school as she was growing up; another had worked as a certified public accountant in the Midwest before returning to do graduate work. Group members' perspectives represented a wide range of views on interracial dating, gender roles, and occupational aspirations. We were certainly a mixed group in many ways.

My understandings of unity were reinforced, though, by what I perceived as a strong feeling of skepticism among the group members for anyone who was not a person of color, and a resulting desire to present what might be called a "facade of unity." As Denise wrote in her reflections, "As a marginalized group of people, we have our own codes for what is to be discussed in public and what is to be kept private. We often feel the pressure to present a united front, despite our disagreements." This façade serves to perpetuate a false unity among certain groups and establish, therefore, that any member of a racial group could be a "representative for the race." In other words, if all members agree, then any member can represent the whole. The rationales for protecting this perceived unity were constructed and deconstructed repeatedly during our group's time together.

In her discussion of black feminist thought, Patricia Hill Collins (1996) establishes that although Black women have certain commonalties, they also are enmeshed in a diversity of experiences and, therefore, in different expressions of their commonalties. Essentialism is especially dangerous for Black women because, "In an essentialist world, black women's experience will always be forcibly fragmented before being subjected to analysis, as those who are 'only interested in race' and those who are 'only interested in gender' take their separate slices of our lives" (Harris, 1997, p. 11). Although perhaps at times useful politically, unity often (dangerously) suggests an essentialism that is potentially harmful to women of color.

So how can we use our own and others' sometimes unitary, sometimes distinct voices to be advocates to change policies, practices, and experiences of and

for those whom we perceive to be marginalized? How can we reclaim the usefulness of our own and others' voices within this quagmire of legitimation, essentialism, and difference? In one sense, group members, as well as scholars such as
Lisa Delpit (1993) and Michelle Foster (1997), insist that people who are seeking to be allies with—or at least understand—others really listen to them. On the
other hand, I have heard group members express their frustration that they are
constantly seen as the source for enlightenment about the experiences of African
American women or other groups with whom they are perceived to be affiliated
(Yamato, 1990). The quandary of trying to learn to be an advocate without assuming unitary difference or, in this case, that group members could be "repre-
sentatives for their race," limited my interactions with group members and
resulted in an ongoing struggle about the processes involved in learning to participate in advocacy education. I struggled with taking up (or wasting?) group
time to ask the question, "How can I frame my participation in this group and in
higher education settings in a way that is useful to women of color?" I wonder,
who should I be listening to if I want to learn to be an advocate? Does advocacy
education truly have to be relearned at an intimately local level each time? If so,
what implications does that have for those who would like to advocate for institutional and educational change at the policy and practice levels?

I learned from these interactions that while tempting to do so, difference is
limiting if it is perceived as all-encompassing, stable or permanent. As several
group members reiterated to me, the way one defines "difference" is (re)con-
structed in relation to others' identities and fluctuating positions, and in constantly changing situations. We pay attention to and emphasize certain aspects
of our identities depending on context. As such:

> Ultimately there are as many differences as selves, and thus our invo-
> cations of difference always risk essentialism, wherein we reify a cer-
> tain identity and proclaim its immutable nature, without attention to
> the differences within the identity itself, or the damage done to the
> new "other" the reclaimed identity leaves in its wake. (Sypnowich,
> 1996, p. 285)

Through the stories I heard from the women in this group, I came to believe that because of their precarious positioning at the intersections of race
and gender, many women of color are constantly renegotiating their identities and figuring out what strategic positions they should choose from among
their various allegiances. As Luoluo Hong, a group member, reminded me in
a personal communication, "Perhaps that is the essence of women of color's
identities in a predominantly White culture. Non-Whites may necessarily do
this negotiation in order to survive, to generate a cohesive self and a connection to community." I wonder about the pain and strength that emerges from
these reconstructed identities, and consider how women of color have so

often embodied the existence of multiple selves to which postmodernism has relatively recently drawn educators' attention.

When we no longer think of identity as stable or unitary, it is more difficult to engage within advocacy education because a fascination of and desire for difference becomes much more complex. Leslie Roman (1993) expressed her concerns about unequal "others" ever being able to know oppressed persons. But, in some sense, as much as this may not be reasonable or realistic, I want to try to know others. From that location, I think that I can be the best possible advocate for and with them. I want to know those I am trying to support and enact advocacy education with. Audre Lorde's (1984) words suggest the necessity of engaging within this dilemma of difference:

> Where the words of women are crying to be heard, we must each of us recognize our responsibility to seek those words out, to read them and share them and examine them in their pertinence to our lives. That we not hide behind the mockeries of separations that have been imposed upon us and which so often we accept as our own. . . . It is not difference which immobilizes us, but silence. (p. 44)

The positioning of scholars in higher education enables them to hear the calls of women of color in their classrooms and on their campuses if they choose to listen. Through conversation and communication, our differences can become sources of strength, rather than only areas of concern.

(De)constructing Inclusion/Exclusion

Throughout the semester, I better understood another motive for my participation. I wanted to be included in the struggle to value women of color in academe. Much of my learning came through Luoluo, an Asian American woman who had requested that we broaden our focus from "Black women in college" to "Women of color in college." In trying to be inclusive, a Black woman in our group said that Luoluo could certainly participate—after all, she was an "honorary sister girl." In other words, she could participate because she was, perhaps, "Black enough" in her actions and attitudes. As Luoluo later pointed out to me, in the South, "women of color" often seems, by default, to mean "Black women." Her identity as an Asian American woman was obscured by this "honorary" membership into a "Black" group. Yet she wanted to assert that as an Asian American woman, she was a woman of color—with or without anyone else's blessing or permission.

When we discussed the problematics involved in this labeling during a subsequent meeting, I wondered how I would have felt had that honorary title been bestowed on me. In some senses, I desired to be an honorary member of a group that my whiteness prohibited me from ever truly entering. In another sense, I shared with Luoluo a concern about the process or practice of honorary inclusion because it seemed like racial gatekeeping to me. I was afraid that I would be left out of related struggles and consequently wondered: How is this gatekeeping related to oppression? Is it a necessary political strategy? Where do those people who are not the "norm" within any group fit in? Must they always (ironically) strive to attain and uphold an honorary status in the struggle against oppression?

Another instance provided me with uncertainties about inclusive and exclusive practices in advocacy education. During a conversation about another Black person who was not part of our group, I was told by a group member that they (group members) generally did not say challenging things about other African American people to others who are not African American. They said I was "different," though, and continued their dialogue. In a later conversation, I was told that group members sometimes felt that they did not need to change their manner of speaking around me as they did around most White people (sometimes referred to as "code switching"). I wondered what types of behavior on my part would allow me to know or hear more than others. Why was I different than other White people? I feared that I might do or say something that would make me "the same" as all other "Whites." An additional undercurrent came to the surface reluctantly in my thinking on this topic. Perhaps I was able to act as an advocate precisely because of the structures that I was trying to deconstruct (those that fostered the development of White and middle-class persons while ignoring others). The irony of this positioning implies both a sharp responsibility and an unnerving feeling of being caught up in wrongful desires. I wanted so much to avoid having my "whiteness"—my "difference"—found out. Why was I at least minimally accepted into this group? And where were the boundaries of my acceptance? How are these boundaries harmful, useful, and malleable, to and by whom?

(De)constructing Speech and Difference

I learned from this experience that what I understood to be "respectful communication" was not uniformly accepted or enacted as such by other group members. Instead, we operated within another system of communication that redefined, for me, understandings of respect. When one member of the group was designated formally or informally as the "speaker" for that part of the session, others rarely interrupted. During discussions, though, several group members often spoke loudly over each other, seemingly to suggest that the volume of their voice would assure them the right and space to speak. I had been taught that respectful speech dictated that I wait until there was a brief pause before I spoke. I had learned that one values others by trying to provide them with the comfort, space, and time to speak. Consequently, during the first several meetings of this group, I did not speak much, even though my presence as a professor lent support for my voice. I learned that communication and, relatedly, conceptualizations of respect for others must be negotiated when attempting to engage in advocacy education. Many times, I was negotiated—by the interactions between and among group participants and myself—right out of verbal participation.

Perhaps my silence is good, I tried to tell myself to smother my discomfort. After all, I was concerned about the establishment of a communication style that privileged my thinking. More specifically, I did not want to impose my version of communication as the norm. As Christine Sleeter (1993) points out, whiteness can often inadvertently be established as the norm, even in multicultural interaction. As the only professor and White person involved in the group, I was quite hesitant to express my views because I was afraid that they would either shut down discussion, be followed with over-attendance to my ideas, or be met with a "how could you possibly understand what we're talking about?" look. While not necessarily more "true" or "valid," the experience of talking about myself is different from the experience of talking or asking about others. I wondered about the boundaries of both my "right" to speak with and about others and the usefulness of such attempts. Even when group members encouraged me to participate more verbally in our group discussion, I hesitated. As I reflect now, I understand that my lack of participation had little to do with the actual discussion. Instead, it portrayed somewhat accurately my own concerns about interrole communication. I found myself circling back to the dilemmas related to difference.

Although my silence greatly shaped my participation, I rationalized these actions in many ways. I wanted to be sensitive to those who have suggested that in others' efforts to empower or advocate for them, they have not been listened to. I knew that I was sorely lacking in my understandings of the lived experiences of women of color in college and wanted to listen to enhance that understanding. I wanted to be sensitive to the question that Leslie Roman (1993) poses when she writes:

> The question for scholars working within [First World European and North American contexts] . . . who now confront the crisis of representation, is *not* whether the subaltern can speak. Instead, it is whether privileged (European and North American) white groups are willing to listen when the subaltern speaks and how whites can know the difference between occasions for responsive listening and listening as an excuse for silent collusion with the status quo of racial and neocolonial inequalities. (p. 79)

Thinking back, I wonder how my silence affected group members and if my lack of verbal participation, lack of exposure of myself, was responsive or merely collusive with the very inequalities I was trying to work against. Had I become the "unknowable other" to them?

In a response to many of the questions I have posed here, I found Adrien Wing's (1997a) assertion that identities are multiplicative, rather than additive, both useful and complicated. For example, she asserts that Black women are assumed to be both "Black" and "woman," although neither of those categories fully includes the unique nature of the interaction between their "blackness" and their "womanness." In her thinking, then, each person is a product, rather than a sum, of the identities that comprise them. As such, our relationships can be both grounded in common factors and shaped by the various elements that our differences infuse into our interactions. Still, how can any of us know the various "multipliers," the identities, at play in the students and teachers we encounter? Without this knowledge, the benefits and detriments of concepts such as "unitary difference," "exclusivity and inclusivity," and "useful speech" quickly become foggy and intertwined. And advocacy education becomes that much more complex.

Splitting the Difference: A Womanist Response

My (Denise's) response to Becky's analysis is a "bottom-up" analysis of our group effort. Essentially, it is my side of the story, which is unavoidably colored by my experiences as an African American female student at LSU between 1994 and 1998. This response is also shaped by my recent experiences as an African American female faculty member who is constantly redefining my own sense of teacher, researcher, and advocate. I have organized my response into three parts. The first deals with the historical legacy that imposes on our group work as well as substantiates the need for it. In the second part, I review inter- and intracultural conflicts that emerge around the notion of "advocacy." And in the third part, I attempt to rethink "advocacy education."

Feminist Disjunctures, Womanist Conjectures

> Black women must have been affected by their experiences during slavery. Some, no doubt, were broken and destroyed, yet the majority survived and, in the process, acquired qualities considered taboo by the nineteenth-century ideology of womanhood. (Davis, 1983, p. 11)

Before I joined the group, I knew there would be tensions, contradictions, and silences. I knew there were many differences in backgrounds, goals, and experiences among other aspects that would set us apart while, at the same time, bringing us—strangely enough—close together. I anticipated the uneasiness that would result, no matter what, from the way raced and gendered legacies would impinge on the present. Yet, I looked forward to breaking through "pc" codes and confronting many things, especially the troubled relationships between White women and women of color. The racial tensions that have shaped even the earliest of feminist movements (Davis, 1983; hooks, 2000) were certainly lurking just below the surface of our initial conversations. Chats that took place on the margins of our collective forays revealed that some of us were indeed suspicious of Becky's relationship to the group. "Suspicious" does not mean we believed that her intentions were unworthy; it does mean, however, that our perceptions were veiled by the remnants of historical circumstance—an age-old distrust of whiteness and authority.

This distrust was not always spoken or explicit or based on personal experience. It was sometimes critically conscious and other times dysconscious; it was sometimes rooted in personal experiences and other times in historical collective experiences. However, whether covert or overt, this distrust was always paradoxical. Our suspicions of Becky had little to do with anything she did or did not do. It was mainly about what she represented historically—a White woman in a position of power, offering her help to us unfortunate women of color. Thus, what was creeping just below the surface of our work was a suspicious air of paternalism.

Historically and in terms of race relations, paternalism has been used to describe the relation between White folk and Black folk as one indicative of a parent–child relationship. In the education of Black people, the notion of paternalism has been significant. Many nineteenth-century advocates of slavery advanced philosophies of paternalism that suggested that slavery was good for Africans because it (slavery by Europeans) taught them how to be "civilized." Also, the missionary efforts of many White organizations in the late nineteenth and early twentieth centuries to educate Black people in the ways of the Bible and other European values, beliefs, and traditions were often rooted in the understanding that Black folk were childlike and needed to be taught the ways of the parent. Paternalism continues to shape the education of Black people in this country. Paternalistic attitudes have supported compensatory programs for, and low expectations of, African American and other children of color. Furthermore, many scholars of color continue to struggle to free themselves from "intellectual paternalism," from the hegemony of Eurocentric paradigms.

It is reasonable, then, to argue that educational advocacy on behalf of African Americans has traditionally been grounded as paternalistic endeavor. Has the White feminist paradigm of advocacy been any different? Although the "parent" now seeks information from the "child," some would argue that paternalism still haunts the mainstream White feminist paradigm. In her essay entitled "Holding My Sister's Hand," bell hooks (1994) attests to how traditional tropes of power manifest in White feminist paradigms:

> [W]ith the increasing institutionalization and problematization of feminist work focused on the construction of feminist theory and the dissemination of feminist knowledge, white women have assumed positions of power that enable them to reproduce the servant–served

paradigm in a radically different context. Now black women are put in the position of serving white female desire to know more about race and racism, to "master" the subject. (p. 103)

In the context of our multiracial and multicultural endeavor, I could not help but wonder what Becky meant by "advocacy." What could she do for us? Some of us gave her the benefit of the historical doubt, yet at least one member of the group remained adamantly suspicious, because she was unnerved by the idea that we were being "used" for the benefit of Becky's research.

Inter- and Intracultural Differences in Advocacy Work

"We are what we know." We are, however, also what we do not know. If what we know about ourselves—our history, our culture, our national identity—is deformed by absences, denials, and incompleteness, then our identity—both as individuals and as Americans—is fragmented. (Pinar, 1993, p. 16)

There is a beautiful irony here. While Becky spent a lot of time reflecting on the challenges she faced in her role as "advocate," I was reflecting on how Becky's style of advocacy was really working for this group of very vibrant, determined, intellectual women of color. Whereas some of Becky's choices contradicted her initial understandings of "advocacy," they were decisions that allowed this diverse group of women to name themselves for themselves. This is an absolutely critical idea, because it displaces anachronistic meanings of advocacy education that have tended to fit nicely into what Freire (1970) has called "banking education." Traditionally, the advocate "helps" her subjects by showing them how to, what to, or when to. Advocacy, in this sense, reinforces hierarchy, domination, and objectification.

Is this kind of advocacy even possible when the advocate is a White feminist trying to "help" a group of women of color who have a historical legacy of self-reliance, independence, and activism on behalf of themselves and others? Whether we were sitting around Becky's kitchen table, a seminar table in Peabody Hall, a folding table in the African American Cultural Center, or the coffee table in Stefanie's apartment, our multiracial and multicultural interactions refused the order of traditional advocacy. As we discussed interracial relationships, racist and sexist professors, relationships with men of color, code switching, and the salience of race and/or gender, we were also problematizing and redefining advocacy.

While Becky worked on debunking the assumption of unitary difference, I was enthralled by the way we managed to hold onto a collective sense of Black womanhood while at the same time being very different from one another. At times we disagreed adamantly with one another. For instance, when we discussed interracial relationships, at least one of us had dated a White man before and did not see much wrong with it. Others (including myself) simply said, "I have nothing against it, but I have never done it." Someone else tied it back to White slave masters' rape of enslaved Black women. And Becky wondered why it would be racist of her to say she would not date Black men, but not racist of us to say we would not date White men. In this conversation as in many others, none of us seemed to change our positions; nevertheless we did have the opportunity to better understand the reasoning behind other folks' choices. In other instances, we agreed more with one another, taking supportive stances and tones. In this sense, advocacy in action suggests that there is no one advocate who can fully understand the group for whom she advocates. We were all advocates. As Becky was learning to advocate for us, we were, indeed, learning to advocate for Becky as well as for each other and for ourselves.

Another implicit assumption of traditional advocacy work is that there is a "right" way for it to unfold. Although Becky admits that she did not have a certain expectation when we began the project, she, as well as we all, had some vision of what this project might look like. For instance, as Becky has already mentioned, her vision of what our talks would be like was quite different, most of the time, from what actually transpired. We were often "womanish" as we sometimes talked loud, strayed from the topic, and interrupted one another. Although Becky notes her reservations about her silence, it was often appropriate. Does it make sense to bring together a group for the purpose of "getting to know" us or advocating with us and insist or expect that we communicate in a style that is not culturally our own and that can be identified with the very structure that defines our oppression? From a cultural standpoint, because of the ways in which we have been denied, we have had to be audacious to even be heard. Essentially, advocacy education in a multiracial or multicultural context that is "liberatory" must be open to difference and differences that will, at times, bring about contradiction, contestation, and conflict within individual selves as well as between selves. Our group dynamics were unfolding because of, and in spite of, raced and gendered selves.

Another underlying assumption driving Becky's vision was that she could "get to know us." However, Becky's attempt to advocate for us depended far less on her getting to know us than it did on her getting to know herself in relationship to us. Although who we were not was challenging for Becky, I found that Becky's efforts to come to terms with who she was encouraged a trust and an openness among the other women. At one night session, we were grappling with the race–gender issue as Erikah Badu sang, "Who gave you permission to rearrange me?" in the background. At an intense moment, Becky asked a question that, for me, became the most significant question of our project: Who am I to question the salience of race to you as women of color without questioning the salience of gender to me as a White woman? It marked the moment when Becky publicly acknowledged what many White feminists resist. Recognizing the salience of race in the lives of women of color is no substitute for interrogating the way it structures White feminist thinking and discourse. As hooks (1994) goes on to point out, White feminist epistemologies often leave whiteness unproblematized:

> Curiously, most white women writing feminist theory that looks at "difference" and "diversity" do not make white women's lives, works, and experiences the subject of their analysis of "race," but rather focus on black women or women of color. (pp. 103–104)

hooks' point here is imperative because it foreshadows the impossibility of White women advocating, in a traditional sense, for women of color. In a society in which whiteness represents a set of "unmarked and unnamed" cultural practices that often deny difference, race and racism mark off that which is not White as untouchable, sinfully desirable, and/or in need of help (Frankenburg, 1993). As Ruth Frankenburg notes, when race and racism are seen as the "other's" problems, it profoundly affects the possibility of who can help whom. She writes:

> For when white people . . . look at racism, we tend to view it as an issue that people of color face and have to struggle with, but not as an issue that generally involves or implicates us. Viewing racism in this way has serious consequences for how white women look at racism and for how anti-racist work might be framed. With this view, white women can see anti-racist work as an act of compassion for an "other," an optional, extra project, but not one intimately, and organically linked to our own lives. (p. 7)

By posing such a self-reflective inquiry, Becky reconstructed her efforts at advocacy. Advocacy no longer meant her "getting to know us" as raced women, but her getting to know herself as a raced woman in ways that subsequently became mutually beneficial, to her and to us.

Becky's willingness to openly think about the significance of her whiteness opened avenues for us to openly discuss the significance of our femaleness. I emphasize "openly" because I believe that, because we are raced and gendered, we always engage the realities of both, even if we do so dysconsciously (King, 1991).

Advocacy in between Feminist Disjunctures and Womanist Conjectures

> As a [classroom] community, our capacity to generate excitement is deeply affected by our interest in one another, in hearing one another's voices, in recognizing one another's presence. (hooks, 1994, p. 8)

As a Black woman I know that the Black women who have loved and taught me both literally and metaphorically what it means, in some sense, to be Black and a woman, have often warned me not to "talk" too much to those White women: "You can't trust 'em. They think they know it all." So I learned to be nice, but not to say too much. What I have come to realize is that folks talk more when they believe they are being listened to. And folks who are good listeners are folks who realize that they do not know everything, no matter who they are or are not. Thus, listening in dynamic ways is vital.

This idea was reinforced for me as I worked with Becky and the other women in the group. It allowed me to clarify my understanding of how we as advocates and teachers let our co-subjects know that we hear them. Today as an African American woman committed to teaching for social justice, I am inevitably always advocating, teaching, and researching with my students. As I reflect on the time I spent with Becky and the other group members, I keep in mind the tensions, the ongoing struggles, and the successful moments, taking away important lessons. First, it has recently occurred to me that our group project was not simply about advocacy education but also about advocacy through education. Although Becky was clearly working through some notion of how to advocate within a multiracial and multicultural group of women, other group members were not thinking about advocacy at all. We were simply doing it by educating ourselves and each other, by engaging in consciousness raising. Second, advocacy education and advocacy through education that happens across racial–cultural lines cannot successfully function absolutely within an assimilationist paradigm. If it is to be multiracial and multicultural, then it must engage and respect the differences that will unavoidably exist, whether they are different communication styles or different values. Third, advocacy education and advocacy through education in a multiracial and multicultural context requires self-reflection by each and every participant. All must be willing to challenge and be challenged by the differences. Fourth, advocacy education and advocacy through education does not "solve" problems; it helps us work through them as we grapple with truly unanswerable questions. The success of our project is difficult to measure because it lingers in the space in between where definite answers were not and are not possible. Our work together was, nevertheless, valuable not because, at last, we defined what race means to gender or vice versa, not because it testifies to the "real" experiences of women of color or a white feminist ally, and not because it makes any more relevant claims about what it means to be a woman. Rather, our work was and is valuable because it is a demonstration of working through difficulties within and between ourselves, without any absolute claims to having worked them out. In this sense, Becky's most important act of advocacy was simply bringing the group together and allowing it to emerge and to evolve on its own terms.

Ultimately, understanding advocacy education and advocacy through education and its benefits arise out of what Sandra Hollingsworth (1994) calls "relational knowing":

The concept of knowing through relationship, or relational knowing, involves both the recall of prior knowledge and the reflection on what knowledge is perceived or present in social and political settings . . . we find that relational knowing does not rest in contemplation but becomes clarified in action. (p. 77–78)

It is in this indefinite space in between differences that learning in multicultural and multiracial contexts has its greatest potential.

FINAL THOUGHTS ON ADVOCACY EDUCATION IN HIGHER EDUCATION

Higher education remains resistant to change, even though there is insurmountable evidence that something is wrong and continues to be wrong despite present efforts to make things right. Glimmers of hope appear, but thus far academia has failed to reach to the heart of the problem. (Turner, Myers, & Creswell, 1997, p. 49)

At least superficially, most higher education institutions today have committed to supporting many forms of diversity. Yet, those who occupy positions that have traditionally been excluded from higher education discourse are still asserting that their voices are not heard, that they are not well represented in leadership positions, and that their working environments are often hostile and unwelcoming (Clark, Garner, Higonnet, & Katrak, 1996; de Castell & Bryson, 1997; Neumann & Peterson, 1997; Tierney & Bensimon, 1996). These testimonies suggest that the "inclusive university" that Turner, Myers, and Creswell (1997) describe as "hospitable, engaging, and supportive providing opportunities for all historically disadvantaged groups" (p. 45) is not yet a reality. We operate in both gendered and raced space that shapes the participation of current and potential participants. It is in everyone's best interests to foster dialogic communities in which we can see, hear, and feel (at least partially) the material effects of each other's life experiences. In this historical moment, higher education needs teachers, researchers, and advocates if we are truly to understand and benefit from the diverse participants and paradigms of which we are a part.

NOTE

1. According to the Coordinator of Minority Student Services, African American students voted to impose a fee upon themselves for the building and maintenance of the Center. This fee was supported after other attempts to generate support for the funding had failed. It is no longer in place.

REFERENCES

Carter, D., Pearson C., & Shavlik, D. (1996). Double jeopardy: Women of color in higher education. In C. Turner, M. Garcia, A. Nora, & L. I. Rendon (Eds.) *Racial and ethnic diversity in higher education* (pp. 460–464). Needham Heights, MA: Simon & Schuster. Originally published in 1987.

Chang, M. (2002). Preservation or transformation: Where's the real educational discourse on diversity? *Review of Higher Education, 25*(2), 125–140.

Clark, V. A., Garner, S. N., Higonnet, M. R. Katrak, K. (1996). *Antifeminism in the academy.* New York: Routledge.

Collins, P. H. (1990). Defining black feminist thought. In S. Madison (Ed.) *The woman that I am* (pp. 578–600). New York: St. Martin's Griffin.

Collins, P. H. (1991). *Black feminist thought: Knowledge, consciousness, and the politics of empowerment.* New York: Routledge.

Collins, P. H. (1996). The social construction of Black feminist thought. In C. Turner, M. Garcia, A. Nora, & L. I. Rendon (Eds.) *Racial and ethnic diversity in higher education* (pp. 115–133). Needham Heights, MA: Simon & Schuster.

Davis, A. (1983). *Women, race, and class.* New York: Vintage Books.

De Castell, S., & Bryson, M. (1997). *Radical in(ter)ventions: Identity, politics, and difference/s in educational praxis.* Albany: State Univeresity of New York.

De La Luz Reyes, M., & Hamlcon, J. J. (1998). Racism in academia: The old wolf revisited. *Harvard Educational Review, 58*(3), 299–314.

Delpit, L. (1993). The silenced dialogue: Power and pedagogy in educating other people's children. In L. Weis & M. Fine (Eds.) *Beyond silenced voices: Class, race, and gender in United States schools* (pp. 119–139). Albany: State University of New York.

Ellsworth, E. (1992). Why doesn't this feel empowering? Working through the repressive myths of critical pedagogy. In C. Luke & J. Gore (Eds.) *Feminism and critical pedagogy* (pp. 90–119). New York: Routledge.

Fine, M. (1994). Dis-stance and other stances: Negotiations of power inside feminist research. In A. Gitlin (Ed.) *Power and method: Political activism and educational research* (pp. 13–35). New York: Routledge.

Foster, M. (1997, June). *Insider research: What counts as critical.* Keynote address at the Reclaiming voice: Ethnographic Inquiry and Qualitative Research in a Postmodern Age conference, Los Angeles, CA.

Foucault, M. (1978). *The history of sexuality: An introduction.* (Vol. 1). New York: Random House.

Frankenberg, R. (1993). *White women, race matters: The social construction of whiteness.* Minneapolis: University of Minnesota Press.

Freire, P. (1970). *Pedagogy of the oppressed.* New York: Continuum.

Greene, M. (1995). *Releasing the imagination: Essays on education, the arts, and social change.* San Francisco: Jossey-Bass.

Gumport, P. J., & Snydman, S. K. (2002). The formal organization of knowledge: An analysis of academic structure. *Journal of Higher Education, 73*(3), 375–408.

Harris, A. P. (1997). Race and essentialism in feminist legal theory. In A. K. Wing (Ed.) *Critical race feminism: A reader* (pp. 11–18). New York: New York University.

Hassard, J. (1993). Postmodernism and organizational analysis: An overview. In J. Hassard & M. Parker (Eds.) *Postmodernism and organizations* (pp. 1–24). Newbury Park, CA: Sage.

Hollingsworth, S. (1994). *Teacher research and urban literacy education.* New York: Teachers College Press.

hooks, b. (1994). *Teaching to transgress: Education as the practice of freedom.* New York: Routledge.

hooks, b. (2000). *Feminism is for everybody.* Cambridge, MA: South End Press.

Hurtado, A. (1989). Relating to privilege: Seduction and rejection in the subordination of white women and women of color. *Signs, 14*(4), 833–855.

Hurtado, S., Milem, J., Clayton-Pederson, A., & Allen, W. (1998). Enhancing campus climates for racial/ethnic diversity: Educational policy and practice. *Review of Higher Education, 21*(3), 279–302.

Kezar, A., & Eckel, P. (2002). The effect of institutional culture on change strategies in higher education: University principles or culturally responsive concepts? *Journal of Higher Education, 73*(4), 435–460.

King, J. (1991). Dysconscious racism, ideology, identity and the miseducation of teachers. *Journal of Negro Education, 60,* 135–145.

Kolodny, A. (1996). Paying the price of antifeminist intellectual harassment. In V. Clark, S. N. Garner, M. Higonnet, & K. H. Katrak (Eds.) *Antifeminism in the academy* (pp. 3–33). New York: Routledge.

Kraemer, B. A. (1997). The academic and social integration of Hispanic students into college. *Review of Higher Education, 20*(2), 163–180.

Ladson-Billings, G. (1997). For colored girls who have considered suicide when the academy's not enough: Reflections of an African American woman scholar. In A. Neumann & P. Peterson (Eds.) *Learning from our lives: Women, research, and autobiography in education* (pp. 52–70). New York: Teachers College.

Lather, P. (1986). Issues of validity in openly ideological research: Between a rock and a soft place. *Interchange, 17*(4), 63–84.

Lather, P. (1991). *Getting smart: Feminist research and pedagogy with/in the postmodern.* New York: Routledge.

Lather, P. (1994). Fertile obsession: Validity after poststructuralism. In A. Gitlin (Ed.) *Power and method: Political activism and educational research* (pp. 36–60). New York: Routledge.

Lerner, G. (1986). *The creation of patriarchy.* New York: Oxford University Press.

Lewis, M. G. (1993). *Without a word: Teaching beyond women's silence.* New York: Routledge.

Linstead, S. (1993). Deconstruction in the study of organizations. In J. Hassard & M. Parker (Eds.) *Postmodernism and organizations* (pp. 49–70). Newbury Park, CA: Sage.

Lorde, A. (1984). *Sister outsider: Essays and speeches.* Trumansburg, NY: Crossing.

Markie, P. J. (1994). *Professor's duties: Ethical issues in college teaching.* Lanham, MD: Rowman & Littlefield.

McCarthy, C. (1990). *Race and curriculum.* New York: Falmer Press.

Minnich, E., Rosenfeld, R. A., & O'Barr, J. F. (1988). *Reconstructing the academy: Women's education and women's studies.* Chicago: University of Chicago.

Neumann, A., & Peterson, P. (1997). *Learning from our lives: Women, research, and autobiography in education.* New York: Teachers College.

Orner, M. (1992). Interrupting the calls for student voice in "liberatory" education: A feminist poststructuralist perspective. In C. Luke & J. Gore (Eds.) *Feminism and critical pedagogy* (pp. 74–89). New York: Routledge.

Pagano, J. (1991). Moral fictions: The dilemma of theory and practice. In C. Witherell & N. Noddings (Eds.) *Stories lives tell: Narrative and dialogue in education* (pp. 193–206). New York: Teachers College.

Pinar, W. F. (1993). Notes on understanding curriculum as a racial text. In C. McCarthy & W. Crichlow (Eds.) *Race, identity, and representation in education* (pp. 60–70). New York: Routledge.

Reinharz, S. (1992). *Feminist methods in social research.* New York: Oxford University.

Roman, L. (1993). White is a color! White defensiveness, postmodernism, and antiracist pedagogy. In C. McCarthy & W. Crichlow (Eds.) *Race, identity, and representation in education* (pp. 71–88). New York: Routledge.

Romany, C. (1997). Ain't I a feminist? In A. K. Wing (Ed.) *Critical race feminism: A reader* (pp. 19–26). New York: New York University.

Ropers-Huilman, B. (1997). Constructing feminist teachers: Complexities of identity. *Gender and Education, 9*(3), 327–343.

Ropers-Huilman, B. (1998). *Feminist teaching in theory and practice: Situating power and knowledge in poststructural classrooms.* New York: Teachers College.

Rosenberg, R. (1992). *Divided lives: American women in the twentieth century.* New York: Hill & Wang.

Sleeter, C. (1993). How white teachers construct race. In C. McCarthy & W. Crichlow (Eds.) *Race, identity, and representation in education* (pp. 157–171). New York: Routledge.

Stanton, D. C., & Stewart, A. J. (1995). *Feminisms in the academy.* Ann Arbor: University of Michigan.

Sypnowich, C. (1996). Some disquiet about "difference." In M. F. Rogers (Ed.) *Multicultural experiences, multicultural theories* (pp. 278–291). New York: McGraw-Hill.

Tierney, W. G. (1994). On method and hope. In A. Gitlin (Ed.) *Power and method: Political activism and educational research* (pp. 97–115). New York: Routledge.

Tierney, W. G., & Bensimon, E. M. (1996). *Promotion and tenure: Community and socialization in academe.* Albany: State University of New York.

Tierney, W. G., & Rhoads, R. A. (1993). Postmodernism and critical theory in higher education: Implications for research and practice. In J. C. Smart (Ed.) *Higher education: Handbook of theory and research* (pp. 308–343). New York: Agathon.

Turner, C. S. V., Myers, S. L., & Creswell, J. W. (1997). Bittersweet success: Faculty of color in academe. Paper presented at the Annual Meeting of the Association for the Study of Higher Education, Albuquerque, NM.

Walker, A. (1983). *In search of our mothers' gardens: Womanist prose.* San Diego: Harcourt Brace Jovanovich.

Wing, A. K. (1997a). Brief reflections toward a multiplicative theory and practice of being. In A. K. Wing (Ed.) *Critical race feminism: A reader* (pp. 27–34). New York: New York University.

Wing, A. K. (1997b). *Critical race feminism: A reader.* New York: New York University.

Wolf, M. (1992). *A thrice told tale: Feminism, postmodernism and ethnographic responsibility.* Stanford, CA: Stanford University.

Yamato, G. (1990). Something about the subject makes it hard to name. In G. Anzaldua (Ed.) *Making face, making soul: Haciendo caras: Creative and critical perspectives by feminists of color* (pp. 20–24). San Francisco: Aunt Lute.

Gender, Race, and Millennial Curiosity

Ana M. Martínez Alemán

In this chapter, the significance and importance of a raced deliberation of gender in higher education scholarship is considered. The failure of higher education research and scholarship to explore the many ways gender and race are interdependent and dynamic elements of identity and thus significant for the development of consciousness and conduct are examined. Given the continued and growing participation of all women in post-secondary education, continuing to disregard gender's racial details and distinctions in higher education research and scholarship is a dangerous trend for this new millennium.

When asked to contemplate for the pages of the *New York Times Magazine* the prospects for the twenty-first century, noted author Stanley Crouch surmised that "race, as we currently obsess over it, will cease to mean as much 100 years from today" (Crouch, 1996, p. 271). Crouch speculated that the "international flow of images and information" would change the realities of lives on the planet, realities that will reflect a material reshaping and ideological reconstruction of race. Crouch rightly predicts (given the demographics of immigration, migration, diaspora, exile, interracial births, and the real and virtual collapse of cultural and national borders) that how Americans have come to know and understand race, how our behaviors have been shaped by this consciousness, will be a historic curiosity.

What is absent from and implied by Crouch's prognostication is itself a "curiosity" of gendered significance. Crouch's view of "race," not unlike those of other writers and scholars of this century, is an experiential schema free of the complications presented by gender. He submits us to an account of "race," meaningfully constructed within present and future politics, that is apparently free of experiential interruptions and that is somehow independent of the effects of gender and gender relations. The realities that will be recast by Crouch's ideological shift in the twenty-first century appear to have no sexual or gender differences, no positions within consciousness other than the specter of "race." Implicit in this view, then, is the supposition that "race" is and will be similarly experienced by all, that such an experience is and will continue to be normative, and that experiencing "race" can be independent of all the ways our bodies are conferred, including appropriate gendered meaning. Based on an explanation of "race" that obscures or ignores other markers of identity, it is a grossly simple and highly suspect prediction. "Race" consciousness without a consideration of such behavioral and experiential realities like gender is misrepresentative and illusory.[1]

Such deception, problematic in any examination of our varied associations, warrants careful scrutiny if post-secondary scholars are to honestly examine how race, or in Crouch's words, "race consciousness," will shape the future of higher education. I am confident that the material and ideological realities that Crouch correctly identifies will alter the place and position of race in the college and university of America's twenty-first century. But as women of color[2] outnumber men of color on college campuses, and as the enrollment of all women in higher education continues to exceed that of men (National Center for Educational Statistics, 1996), can we in American higher education validly speculate the future of "race consciousness" in higher education without accounting for gender? If women of color now account for a quarter of all professional degrees (Babco, 1997), can we accept a configuring of race on campus that does not weigh the significance of gender?

But the growing number of women of color on college and university campuses should not be the sole reason for a deliberate inquiry into the intersection of race and gender. As systemic arrangements for relations between individuals and between individuals and institutions, race and gender can provide higher education scholars with an example of the varied and complex ways campus life is experienced. How, for instance, as challenges to affirmative action marked the end of the twentieth century, is African-American women's access to higher education differently impacted from that of European-American women? If such antiaffirmative measures as California's Proposition 209 are deemed attempts to decrease minority enrollments at selective colleges and universities (Bowen & Bok, 1998, p. 32; Burdman, 1997, p. 32), are Black women applicants subject to further discrimination because they are also women? Are such antiaffirmative action policies also inherently sexist? Are women of color "under the double jeopardy of gender and race discrimination" (Busenberg & Smith, 1997, p. 150)?

Examining the links between gender and race in higher education also enables us to reveal discriminatory practices that would otherwise go undetected. For example, Patricia Hill Collins (1991) notes that within the academy many Black women scholars find their work deemed invalid because their claims challenge both masculinist and racist views. Because this scholarship demands a view of the nexus of race and gender in a way that neither obscures nor assumes a static relationship between these two markers of identity, it is often unsupported in academic settings. Scholarship that posits the kinds of questions and explanations that dispute accepted knowledge of Black women's realities is often rejected within the academy. In a profession in which professional opportunities and reputations are anchored to the credibility of one's research, the Black woman academic is oftentimes dismissed as an inadequate or irrelevant contributor. Thus, if we as higher education researchers and scholars were to examine a Black academic woman's presence across faculty ranks, we would necessarily have to ask ourselves how her peculiar position as both raced and gendered researcher impacts her participation.

How have we in higher educational research and practice come to understand race? Do we assume it to be a universal and essential marker of identity? Has post-secondary scholarship come to accept a view of race free of the effects of gender and gender relations?

RACE AS "HISTORIC CURIOSITY" IN HIGHER EDUCATION

In the twentieth century, the view of race in America as universal enabled higher education scholars to think about race as gender-free. As higher education scholars, we typically regard "race" as a genderless experience always in binary opposition to whiteness. In other words, when we invoke "race" in our scholarship or research, we do not ordinarily mean whiteness, and we presume no apparent effects from gender. The presumption of a genderless race, however, is inaccurate despite the attempts to universalize its claims. As noted anthropologist Franz Fanon dictates in "The Fact of Blackness" (1998), "For not only must the black man be black; he must be black in relation to the white man" (p. 62). "Race" here is gendered but presumes (by implication) no significant effect from its gendered status. The "black man" here implies several things. First is that by using the term "man" to include both men and women, Fanon does not believe that gender difference matters when considering race. Fanon's "race" seems an overarching cultural construct in opposition to whiteness and independent of all else. But let us recall that Fanon's view of race is that of "the black *man*" in opposition to the "white *man*" (emphasis mine). So is a fact of "race" gender after all?

It appears that in Fanon's definition of blackness is a common ontological error regarding gender. Gender difference in a view of race like Fanon's is impossible because gender difference is rendered irrelevant by either patriarchal or racist predilections, or both. To have "race" is to be not-White and not-female. Fanon's "black man" is a reflection of societal disregard and discounting of women, a linguistic convention that acts as a social mirror, "reflecting the organization and dynamics of the society of which it is a part" (Adams & Ware, 1989, p. 470). Situating women's experiences obscurely within men's experiences constructs women as men's derivative, consequently composing women's lives "in essentially male terms, from a male point of view, or with male interests in mind" (p. 472). Such a generic view of our realities resonates with many cultures' conceptual views of women, often suggesting an accepted view that it is natural or inevitable. Thus, Fanon's "black man," generic and inclusive of Black women, sounds reasonable within patriarchal societies. And within these same societies there will be an understanding and acceptance of "race" as a genderless category.

A similar ontology can be observed in poet Nikki Giovanni's (1993) "Black is the Noun." In response to threats of assimilation she writes that "[t]he noun is "black"; American is the adjective" (p. 122). In saying that "Black is the noun" and that all other objects of its hyphenation are simply its dependent modifiers, Giovanni demands an understanding of race in America that is elemental, binary and gender-free. Such an understanding of race epitomizes what Darlene Clark Hine (1993) argues is the problematic nature of race consciousness in America. Clark Hine asserts that Black identity has been understood in this country as a phenomenon in which "Blackness"(or the racial difference from Whites) is its subjectivity, leaving no room for such constructs as gender or socioeconomic class (p. 351). A consequence of the impact of W. E. B. Du Bois' 1903 landmark treatise on race in America, *The Soul of Black Folk*, to be "Black" is to be understood as universal. Du Bois, asserts Clark Hine, "gave the term "Negro" a generic meaning" (p. 338) and in doing so, firmly rooted race consciousness (minimally) as genderless and classless. The meanings given to being "Black" in America, by virtue of this universal and nonspecific construction of race, have helped to conceal the effects of gender. Du Bois' "Negro," according to Clark Hine, allows for the omission of the impact of gender because it reinforces a uniform construction of race not subject to the sociopolitical forces of sexism, homophobia, and so on. "Black" becomes a noun needing modification, a pure and universal position premised on patriarchal norms. "Black" comes to be understood as inclusive of both men and women, particular to neither but reflecting solely the view of the former. The fact that Black women's experiences may differ from those of Black men is unaccounted for here and, consequently, leaves the discourse of race free of the contamination of gender. As African-American feminist Kristal Brent Zook (1995) notes:

> Many in my generation intuitively understand that black women don't always think or feel or even look black in the "authentic," stereotypical sense of the word. We don't always think or feel or look like "women." But we are black. We are women. (p. 89)

Thus, "race" is considered and investigated in our institutions and social arrangements as a unitary entity, a sterile representation of reality that is false, or at best, partial. Simple and absolute, our consciousness about "race" confines us to facile and inaccurate accounts of existence.

These same concerns arise in the writings of Latinas,[3] Native Indian, and Asian American women. Tracy Lai writes of the specifically gendered realities of Asian American women. Lai (1991) reminds us that all of the forces that shape the experiences of Asians in the United States exact a gendered effect. For example, although Asian men have historically been used as a means of cheap labor, Asian women were not as desirable because "women would bear children who could legally claim citizenship rights in the United States" (p. 127). This dubious and racist double standard in labor practice prevented many Asian women from immigrating to, and making economic claims on, America, yet these same views enabled Asian women to immigrate as mail-order brides (p. 129). Sold to U. S. men as docile and subservient, many Asian women found themselves in the crosshairs of misogyny and racism, having to endure degradation and sexual humiliation. Simultaneously experiencing their own cultural estimations of the secondary status of their sex and the exoti-cization of their race by American White men, these Asian women struggled under the accepted cultural renderings of race and gender. Recent Asian refugee women endure a similar reality. Treated as property in their native countries, they may not consider domestic violence as an intolerable offense, and may not report the abuse to authorities for fear of racist and anti-immi-grant prejudices (Dubois, 1991, p. 357). Thus, handcuffed by gender and race, these women live at the intersection of sexism and racism.

Indian women in the United States, finding themselves at a peculiar in-tersection of gender, race, and colonization, enact performances accordingly. In 1981 Indian and other women gathered in Tahlequah, Oklahoma to ad-dress the educational opportunities of Indian girls and women. In these re-search sessions and invited talks, scholars and activists argued for recognizing and addressing Indian girls' and women's distinctive race and gender positions. In a discussion of Indian women's omission from educational textbooks, Rayna Green (1981), a Cherokee woman, reminds the audience that Whites perpetuate a gendered view of Indians that, when coupled with their view of Indians as racial other, can be psychically dangerous for Indian women. Green rightly understands that the dominant image of Indian women found in text-books is that of gendered race traitor. Much like the Aztec princess Mali-nitzin, whose historical image is that of a woman who "sells out" her race to the invading Hernán Cortés, Indian women like Sacajawea and Pocahontas (the only Indian women typically found in schoolbooks) are valued for their contributions to Whites or, better put, for aiding the enemy. Whites construct these images of Indian women that suggest to her that her only worth is her ability to serve them, a demoralizing prospect for her self-worth. Such a con-ceptualization can leave Indian girls confused about their worth as Indian women, as tribal women. Her Indianness, coexisting with and inextricably bound to her gender, acquires a contestable quality rendering her gender equally suspect. In this conception, her most salient attributes—her gendered race—(she is only a gender and a race; she is not a personality) acquire perni-cious relevance.

As Green (1981), Lai (1991) and other women of color attest, understanding their lives requires acknowledging the ways their identities are multiple, fluid, and dynamic. Employing a "plural consciousness" (Mohanty, 1991, p. 36), these women remind us that their lives require a negotiation of multiple oppressions and relations of power in daily life. Positioned as historical identities and thus subject to the meanings assigned to their bodies and behaviors, these women speak of lives in which no one facet of their identities can adequately explain them. Further, each makes it clear that to understand her as a "raced" individual is to locate her within one particular condition in association with and against other conditions, and not as a generic existence. Even when she can annul racial difference by passing as White, she is still a gendered body that "could be beaten on the street for being a dyke" (Moraga, 1983, p. 29). In other words, these women of color are not just nouns, "Asian" or "Black," not just race.

It is evident, then, that these are not lives in which facets of identity are ranked, held in isolation, or considered additive. Race, gender, sexuality, class, and so on, function as concomitant and coexisting attributes that invariably have bearing on identity. Properties of culture implicitly historical, these markers of identity are always relevant and their stratification falsely assumed. Moraga is not ethnicity first, sexuality second. Green is not first a woman and then Indian. Each condition of her identity is never really taken to be independent of any other, despite transitory importance given solely to one. African-American legal scholar Patricia J. Williams (1991) may subscribe to an Afrocentric critique of legal education in the United States, but the reproach is also gendered:

> My abiding recollection of being a student at Harvard Law School is the sense of being invisible. I spent three years wandering in the murk of unreality. I observed large, mostly male bodies assert themselves against one another like football players caught in the gauzy mist of intellectual slow motion. (p. 55)

Williams, a Black woman, finds herself in a man's game (played by both Black and White men), its rules, strategies, and comportment all bearing an alien gender temper.

Julia Alvarez's exiled Dominican protagonist, Yolanda García in *How The García Girls Lost Their Accents* (1992) and its sequel, ¡*Yo!* (1997), crafts an identity within and against a confusing state of simultaneous gender and ethnic determinations. Resisting and negotiating the gender and ethnic expectations put on her by two contrasting cultures, Yolanda García must be *Dominicana*, woman and Dominican; and *americanizada*, Americanized Latina. Yolanda employs a self-decided and mediated life of gendered expectations and ethnic performances. Never can she exist without the pluralities of ethnicity and gender, never can she be "Yo" in cultural or gendered stasis and never can she be just one thing or just the other.[4] Yolanda, like Moraga (1983) and Williams (1991) know their lives to be about the junctures of imposed and consequential meanings, positions they attend to selectively as well as collectively. Listening to her aunts' directives that Yo must adhere to the gendered rules governing the behavior of upper-class Dominican young ladies, Yolanda García, now Americanized and critical of these gendered restrictions, ponders her moment of ethnic acquiescence:

> She sat back quietly, hoping she has learned, at last, to let the mighty wave of tradition roll on through her life and break on some other female shore. She plans to bob up again after the many *dont's* to do what she wants. (Alvarez, 1992, p. 9)

Feminist philosopher Elizabeth Spelman (1998) argues that any analysis of race or gender requires not an additive analysis, nor one in which markers of identity are treated in isolation. Rather, writes Spelman (1998), the lives of women must be understood as embodiments of an extensive network of concrete experiences. These experiences, historical and cultural, determine identity not by their very existence but by the significance attached to them (p. 30). The significance given to her gender, or her sexuality, or her race is not ordered or tiered to suggest primacy or preference. To engage in such an establishment of hierarchical identities, asserts Spelman (1998), is to believe that "one form of oppression is merely piled up upon another" (p. 27), thus concealing and de-emphasizing the effects that race and gender have on one another (p. 23). For example, Black women, according to Spelman (1998), experience racism not in the same way as Black men experience it and they do not experience sexism in the same way that White women do (p. 27). She writes:

> How one form of oppression is experienced is influenced by and influences how another form is experienced. An additive analysis treats the oppression of a Black woman in a society that is racist as well as sexist as if it were a further burden when, in fact, it is a *different* burden. (p. 27) (emphasis mine)

According to Spelman (1998), it is this difference in her "burden"[5] that is the critical issue in theorizing and researching the experiences of women of color, and thus "the crucial question is how the links between them are conceived" (p. 23). The intersections of race and gender for women on our campuses must also bring about differences in accountability, differences in development, differences in comportment. But do higher education scholars and researchers attend to the confluence of race and gender and its significance? Do those of us who study and theorize higher education policies and practices engage in appraisals of the concomitant identifications of race and gender in such a way as to understand the significance of their coexistence? As researchers and scholars, do we miss the significance attached to their intersection and, in doing so, overlook and disregard the difference in this "burden"?

GENDER AND RACE IN HIGHER EDUCATION RESEARCH AND SCHOLARSHIP

Since the 1960s, scholars for whom higher education in the United States has been an object of study have investigated race and gender, albeit in problematic ways. The vast majority of literature on higher education in the last 40 years has not attempted to understand how race and gender are linked and consequential for the educational lives of women. Rather, the last four decades of scholarly work in the twentieth century have resulted in empirical projects that typically have not been mindful of the importance and consequence of this shifting and vacillating positionality. The mutual dependence of race and gender and their confluence has often been ignored in these studies. When they are the focus of investigation, these sociocultural positions are invariably configured as independent constructions. There is little discussion of the influences that race and gender have on each other, nor on how these impact women's participation and experience in higher education. There is little inquiry into the fact that the intersection of gender and race presents lived collegiate experiences with special and verifiable truths about post-secondary life.

The post-secondary research literature of the 1960s began our formal conversation about race and gender in at least two ways. First, this literature discussed White women's historic place in American higher education. Second, it considered race framed largely by prognostications about the effects of the 1964 Civil Rights Act and Title VII's inclusion of higher education. It was not until the 1970s that we began to see scholarly focus on race and gender, even if solely as factors to be measured in relation to enrollment patterns, attrition and retention, and financial aid. In this decade, researchers primarily concerned themselves with demographic shifts within the collegiate population of women and racial and ethnic minorities, and not with environmental factors or affective conditions impinging on women's and non-White students' campus experiences. It was not until the later years of the decade and the beginning of the 1980s that the discourse of diversity and multiculturalism, feminism and gender studies suggested that race and gender should be incorporated into research. Additionally, perhaps reacting to the social and fiscal conservatism of the 1980s, researchers and scholars of higher education began to thoughtfully engage in questions about the quality of campus life for women and minority students as a consequence of these policies. For example, the 1987 Commission on Women in Higher Education-sponsored report, "The New Agenda of Women for Higher Education: A Report of the ACE

Commission on Women in Higher Education," asserted that the 1980s were a time in American history in which "women's issues" were as "compelling" as they had ever been (1988, p. iii). Experts who contributed to the report were asked to consider how a college or university could "commit itself fully to meeting the educational needs of women" (p. v). These educational needs, the Commission reported, were informed by the sociocultural and economic changes that prevailed in the 1980s: the "superwoman" who must be both the nontraditional professional wage earner and traditional mother and wife; the paucity of women in top leadership roles across all professional fields (the glass ceiling phenomenon); salary inequities; and sexist policies (e.g., maternity leave as "disability leave;" sexual harassment).

The idea that there was a campus "climate" that could be assessed, especially in relation to the college and university's new and nontraditional participants, took hold during the 1980s with race and gender remaining separate analytical categories. Hall and Sandler's (1982) groundbreaking study on "classroom climate" presented higher education with a gendered view of pedagogical experience. Suggesting that as a consequence of preferentially gendered teaching and curricula the college and university classroom can be a "chilly" one for women students, Hall and Sandler (1982) challenged higher education researchers to critically examine the values and assumptions of higher learning. Long-held views about the value of argumentative classroom speech, the indictment of women's classroom silence, the implicit and explicit communication of expectations for women students on the part of faculty and administrators, curricular exclusion and/or stereotyping of women's contributions, and outright hostility toward women's participation in the intellectual enterprise were foreground and, consequently, deemed important for research.

But despite the impact of the "chilly climate" study and other scholarly critiques (e.g., poet and author Adrienne Rich's [1985] supplication that higher education must take all women "seriously" and Carol Gilligan's [1982] challenge to the application of masculinist views of developmental progress to women), the study of gender continued to focus on comparative analyses of women's participation, whether as students or faculty, their academic segregation, professional choices, and the newly articulated "sexual harassment." In the 1990s researchers expanded their view of the "chilly climate" issue, considering such things as the relationship between power and pedagogy and gender, and the cognitive needs of women. Studies examined women and mentoring, women faculty and tenure, testing and gender, leadership and gender, women students' persistence and aspirations. Feminist scholarship, despite its clear message about the intersection of race and gender, seems not to have made a substantive impact on the research decisions at this time despite the growing acceptance and expansion of qualitative research methodology. "Women," a subset of the category "nontraditional" student (the others being "minorities," "foreign," "older," "part-time," "disabled," and "academically underprepared"), was in the 1990s largely conceptualized as a static research variable. It is only in qualitative, naturalistic, or ethnographic studies that participants were asked to also consider their racial or ethnic particularity. Yet even in those studies of the 1990s that presented the intersection of race and gender, the critical examination of that epistemological position was an infrequent exercise. Often our qualitative studies in the 1990s acknowledged the intersection of race and gender in particular phenomena, but rarely did we as researchers engage in epistemological scrutiny of the meanings inherent in those intersections.

Like studies on gender, the research on race in the 1970s attended to enrollment, attrition, and retention patterns with little concern for the affective variables that makes race salient in American society. It was not until the 1980s that studies on the implications of race were guided by the possibility that institutional cultures may thwart the progress of its non-White students and faculty. The rise in enrollment of non-White students and its consequent anxieties over support services, curricular relevance, and organizational policies also triggered an investigative interest in race. Trend analyses such as Daryl Smith's (1989), *The Challenge of Diversity: Involvement or Alienation in the Academy*, were representative of the research of the era. Framed as a response to the challenges that racial and ethnic minorities and women were bringing to higher education, the principal objectives of studies like this were often organizational and functional. They were not attempts to understand race in any subjective way. The challenges to the neutrality of knowledge brought to academic research by critical, postmodern, and feminist theories found limited expression in race studies in higher education and as a consequence, race remained presumed as static and as singular as gender. Even in the decade of the 1990s when we in post-secondary research concerned ourselves with the relationship of race to campus climate and student satisfaction, we often failed to systematically scrutinize race from other than dominant epistemological paradigms. Studies that considered the transmission of tacit knowledge and its relationship to college success, studies that tried to understand the role of race in post-secondary socialization, like the studies of gender, failed to render the category dynamic, multidimensional, and epistemologically politicized. Even in our aggressive attempts to combat the antiaffirmative policies of the late 1990s, higher education researchers and scholars invoked race as a stable and generic condition. It did not occur to us to wonder if policies such as California's Proposition 209 exacted a uniquely tangible effect on women of color and how their educational lives were modified.

In the decades since 1960, American post-secondary scholarship on race and gender reveals that the principal research concerns have been enrollment, persistence, and the participation patterns of women and minorities as separate categories of analyses or as categories to be compared to men or Whites. Whether considered as variables in quantitative analyses or as dimensions of experience in qualitative research, race and gender are most often either compared to the referent group—Whites or men—or methodologically brought together as finite categories momentarily coexistent. It is methodology that forces the intersection, implying that their concrete coexistence matters only as a consequence of methodological manipulation, that a simultaneously raced and gendered reality is not a formal or guiding unit of analysis. It is as if to say that the moment of being both raced and gendered holds no important research consideration. In part this is largely due to the governing epistemological positions that place race and gender as derivative categories. As variables for analysis, race and gender are each set in comparison to the usual or the normative type, White (implicitly not raced) and men (inherently not gendered). Consequently, their concomitant peculiarity is rendered subordinate and dependent on the referent. Race and gender become succeeding terms in a proposition in which maleness and whiteness are the benchmark events.

Take, for example, Nora, Cabrera, Hagedorn and Pascarella's (1996) important investigation of precollege factors and their impact on college persistence "*across* different ethnic and gender groups" (emphasis mine). Nora, et al. (1996) set out to better understand "factors affecting student retention" (p. 428) through a framework that is both comprehensive and integrated. These researchers rightly point to the limitation of the conceptual model of persistence used in previous research, a model that "would not be the same for different groups of students (e.g., males versus females, minorities versus nonminorities)" (p. 431).

Despite its critique of previous conceptualizations of persistence that may not have taken into account race and gender factors that affect student retention, this study stays the course in the conceptualization of the categories themselves. Here, race and gender remain discrete and detached realities of personhood coming together only in comparative or disaggregate analyses or "across" each other. As variables, they come into contact only at the moment of disaggregation, a statistical move that suggests that the variables are understood as isolated, removable from other variables, and deliberately brought back into contact through conditional manipulation. Not only are gender and race not problematized in any significant way by the researchers, but even in the brief moment when the intersection of gender and race is deemed significant—when minority status has a positive effect on maleness (p. 445)—it is maleness, the normative variable, that is given value. The same sort of analysis is absent when the researchers note that interaction with faculty is significant for the educational persistence of women (p. 446). Here they caution that faculty are predominantly male, thus rationalizing the likelihood of significance. What one wonders is whether the faculty's race, together with their gender, would exert significant effects on Black women students and White women students, and so on. If the researchers had conceptualized the faculty as simultaneously raced and gendered, would their interactions with women, also concurrently raced and gendered, yield significance? Would an analysis that understood faculty and student interaction as complex and dynamic race and gender performances change the prescriptive results of the study, and as a result would we as researchers see, assess, and manage our contact with students in more comprehensive and meaningful ways?

Even noteworthy projects like those sponsored by the American Educational Research Association (AERA) and the Center for the Comparative Study of Race and Ethnicity at Stanford University that sought "to examine the existing professional knowledge in higher education research regarding race relations and make explicit the underlying assumptions and theories" (Chang, Witt-Sandis, & Hakuta, 1999, p. 12) fail to critically address the fact that gender is embedded and often disregarded by many race studies, and that it could be a consequential factor. Although the project correctly understands the issue of fairness and race in the affirmative action debate, it neglects to speculate whether anything in addition to "racism in various forms is still prevalent among individuals and institutions in the United States" (p. 13). Are individuals and institutions free of sex discrimination and gender bias? The National Education Association (NEA) and the American Association of University Professors (AAUP), in an effort to describe "key features" of effective mentoring programs for minority students and faculty, also ignore the impact of gender in their "Mentoring Minorities in Higher Education: Passing the Torch" report (Leon, 1993). Here, though defining mentoring as usually involving "two persons with similar backgrounds, interests and perspectives" (p. 18), the authors discuss women as a correlate of minority status because they "suffer the effect of similar prejudices," and "this includes minority women" (p. 19). Although this last qualification is an important one, little else is said about the distinctive condition of being both female and a racial or ethnic minority in higher education. The simultaneity of being female and racial other seems only important as it relates to sexual harassment and not to such things as motivation, persistence, and relational factors, contingencies one would normally deem important in a prescription for effective mentoring.

Generally, in higher education research we have not effectively conceptualized faculty, administrators and students as simultaneously raced and gendered, but there are signs of change. Inspired in part by the infusion of feminist critiques and naturalistic methodologies, higher education scholars are beginning to struggle with the messy research considerations of gendered race, or raced gender. Recently, for example, I reviewed two research proposals for the major educational research annual conference and was happily surprised at the deliberate investigation of the intersection of race and gender.

The most significant changes to our research will come from the psychological and developmental research on identity. Exploratory studies such as Shorter-Gooden and Washington (1996) that seek to establish the intersection of race and gender as an ego domain in the identity construction of African-American women in college warn about the limitations of quantitative analysis in this area. Markus and Kitayama (1991) supply us with an understanding of race and ethnicity as critical variables in the development of self-worth and positive identity construction among women and men of color. Phinney and Alipuria (1990) note that racial identity is a discernible and primary condition of racial and ethnic minority college women's identity, a phenomenon I, too, uncovered in research that explored the value of their female friendships.

In this qualitative investigation of the cognitive value of female friendship among women of color, race and/or ethnicity played a principal developmental role (Martínez-Alemán, 1999). On a campus at which the salient features of their identities are race and/or ethnicity, these women appeared to require a sororal "relationship familiarity largely determined by those very features" (p. 138). Unlike their White counterparts, women of color in this study engaged in self-development and identity construction with a peer who was acquainted with and aware of the stresses, pressures, and anxieties that are the consequence of race and/or ethnicity. Yet, I was stymied by my inability to adequately conceptualize the bearing of the gender–race dynamic on the identities and collegiate relationships of these Latinas, and African and Asian American women.

STUDYING RACE AND GENDER IN HIGHER EDUCATION: METHODOLOGICAL CONSIDERATIONS

How can we in higher education begin to critically theorize and research the links and intersection of race and gender? How can researchers and scholars begin to conceptualize "race–gender" so that its effects on collegiate populations can be analyzed far more accurately?

Attinasi and Nora (1996) argue that the "extreme diversity of today's college students cannot be studied adequately through the use of the structured survey alone," that alternatives to quantitative analyses are needed (p. 545). The researchers survey their own work on the persistence of Hispanic students and conclude that students' racial and ethnic diversity requires researchers "to be sensitive to diverse frames of reference, many of which may be different from the investigator's own" (p. 552). Attinasi and Nora (1996) assert that the increasing number of racial and ethnic minority students on our colleges and universities require college student researchers to question and assess the epistemological assumptions and positions of the survey instruments employed. These positions, the authors correctly insist, can result in data that do not adequately represent "the experiences of diverse students in institutions of higher education" (p. 547). Attinasi and Nora (1996) call for a research strategy that combines naturalistic and quantitative approaches. They submit that by integrating these two approaches the "unexplained variance in quantitative models" can be addressed (p. 552).

On the surface the proposition that Attinasi and Nora (1996) offer seems appropriate for our desire to understand the dynamic of race and gender, or "race–gender," but a careful inspection of the hypothesis reads differently. The combination of methods proposed is one of unscrutinized amalgamation. Ethnography is presented as the form of naturalistic inquiry that will infuse quantitative analyses with the necessary relational data between factors. Ethnography, and in particular, Wolcott's (1988) version, is presented as methodology uncomplicated by the very thing that concerns the authors, access to the "diverse frames of reference" (p. 552) often in opposition to those of the researchers'. Could Attinasi and Nora's (1996) comfort with ethnography as the epistemological plug for quantitative survey instruments be the consequence of their inability to consider that other "diverse frame of reference," gender? Is male bias in ethnography ignored here?

Feminist critiques of ethnography shed some light on this issue. In her examination of gender in the context of the student uprisings in Tiananmen Square in 1989, Rey Chow (1991) reminds us that the Western tradition of ethnography, whether feminist or not, can render the analysis suspect because of the power imbalance between West and East, between the colonized and the colonizer (p. 93). Chow (1991) echoes feminist anthropologist Ruth Behar's (1993) claim that "the ethnographic relationship is based on power" (p. 6) and as such, the researcher must be aware of the privileges of his or her authorial position whether "constituted by gender, sociohistorical background, and class origins, or lately class Diaspora" (p. 338).

What both Ruth Behar (1993) and Rey Chow (1991) raise is the matter of representation as a function of epistemological perspective, a position that could furnish a view of identity that is unitary, fixed, coherent, and singular. If the ethnographic view of women of color on our college and university campuses is such that we will only "see" what is the result of the consciousness of the researcher—his or her subjectivity—and if that subjectivity is an atomistic consciousness, then we will be asked to "see" race as simply, universally and essentially race, and gender as somehow purely, wholly and only itself. If, on the other hand, we investigate questions of identity with a view of consciousness on both the part of the researcher and the informants as "plural or collective" (Mohanty, 1991, p. 37), then our view is one in which the "multiple" and "often opposing ideas and knowledges" (p. 36) that are the embodiment of simultaneously raced and gendered selves could be made evident.

To effectively research the intersection of race and gender, then, is to understand subjectivity as it is: nonunitary, collective and relational. If the postsecondary community desires an accurate understanding of how Asian women negotiate the demands of tenure, or how Black women students choose academic majors and careers, then as higher education researchers we can not persist in analytical practices that separate identities into component parts, parts assumed homogeneous prior to analysis. Nor can we assume that their unequivocal analytical separation tells us the whole story. Race and gender may not be epistemologically eligible for dependent or independent variable status. Race and gender may not be eligible for an unproblematized and uncontested inter-dependence in naturalistic inquiry. Race and gender, as collective and relational subjectivity, may in the end be best understood as an "epistemological commu-nity" (Nelson, 1993, p. 121), a community in which how a person knows and how she or he behaves is derivative of "multiple, historically contingent, and dynamic" evidence with "fuzzy overlapping boundaries" that "evolve, dissolve, and recombine" (p. 125).

GENDER, RACE, AND MILLENNIAL CURIOSITY

Stanley Crouch's (1996) prediction of race as a "historic curiosity" is more cor-rectly an event that cannot transpire without the eradication of the signifi-cance of gender on subjectivity and thus on consciousness. Before race can take on its millennial multiplicity and consequent insignificance, it is impera-tive to first tend to the tangible and unresolved matters of gender. As higher education researchers and scholars, we need to theorize and then empirically represent race–gender both as a force that affects the development of con-sciousness and motivates a stable yet variable subjectivity, and as an embodi-ment that though produced through elaborate and involved historical realities, is salient and comprehensible.

Race–gender or gender–race (I do not mean to give either category episte-mological preference or priority) needs to be understood not as a hybridity or consolidation but as a hyphenation of mutuality. It is the hyphen, in my view, that may give us a way to empirically understand the "fuzzy overlaps" that func-tion to produce a consciousness and subjectivity that is powered by its very multifariousness. The hyphen, as a purely symbolic tool, directs the researcher not to a depiction of college and university lives that are artificially raced and gendered at the moment of disaggregate analysis or naturalistic description. In-stead, the representative hyphen enables us as researchers to see the relevance of gendered understanding in race and the consequence of race consciousness in the gendered actualities of post-secondary life. The hyphenation may help us see and comprehend the multiplicity of identities and their consequent perfor-mances as tangible and unmistakable, as truthful and undismissable.

Let us return to Stanley Crouch's claim that the twenty-first century will be a century in which how Americans have thought about race will become "historic curiosity," that "race" will become a trifling interest, a matter of no concern. It seems to me that if the scholarship and research on higher educa-tion is reflective of the knowledge necessary to reach a consciousness in which the matters of race in America are insignificant, we as a community of post-secondary researchers and scholars are far from achieving that consciousness. In fact, to achieve Crouch's consciousness ideal, we would pay much more atten-tion to race matters at the outset, at those times when race and ethnicity does matter. The history of our curiosity about race on campus tells us that we have not paid careful attention nor given care to many of the details of race, in particular the detail of gender. Our lack of curiosity about the constituent nature of race, especially with regard to gender, has confined us to old questions and uninspired research.

One of the most important goals of higher education scholarship and research is to inform practice. Student affairs professionals, campus administrators, and state and federal policymakers look to higher education scholars to provide them with ever-expanding knowledge about students. As more and more women of color enter higher education and challenge the norms of academic culture, higher education professionals need knowledge borne of research that reflects these identities. Research on higher education that does not take into account the gendered nature of race or the raced nature of gender can limit the scope of post-secondary policy and practice. For example, one could stipulate that the usefulness of recent post-secondary research on women's participation in science, mathematics and engineering curricula for faculty and administrators is in its ability to suggest positive change as a consequence of evidence (Sax, 2001; Colbeck, Cabrera, & Terenzini, 2001). But in cases such as these, the conceptual framework and inadequate review of the sociological and psychological research literature render the research findings ineffectual. Research designed to consider student confidence and self-esteem, as these two studies are, needs to formally consider how gender and race are interdependent variables and how this interdependence is both manifested and addressed on campus. Simply saying (almost as an investigative afterthought) that "being non-White had a negative effect" (Sax, 2001, p. 164) serves no fruitful purpose given the realities of campus life and, ironically, the desired goal of such research: to inform practice.

Studies of this sort are typical in higher education—typical in that they lack the theoretical and cross-disciplinary literacy to truly enlighten practice. For example, rarely does post-secondary research and scholarship draw on the extensive psychological literature on race–gender and identity formation that can help reconceptualize design and methodology to more accurately reflect the realities of students' lives. Our research habits in higher education often limit the breadth of our literature reviews so that we are often unaware of the advanced and forward-looking scholarship in the humanities and social sciences. Our research literacy in higher education often reflects how we are uninformed by and unacquainted with the complex, critical and challenging theoretical work on gender–race done in philosophy, feminist theory, and cultural studies. As a result, much of our research and scholarship in higher education is staid, unexciting and uninspiring, and consequently of limited value to the professions we seek to serve.

In the twenty-first century our research and scholarship on higher education should be informed by the curiosities of race, gender, sexuality, class, and so on. These are the curiosities that matter on college and university campuses; these are the curiosities that shape our behaviors and that populate our class-rooms. In 1993, the number of bachelor's degrees conferred on Hispanic women experienced a 131% increase, compared to the 83.8% increase for His-panic men. That same year, both African-American and Asian-American women also outpaced their male counterparts in the attainment of bachelor's degrees from American post-secondary institutions. In 1995, nearly two-thirds of Black students enrolled in college were women, while of the Hispanic un-dergraduates, 53% were women (National Center for Education Statistics, 1999). The following year saw the number of Asian women in higher educa-tion climb to 51% of the total Asian enrollment (*Chronicle*, 1999, p. 24), yet only 36% of the doctoral degrees granted to Asian Americans belonged to Asian-American women (p. 32). Latinas made up only .8% of the full-time faculty in 1992 (p. 36), and in 1995, of the 2,610 Latinas who were full-time tenure-track faculty, 63% were at the rank of assistant professor (p. 38). In all, approximately 4% of the post-secondary teaching faculty in the United States are women of color (Busenberg & Smith, 1997, p. 162). In 1995, the mean earned income for Black women graduates from selective colleges and univer-sities was $20,300 less than their Black male counterparts, and $37,200 less than White men (Bowen & Bok, 1998, p. 124). How curious is that?

NOTES

1. I do not mean to imply that gender is the only such experiential reality to be absent from this discourse. The effects of sexuality, economic class, and so on are also integral in the consideration of racial realities.

2. I will use this designation to refer to women whose racial and/or ethnic identity fall within the "non-White" categories listed by the U.S. DOE. The categories are the following: Black, non-Hispanic; Hispanic; Asian or Pacific Islander; and American In-dian or Native Alaskan.

3. It is important to note here that the term "Latina" is explicitly gendered. A characteristic Romance language, Spanish requires gendered forms and assumes that masculine versions represent both men and women. Thus, when we say "Latinos," we can assume that either we are speaking solely about Latin men or about both Latin men and Latin women.

4. It is worth mentioning the significance of the name "Yo" for Julia Alvarez's pro-tagonist. In Spanish, the word "yo" is the personal pronoun, "I"; it is also used to mean "ego" and "self".

5. I do not mean to imply that racial or ethnic difference from Whites or that gen-der difference from males is essentially burdensome and oppressive. Nor do I think that Spelman believes this to be the case. To assign the characterization "burden" to racial and/or gender difference reifies a racist and sexist meaning.

REFERENCES

ACE Commission on Women in Higher Education. (1988). *The 1987 Commission on Women in Higher Education Special Report Commission on Women in Higher Education.* Washington, DC.

Adams, K. L., & Ware, N. C. (1989). Sexism and the English language: The linguistic implications of being a woman. In J. Freeman (Ed.) *Women* (4th ed.) (pp. 470–484). Mountain View, CA: Mayfield.

Alvarez, J. (1992). *How the García girls lost their accents.* New York: Plume Books.

Alvarez, J. (1997). ¡*Yo!* New York: Plume Books.

Attinasi, Jr., L. C., & Nora, A. (1996). Diverse students and complex issues: A case for multiple methods in college student research. In C. Turner, M. García, A. Nora, & L. Rendón (Eds.) *Racial and ethnic diversity in higher education* (pp. 545–554). ASHE Reader Series. New York: Simon & Schuster.

Babco, E. L. (1997). *Professional women and minorities: A total human resources data compendium, 12th edition.* Washington, DC: Commission on Professionals in Science and Technology.

Behar, R. (1993). *Translated woman: Crossing the border with Esperanza's story.* Boston: Beacon Press.

Bowen, W. G., & Bok, D. (1998). *The shape of the river: Long-term consequences of considering race in college and university admissions.* Princeton, NJ: Princeton University Press.

Burdman, P. (1997, June–July). The long good-bye: The University of California bids farewell to affirmative action. *Lingua Franca, 7,* 28–39.

Busenberg, B. E., & Smith D. G. (1997). Affirmative action and beyond: The women's perspective. In M. García (Ed.) *Affirmative action's testament of hope: Strategies for a new era in higher education* (pp. 149–180). Albany, NY: State University of New York Press.

Chang, M. J., Witt-Sandis, D., & Hakuta, K. (1999). The dynamics of race in higher education: An examination of the evidence. *Equity & Excellence in Education, 32*(2), 12–16.

Chow, R. (1991). Violence in the other country: China as crisis, spectacle, and woman. In C. T. Mohanty, A. Russo, & L. Torres (Eds.) *Third world women and the politics of feminism* (pp. 81–100). Bloomington: Indiana University Press.

Chronicle of Higher Education. (1999, August 27). Almanac Issue, *46*(1).

Clark Hine, D. (1993). In the kingdom of culture: Black women and the intersection of race, gender, and class. In G. Early (Ed.) *Lure and loathing: Essays on race, identity and the ambivalence of assimilation* (pp. 337–351). New York: Allan Lane/Penguin Press.

Colbeck, C. L., Cabrera, A. F., & Terenzini, P. T. (2001). Learning professional confidence: Linking teaching practices, students' self-perception, and gender. *Review of Higher Education, 24*(2), 173–192.

Collins, P. H. (1991). *Black feminist thought: Knowledge, consciousness, and the politics of empowerment.* New York: Routledge.

Crouch, S. (1996, September 29). Race is over: Black, white, yellow—same difference. *New York Times Magazine,* 170–171.

Du Bois, W. E. B. (1996). *The souls of Black folk.* New York: Penguin Books. Originally published in 1903.

Dubois, C. (1991, July). The many faces of Asian women. *Washington Women News,* 355–357.

Fanon, F. (1998). The fact of blackness. In N. Zack, L. Shrage, & C. Sartwell (Eds.) *Race, class, gender, and sexuality: The big questions* (pp. 61–66). Malden, MA: Blackwell.

Gilligan, C. (1982). *In a different voice: Psychological theory and women.* Cambridge, MA: Harvard University Press.

Giovanni, N. (1993). Black is the noun. In G. Early (Ed.) *Lure and loathing: Essays on race, identity, and the ambivalence of assimilation* (pp. 113–126). New York: Penguin Press.

Green, R. (1981). Indian women and textbook omission. In S. Verble (Ed.) *Words of today's American Indian women: Ohoyo makachi* (pp. 117–121). Addresses from the 1981 Ohoyo Resource Center Conference on Educational Equity Awareness, Tahlequah, OK.

Hall, R. M., & Sandler, B. R. (1982). *The classroom climate: A chilly one for women?* Project on the Status and Education of Women. Washington, DC: Association of American Colleges.

Lai, T. (1991). Asian American women: Not for sale. In J. Whitehorse Cochran, D. Langston, & C. Woodward (Eds.) *Changing our power* (pp. 126–133). Dubuque, IA: Kendall/Hunt.

Leon, D. (1993). Mentoring minorities in higher education: Passing the torch. National Education Association, Office of Higher Education, Washington, DC.

Markus, H. R., & Kitayama, S. (1991). Culture and the self: Implications for cognition, emotion, and motivation. *Psychological Review, 98,* 224–253.

Martínez-Alemán, A. M. (1999). Race talks: Undergraduate women of color and female friendship. *Review of Higher Education, 23*(2), 133–152.

Mohanty, C. T. (1991). Cartographies of struggle: Third World women and the politics of feminism. In C. T. Mohanty, A. Russo, & L. Torres (Eds.) *Third World women and the politics of feminism* (pp. 1–50). Bloomington: Indiana University Press.

Moraga, C. (1983). La güera. In C. Moraga & G. Anzaldua (Eds.) *This bridge called my back: Writings by radical women of color* (pp. 27–34). Latham, NY: Kitchen Table, Women of Color Press.

National Center for Education Statistics. (1995). Minority undergraduate participation in postsecondary education. Retrieved August 23, 1999, from <http://nces.ed.gov/pubs95/95166.html>

National Center for Education Statistics. (1996). Digest of Educational Statistics. Fast Facts. Degrees conferred by sex and race. Retrieved August 5, 2002, from <http:// nces.ed.gov/fastfacts/display.asp?id=72>

National Center for Education Statistics. (1999). Digest of Educational Statistics. Bachelor's degrees conferred by degree-granting institutions, by racial/ethnic group and sex of student: 1976–77 to 1997–98. Table 265. Retrieved August 5, 2002, from <http://nces.ed.gov/pubs2001/digest/dt265.html>

Nelson, L. H. (1993). Epistemological communities. In L. Alcoff & E. Potter (Eds.) *Feminist epistemologies* (pp. 121–160). New York: Routledge.

Nora, A., Cabrera, A., Serra Hagedorn, L., & Pascarella, E. (1996). Differential impacts of academic and social experiences on college–related behavioral outcomes across different ethnic and gender groups at four-year institutions. *Research in Higher Education*, *37*(4), 427–451.

Phinney, J. S., & Alipuria, L. (1990). Ethnic identity in college students from four ethnic groups. *Journal of Adolescence*, *13*, 171–183.

Rich, A. (1985). Taking women seriously. In M. Culley & C. Portugues (Eds.) *Gendered subjects: The dynamics of feminist teaching* (pp. 21–28). Boston, MA: Kegan Paul.

Sax, L. J. (2001). Undergraduate science majors: Gender differences in who goes to school. *Review of Higher Education*, *24*(2), 153–172.

Shorter-Gooden, K., & Washington, N. C. (1996). Young, black, and female: The challenge of weaving an identity. *Journal of Adolescence*, *19*, 465–475.

Smith, D. (1989). *The challenge of diversity: Involvement or alienation in the academy.* ASHE-ERIC Higher Education Report, No. 5. Washington, DC: George Washington University.

Spelman, E. V. (1998). Gender and race: The ampersand problem in feminist thought. In S. Ruth (Ed.) *Issues in feminism: An introduction to women's studies* (4th ed.) (pp. 22–34). Mountain View, CA: Mayfield.

Williams, P. J. (1991). *The alchemy of race and rights: Diary of a law professor.* Cambridge, MA: Harvard University Press.

Wolcott, H. F. (1988). Ethnographic research in education. In R. M. Jaeger (Ed.) *Complementary methods for research in education* (pp. 187–206). Washington, DC: American Educational Research Association.

Zook, K. B. (1995, November 12). A manifesto of sorts for a black feminist movement. *New York Times Magazine*, 86–89.

Contributors

Jana Nidiffer is an Assistant Professor in the Center for the Study of Higher and Postsecondary Education at the University of Michigan, Ann Arbor. Her areas of specialization include both history and gender issues in higher education. Specifically, her research interests focus on access, particularly how higher education serves previously underserved populations, especially women and the economically disadvantaged. She has published many books and articles, the most recent of which is entitled *Women Administrators in Higher Education: Historical and Contemporary Perspectives*.

Lisa Wolf-Wendel is an Associate Professor in the Higher Education Program within the Department of Teaching and Leadership at the University of Kansas. She earned her doctorate in 1995 from The Claremont Graduate School and her bachelor's degree from Stanford University in 1987. Her research focuses broadly on equity issues concerning women and people of color in higher education.

Laura G. Hensley is an Assistant Professor in the Department of Educational Leadership, Research, and Counseling at Louisiana State University. She is a Licensed Professional Counselor with an emphasis in college counseling. She has researched and published in the area of college student development, wellness, and college women's issues in counseling.

William F. Pinar teaches curriculum theory at Louisiana State University, where he serves as the St. Bernard Parish Alumni Endowed Professor. He has also served as the Frank Tabott Professor at the University of Virginia and the

A. Lindsay O'Connor Professor of American Institutions at Colgate University. He is the editor of *Queer Theory in Education* (Lawrence Erlbaum, 1998).

Judith Glazer-Raymo is a Professor of Education at the C.W. Post Campus of Long Island University. She is the author of *Shattering the Myths: Women in Academe* (1999), and of books, monographs, and articles on gender, public policy, and faculty issues in higher education. In 2001, she received the Willystine Goodsell Award from AERA and the Trustees Award for Scholarly Achievement from Long Island University.

Kelly Ward is an Assistant Professor of Higher Education at Washington State University in Pullman. Her research interests are in the area of faculty work and family life, faculty roles and rewards, and service learning. She has held faculty and administrative positions at Oklahoma State University and the University of Montana. She is co-author of *The Department Chair's Role in Developing New Faculty into Teachers and Scholars*.

Becky Ropers-Huilman is an Associate Professor at Louisiana State University where she is affiliated with the Department of Educational Leadership, Research, and Counseling and the Women's and Gender Studies Program. Her scholarly interests include race and gender issues in higher education, as well as collegiate teaching and learning. She has published her work in several articles and books, including *Feminist Teaching in Theory and Practice* and *Women in Higher Education: A Feminist Perspective*.

Monisa Shackelford is a doctorate candidate in sociology at Louisiana State University. Over the past decade, her work has focused on stigma and impression management, particularly in relation to disability, mental illness, and non-traditional families.

Denise Taliaferro is an Assistant Professor of Education at Miami University of Ohio. Her research and teaching interests focus on the historical, political and philosophical foundations of race, identity and difference as well as their influence on pedagogical philosophies and practices.

Ana M. Martínez Alemán is an Assistant Professor of Education at Boston College. Her research activities focus the impact of gender, race and ethnicity on higher education. Her recent publications include "Identity, feminist teaching, and John Dewey" in C. H. Seigfried (Ed.) *Feminist Interpretations of John Dewey*, and "Community, higher education, and the challenge of multiculturalism" in *Teachers College Record*.

Index

201